Saint Francis of Assisi

A Guide for our Times

The Fiery Arrow Collection

Editors: Hein Blommestijn and Jos Huls of Titus Brandsma Institute

Advisory Board:

Elizabeth Dreyer, Silver Spring, U.S.A.
Christopher O'Donnell, Dublin, Ireland
Helen Rolfson, Collegeville, U.S.A.
V.F. Vineeth, Bangalore, India
John Welch, Washington, U.S.A.

The *Fiery Arrow series* aims at the publication of books which connect their readers with the legacy of great teachers of spirituality from the distant and more recent past. Readers are offered a language and conceptual framework which can lead them to a deepened understanding of the spiritual life. The treasures of the spiritual tradition form a veritable "school of love", which is accessible to all who in contemplation desire to be touched by the fire of divine love. In 1270 A.D. Nicholas of France, former prior general of the Carmelites, wrote a letter bearing the title *Fiery Arrow* to his fellow brothers to urge them to call to mind again the fire of the beginning in which, in silence and solitude, they were consumed by the inescapable claim of the One. Based on the Carmelite tradition, this series seeks to share this spiritual legacy – which presents itself in a multiplicity of cultures and traditions – with all those who in a great variety of ways are in search of interior life and the fire of love. The series, which is grounded in scientific research, is aimed at a broad public interested in spirituality.

The Titus Brandsma Institute is an academic center of research in spirituality founded in 1968 by the Catholic University of Nijmegen and the Carmelite Order. Titus Brandsma, who from 1923 on was a professor of philosophy and the history of mysticism, especially that of the Low Countries, died in 1942 as a martyr in the Nazi death camp of Dachau and was beatified in 1985. The Institute continues his research in spirituality and mysticism with a staff of assistants and in collaboration with other researchers. In addition to this and other series, the Institute publishes the international periodical *Studies in Spirituality* and the series *Studies in Spirituality Supplement* (Peeters, Louvain).

Already published in this series:

SAINT FRANCIS OF ASSISI:

A GUIDE FOR OUR TIMES

by
Theodore H. ZWEERMAN O.F.M.
Edith A.C. VAN DEN GOORBERGH O.S.C.

Translated by
Maurits SINNINGHE DAMSTÉ

PEETERS
LEUVEN – PARIS – DUDLEY, MA
2007

A CIP Record for this book is available from the Library of Congress.

Franciscus van Assisi. Over zijn evangelische bezieling en de betekenis ervan voor onze tijd,
Nijmegen, 2003. Originally published by Valkhof Pers, Nijmegen, The Netherlands.
ISBN 90 5625 157 0

ISBN 978-90-429-1955-6
D. 2007/0602/97

© 2007 – Peeters, Bondgenotenlaan 153, B-3000 Leuven

Table of Contents

Foreword

This book was conceived as a fruit of our meditations on the writings of Saint Francis of Assisi. If one is intent on discovering his deepest inspiration as a seeker of God, there is no better place to look than in these. We have especially tried to relate Francis' biblical spirituality of 'thanking, serving and bearing' to the issues concerning our own day and age.

In a small way, this book endeavours to contribute to the actualisation of Francis' charisma: a freely chosen life-style characterised by having no possessions as well as by courageous service and courteous respect to others. What can his biblical 'art of living' signify for the modern individual who jealously guards his or her freedom in a world marked by excessive planning and omnipresent technology, and who at the same time is usually not quite sure for whom or for what he or she is actually free?

We would like to thank Maurits Sinninghe Damsté for his translation of this book. Without his enthusiasm and attentiveness, this English edition would not have been possible. We would also like to thank the governing body of the Dutch Province of the Order of the Friars Minor, which supported this translation-project.

It was Brother Bonaventure Lee O.F.M., a member of the Korean Province of the Friars Minor in Seoul, who took the initiative for an English translation. As a friar minor he received a degree at the Department for Franciscan Spirituality at the Anthonianum in Rome. He was very much in favour of our approach to Francis' spirituality, which is based on a thorough reading of a number of Francis' own writings. This is why he urgently requested an English translation of our book in order to facilitate an introduction to Francis' biblical spirituality for the members of the Franciscan Orders and Congregations in Asia.

This work was realised during the period that Brother Theodore Zweerman O.F.M. felt his energy diminishing as the result of a taxing and incurable disease. He therefore personally experienced what he was writing about in this book. Right up until his death he remained fascinated by the mystery of God's being the pre-eminent Humble One. It can therefore be no coincidence that two days prior to Theodore's passing away, we spent some time together proof-reading the English translation of the passage about God's humility: the final chord to a great number of inspiring years of working together.

Theo considered the actualisation of Francis' biblical charisma for modern-day people to be his life's work. If this book can contribute to this, then his greatest desire will have been fulfilled. Praise be to God!

Megen, Epiphany of the Lord, 2007

(†) Theodore Zweerman O.F.M.
Edith van den Goorbergh O.S.C.

Introduction

The name of Francis of Assisi is well-known throughout the world. Children are captured by his enthusiasm for animals. On the world-wide-web, there are many web-sites devoted to him. His name is often mentioned when the care for the environment and peace are at issue. Why is it that someone who lived eight centuries ago, still receives so much attention from Catholic and Protestant alike, from Christians and non-Christians, from people striving for the improvement of society and from those who are especially interested in spirituality and mysticism? Who is he? What inspired him?

The external facts concerning Francis' life are easily summarised: born in 1181, the son of a rich merchant, he was the centre of the young party-crowd in Assisi. In his twenties, he went through a spiritual crisis which resulted in his decision to radically follow in the footsteps of Jesus Christ. Irresistibly generous and happy-go-lucky before his conversion, he thereafter refused to be hemmed in by the trappings of a safe and secure bourgeois lifestyle. Lavishly bestowing his talents, he was not afraid to seem eccentric and to permanently withdraw from an existence that was caught up in chase of property, power and fame.

Within a short matter of time, there was a steadily growing group of people who wished to lead a different life together with him. They shared their life with the very poorest, travelled around as troubadours, sang their praises of God's goodness and proclaimed what inspired them in the Gospel. Not long afterwards, the aristocratic Chiara (Clare) di Favarone di Offreduccio, also from Assisi, was struck by the same challenge given by the Gospel. As Francis' first female disciple, she chose, just as he did, to live a life without having any possessions whatsoever. She quickly inspired many women to open themselves in the same way to the mystery of God. From the moment of her first encounter with

Francis, her voice, paradoxically through voluntary silence and seclusion, also helped mould this Gospel-inspired way of living.

Living according to the Gospel in a new urbanised culture

Francis preferably referred to himself as a 'lesser' brother and desired to be nothing more than a sign pointing to Christ. He had nothing of the scholar about him and held no great theories concerning social improvement. However his enthusiasm, inspired by the Gospel, has an unequalled power of attraction right up to our own day. What is its secret?

This merchant's son had come to view the boundaries delimiting the social classes as massive walls which were used to shield one individual from the other. Property, acquired in order to provide in one's needs, can quickly become a point of contention which makes an authentic spirit of community impossible. This is why Francis and his disciples literally descended from the rich town-centre, which was usually situated higher up, leaving it in order to share the life of those who were trying to make ends meet further down and on the margins of society.

They knew perfectly well that in doing so they were turning their world upside down. Of course, what the 'done' thing is, is to endeavour to become 'accepted' and to climb the social ladder. However, wasn't the drive to work oneself upwards – often at the expense of others – unmasked by Jesus Christ who himself had chosen the lowest and least place? What touched them most in Jesus, was that God's abundance did not become evident through abundant possessions and fame when it manifested itself within the boundaries of his humanity. Neither did this happen through a manifestation of superior power which would blind and command submission. Something completely different occurred; something that the apostle Paul referred to using the sober and profound words 'self-dispossession' and 'self-humbling' (see Philippians 2:6-11).[1] Of course this is not easy language – just as much then as it is

[1] The bible-citations are taken from the *Holy Bible, New Revised Standard Version*, Anglicized Edition with Apocrypha, Oxford, 1998.

now. Francis and Clare tried to crack open these difficult words and what they discovered was the unheard of: that the Son of God does not act as a possessor, but as the pre-eminent giver. Not as the ruler, but rather as the servant of all. They wanted him to be the measure for their life. They desired to be led by his Spirit.

Francis and Clare: people of their own day and age, as well as people who courageously travelled new roads. In this way their significance transcended the boundaries of their own era. They radically distanced themselves from new social trends which they experienced as contradictory to Jesus' life and teaching. They did, however, remain engaged with the new urbanised culture.

As has been said, Francis and his brothers were to be found on the edge of the towns, preferably associating with the poor, the outcasts and the underdogs. They stood up for the lepers and lived with those who didn't belong anywhere. Without any possessions, they wandered around preaching and tried to arouse people from their rose-coloured day-dreaming: dreams of cash and hard currency.

Clare and her sisters gave their own form to Francis' charisma. They did this in the seclusion of the little cloister of San Damiano, which lies in the immediate vicinity of Assisi. Through intense prayer and their concrete living of the Gospel, they radiated God's presence to the many coming to seek advice and help. In doing so they kept in touch with the common folk and with what was happening in town. The courage to entrust yourself to God's Spirit again and again everyday, without any basic security, and to believe that there is Someone concerned with you in good times as well as bad, has much to say, also to us here and now. The focal points of the Gospel-spirituality of these *poverelli* – the 'little poor' – may throw some light upon the issues surrounding our own manner of dealing with property. In the central themes of Francis' spirituality, 'thanking', 'serving' and 'bearing', we will seek an orientation for those who endeavour to live in the spirit of this blessed man and woman. For example: where do the boundaries concerning security and safety lie? What is the deeper-lying reason for terrorism and 'meaningless violence'? What is the status quo concerning respect for human dignity? Is the discussion surrounding

justice, peace and the conservation of Creation really only a recent
one?

Seeker of God

Francis is most of present interest when it comes to him being a
seeker of God. Whoever wants to understand what moved him
most inwardly cannot ignore this fact. Many facets of his life can
be viewed in this way. However, how does one begin to discover
his deepest motivation?[2]

An attempt was made by Hélène Nolthenius to do just this
very thing.[3] She used the stages of mystic growth as a 'viewer'
through which she studied her subject. In this way she managed
to recognise, in the facts and phases of Francis' life which are
known to us, the stages in his growth towards God. The title of
her book demonstrates this: she sketched Francis not only as
someone from the thirteenth-century who came from the valley of
Spoleto, but she also showed how he climbed up out of that valley through his unique engagement with God and with his brothers and sisters.

Like her, we are also concerned with his orientation towards
God. For us, however, Francis' *own* writings are of prime interest.
These are the fruits of his constant meditation. They prove to be
of surprising content when approached in a meditative manner.

Francis and Clare: meditating people

Our view of Francis and Clare as writers — and therefore our manner of reading — constantly oscillates between two rocks which
both form an obstacle to the correct understanding of their texts.
The first appears when the merchant's son and the aristocratic

---

[2] Octavian Schmucki, 'Mysticism of St. Francis in the Light of His Writings'.
In: *Greyfriars Review,* 3:3 (1989); 1-266.

[3] Hélène Nolthenius, *Un uomo dalla valle di Spoleto. Francesco tra i suoi con-
temporanei,* Padova, 1991, particularly Part III.

young lady are depicted as people who were academically formed. The second is the possibility that the contents of their writings could be considered to be 'associative'. This characterisation could be defended – 'to associate' of course means much the same as 'to bring together', and what does a writer do otherwise? – if only 'to associate' were not almost always understood to be the random collection of intuitions, thoughts, bible-fragments, et cetera. This way of thinking has contributed much to the inflexible view of a freely associating Francis, as well as to the 'academic' pronouncement that it is impossible that such a simple woman as Clare would have been able to produce such ingenious letters. Leaving these two rocks behind us, we will start from the principle that Clare and Francis were meditating people – even though they meditated under various different circumstances.

What did meditation entail in those times?

Clare and Francis undoubtedly understood meditation in the same way as those in the thirteenth-century understood it to be. When Francis withdrew himself into caves for prayer – sometimes for weeks at a stretch – or when, during his long journeys, he travelled silently or whilst singing through the countryside, he did not have to invent meditation. Clare also did not have to do this in the seclusion of San Damiano. As far as meditation goes, there was already a rich tradition which they must have known of. We may surmise that they must have discussed these matters which were so very important to them.

As to the question of how this meditation was actually done, we have restricted ourselves to a small number of moments. We base ourselves on the fact that for Francis and Clare, the daily celebration of the liturgy was important nourishment. They held fast to the words that had touched them, while praying in their heart.

This manner of using the Bible is made up of attentive 'reading' or 'listening' (*lectio*) – 'assimilation' (*meditatio*) – 'replying' (*oratio*) – 'dwelling upon' (*contemplatio*). Many have rediscovered this manner of prayer. This way of praying offers forms for people

of all types and levels of spiritual development. Meditation therefore entails searching for and discovering what is offered in God's
word: boiling it down and receiving it in one's own heart. To start
with, this often means the repetition of certain words. By letting
such words function as a mantra – a term often used these days –,
they can sink into one's inner being. In mediaeval times this was
called 'ruminating' (*ruminare*): a process of assimilation or diges-
tion, through which the essentials of a bible-fragment could be
released and enter oneself. Or, to put it differently: by constantly
circling around its essentials, the profound meaning of the bible-
fragment could be got at and its nucleus discerned from what was
of less importance.

The plumbing of these essentials can be compared to a distilla-
tion-process. In doing so, a cursory reading becomes, so to speak,
more and more concentrated. As far as this is concerned, meditation is rather like writing poetry. Great poetry, being the fruit of
the intense assimilation of experiences, does indeed contain a high
degree of concentration. It offers the 'essence' of observed reality.
Such a strong concentration can be tasted in Francis' and Clare's
texts. They offer a liqueur, so to speak, which cannot be quickly
gulped down as instant information.

Meditation is also, from another viewpoint, 'collective reading'
and 'bringing together' (therefore indeed 'association'!). One can
think of the discovery of internal connections between the mysteries of faith, between these mysteries and our own existence –
who we are (and hope to become). However, this is perhaps a
much too active way of looking at things. The reality of meditation is done more justice by realising that the meditating individual sometimes sees connections which throw light on what is really of value.

Most important is the way in which an individual gives an
answer to what has spoken to him.[4] Sometimes this will be a
prayer of supplication, at other times a prayer of thanks and
praise.

---

[4] Wherever we use he/him/his, we refer to both men and women.

Once all considerations and reflections have come to rest, there is 'only' *silent openness*. This often means exercising humility and patience. These are, by the way, two virtues with which Francis and Clare denote the mystery of God.

While meditating with an ever more finely tuned sense for what was essential in the life of Jesus, Francis and Clare composed their texts. By reading these and meditating in our own turn, we can gradually discover their wisdom.

Francis as a writer

When Francis died in 1226, he left us a handful of writings: prayers, letters, admonitions (kernels of wisdom), an Earlier and a Later Rule for the brotherhood which had come into existence around him and a unique song of praise concerning the Creation, which has remained much loved right up to our own times as the Canticle of the Creatures. If one only considers the quantity of his writings, this is not much. Most of his texts were only composed during the last years of his life, when he was often forced by illness to stay put wherever he was. However the fact that he wrote a compact rule for Clare and her sisters already in 1212/1213, says a lot about his relationship and engagement with them.

Francis was much like Clare: they could both write in a captivating manner, and we know that he was a clever story-teller. They both however, didn't consider their vocation as being writers. Above all, these two were engrossed with the formation and inspiration of communities based on the spirit of the Gospel. This is what they have left us. This does not however mean that their writings are not a goldmine for those seeking an authentic Gospel-inspired spirituality. On the contrary: for nowhere else other than in their writings, even though these were mostly written for specific occasions, is one able to discover their most profound inspiration.[5]

---

[5] Compare Leonhard Lehmann, *Tiefe und Weite. Der universale Grundzug in den Gebeten des Franziskus von Assisi* (Franziskanische Forschungen, 29. Heft),

What inspires us, who live under such more distracting circumstances, in the simple life of Francis and Clare? Is it perhaps their radical stance; the fact that they uncompromisingly wished to follow in the footsteps of Jesus Christ? In doing so Francis indeed became a 'prophet' and Clare 'the new leader of women'.[6] This, despite the quickly developing tendency within the brotherhood to seek security in scholarship and clerical positions.

Through this orientation, these 'poor in spirit' were, thanks to the light of Christ, able to see through the society of their day and age which had been cast adrift. The clarity of this light, however, encompasses much more than mere simplicity, let alone simple-mindedness. Whoever lets daylight shine through a prism sees all the colours of the rainbow. In the same way, behind the simplicity of the charisma of these two people, lies a great colourfulness. We, who live in a pluriform culture and often thirst for simplicity, would be well advised to look for the tensions within the simplicity of these 'little poor', which make up its richness. Francis and Clare were humble as well as frank. They were interested in the individual human-being as well as in the Church as the Body of Christ. Francis wanted to be a disciple of Jesus, associating with dropouts and underdogs, whilst also seeing the journey through the ages which Christ is undertaking with his Church. He was socially and ethically motivated and at the same time strongly

Werl-Westfalen, 1984; 33; Thaddée Matura also points out that there is a difference between the message of Francis' writings and that of his biographers. Compare idem, *François d'Assise "auteur spirituel": Le message de ses écrits*. Paris, 1996; 8 ff. English translation, *Francis of Assisi: The Message in His Writings*. St. Bonaventure, NY, 1997.

  [6] *The Remembrance of the Desire of a Soul by Thomas of Celano* (= 2 Celano); 2 Celano 54. In: *Francis of Assisi: Early Documents. Volume II. The Founder*. Edited by Regis J. Armstrong, O.F.M. Cap., J.A. Wayne Hellmann, O.F.M. Conv., William J. Short, O.F.M., New York – London – Manila, 2000; 283; Niek van Doornik, *Francis of Assisi. A Prophet for Our Time*. Trans. Barbara Potter Fasting, Chicago, 1979; Clare of Assisi. *Early Documents*. Edited and translated by Regis J. Armstrong O.F.M. Cap., (revised and expanded), Saint Bonaventure, New York, 1993, 'The Legend of Saint Clare': Preface; 252.

engaged with all Creation. His engagement with all creatures was with every single animal as well as with the entire cosmos, which he saw as a mirror of the Creator.

No longer could he live as someone who treated nature as something to be ruled over. He addressed the animals and even the elements as sisters and brothers, all originating from the same creative hand of God. Above all, he respected the mystery of God: that Humility which is so very close to us in every outcast and which is as sublime as the silence and grandeur of the mountains. As long as his physical condition allowed, he travelled around as an inspired preacher, however again and again he took the time to seek seclusion in often lofty hermitages and caves in order to let himself be refreshed by the Source of all that is good.

Restraint

Francis stood in a long tradition of writing, which exercised restraint in speaking openly about God. This is the reason why a veiled manner of speaking was often used, especially where the hidden and intimate relationship with God was concerned. It was careful not to infringe upon the awe which God is due.[7] This restraint, based on awe, is also due even if the intimacy proffered by God is not accompanied by paranormal phenomena – which mystics usually blame on their own weakness. The term 'mysticism', by the way, evokes a certain 'closing' and an attempt at concealment. The Greek word *muein* (to be silent), from which the term is derived, traditionally expressed this. In his twenty-eighth Admonition, Francis explicitly praises the servant 'who does not endeavour to make (...) the mysteries of the Lord known'. This conclusion to the collection of Admonitions clearly functions as a sort of *seal* securing what the Lord revealed to him: a lock requiring a certain key.

[7] Compare Joseph Sudbrack, 'Erfahrungsräume geistlicher Scham'. In: *Geist und Leben* 49 (1976); 46-60; 47 and 60; compare Reinhold Haskamp, *Ich schäme mich. Ein Plädoyer gegen die Unverschämtheit*. Würzburg, 1989: part 3: 'Ehrfurcht und Scham vor dem Geheimnis Gottes'; 113-116.

Along the same lines, the concluding words to the Golden Epistle by William of Saint Thierry also function as a type of *seal*.[8] It is true, he says, that it is God's love, or the love of his Love, which spurs us on to speak of Him. However, it remains important not to proclaim this priceless truth in a completely open manner, but to rather 'hide it in one's cell and to give it a place in one's innermost being'. And as an inscription above one's innermost being and cell should always be the words: 'my secret is mine, my secret is mine'– words that Francis would also use at some stage to shield the intimacy of his prayer-life.

The genre of 'clothing' in which a deeper meaning was hidden, functioned as a cover: this in the sense of protection and of veiling. All sorts of forms of allegory and speaking in parables belonged to this genre. The symbolism of numbers was a way to denote certain matters in a veiled manner. Bernard of Clairvaux, for example, composed syllable-cryptograms which he hid in, amongst others, one of his sermons on the Song of Solomon. The fact that he did this in a text which is 'undoubtedly one of the most mystic of his writings' says much about the connection between mysticism and concealment.[9] Bernard mentions his conviction that 'the Holy Spirit wished to protect the forms of the mysteries in divine Scripture and not to offer them openly'.[10] Typically mediaeval? We know for a fact that the twentieth-century philosopher Wittgenstein used a secret alphabet to pen his notes on God and ethics.[11]

---

[8] William of Saint Thierry (1075-1148), a friend of Bernard of Clairvaux, had a great influence on the mystic theology of his time. The famous Golden Epistle was written for the Carthusians of Mont-Dieux.

[9] A. Bredero, *Bernhard von Clairvaux im Widerstreit der Historie*. Wiesbaden 1966; 58.

[10] J. Deroy, *Bernardus en Origenes. Enkele opmerkingen over de invloed van Origenes op Sint Bernardus' sermones super Cantica Canticorum*. Haarlem, 1963; 150 ff. A couple of times Bernard worked with the number 99, in Roman numerals IC, to denote *Iesus Christus*. Into one text he wove the name *Claraevallis*, the Latin name for Clairvaux.

[11] 'All that really matters in life is precisely what we must be silent about.'(Wittgenstein). Quoted by Damien Isabell O.F.M., 'The "Virtues" in

Could Francis, who considered himself to be illiterate, have also used a similar secret language which could only be deciphered after the necessary sleuthing? The answer to this question depends on the image one has of him as a person and a poet. If the romantic image of him as being an inspired extravert and freely associating writer figures most prominently, then the answer must be no. Recent research has however demonstrated that he composed some of his writings extremely carefully.[12] Moreover, the testimonies of his biographers concerning his penchant for secrecy, especially as to his prayer-life, are very clear on the matter.

One can be very sure of the fact that Francis was so affected by the vision that he had on Mount La Verna two years before his death, that what Nolthenius remarks upon in her book, must have applied to him: 'Whoever is authentically inspired by the urge to create, cannot remain silent about what has touched him, even out of humility.'[13] We do not, however, share her opinion that he – apart from the Praises of God which he wrote after having received the stigmata and apart from the Canticle of the Creatures – did not leave behind anything regarding his mystical experiences. As far as we know, he indeed did not do this in the form

Admonition XXVII of the Writings of Francis of Assisi and their Usefulness in Spiritual Discernment.' In: *The Cord, A Franciscan Spiritual Review*, 38 (1988); 35-57; 52; compare Emily Dickinson's poem: 'Embarrassment of one another / And God / Is Revelation's limit / Aloud / Is nothing that is chief, / But still, / Divinity dwells under seal.'

[12] Compare e.g.: Leonhard Lehmann, *Tiefe und Weite*; passim.

[13] Hélène Nolthenius, *Un uomo dalla valle di Spoleto*; 369; Ib. Kurt Ruh is also of the opinion that Francis offers "keine gewortete, sondern gelebte Mystik": 'Zur Grundlegung einer Geschichte der franziskanischen Mystik'. In: *Vita Seraphica, Anregungen und Mitteilungen aus der Sächsischen Franziskanerprovinz vom Heiligen Kreuz*. (Hrsg. vom Provinzialat Werl); 61 (1980) Heft 1/2, 3; Kurt Ruh, *Geschichte der abendländische Mystik. Band II: Frauenmystik und franziskanische Mystik der Frühzeit*. München, 1993; 380: 'Francis... never saw himself as a mystic. Indeed, he never speaks about his inner life'. In an important and convincing study on Francis' mysticism, Oktavian Schmucki does justice to some of the writings which bear witness to this dimension of his life. In: 'Mysticism of St. Francis in the Light of His Writings'. In: *Greyfriars Review* 3:3 (1989); 241-268.

of a direct autobiographical missive. He did do so, however, by way of encryptions in the form of veiled writings which could be decoded. The task which he saw for himself, was to, on the one hand, do justice to the awe and respect which were due, and on the other to communicate what had been entrusted to him for the benefit of others. He fulfilled this task by concealing his vision using well-known genres – amongst others, as we shall see, the genre of drawing a contrast between virtues and vices.

In some of his writings, like in a palimpsest – parchment on which another earlier-written text can be discerned – Francis let a deeper meaning shine through by using number-symbolism and by discretely referring to biblical and liturgical texts.[14] The sometimes striking position of the vowels *A* and *O* and the weaving in of Christogrammes completed this game of concealment and revelation, as if again and again he was trying to communicate for Whom and with Whom he desired to live. In Chapters 6 and 7 we will follow this game more closely.

The purpose of this book

Our choice to mostly concentrate on Francis' own writings has its limitations. The colourful stories which his contemporaries told about him are undoubtedly important as to what kind of a man he was and they demonstrate how he was part of, yet at the same time transcended his own era. The best gateway to what he cared about most lies however in the careful reading of his own texts. For a large part, these are about being with God, Who revealed himself pre-eminently in Jesus Christ and in his lowliest brothers and sisters. The qualitative difference between the biographies and what he wrote down himself or dictated is therefore important to us. By taking the fruits of his meditations seriously, we can best

---

[14] Edith van den Goorbergh and Theodore Zweerman, *Respectfully Yours: Signed and Sealed, Francis of Assisi. Aspects of His Authorship and Focuses of His Spirituality.* The Franciscan Institute, St. Bonaventure, NY, 2001 (= *Respectfully Yours*), compare 'Appendix: The Symbolism of Numbers'; 397 ff.

discover the spirituality of this seeker of God. This does not mean that we will not take the biographies into consideration. Instructive as they are, they are of incomparable value to us.

In view of all this, it is an important discovery that the interpretation of one text sheds light upon the interpretation of a second. In the words of Pascal: 'All this evidence is self-supporting. If one thing is true, then it follows that the rest is as well.' [15] Mutual comparison usually confirms our expositions of Francis' texts.

In this book we will make use of two of our earlier studies: *Light Shining through a Veil. On Saint Clare's Letters to Saint Agnes of Prague* and: *Respectfully Yours: Signed and Sealed: Francis of Assisi. Aspects of his Authorship and Focuses of his Spirituality.* In these works we pay much attention to the structure of both their writings and in doing so, have discovered a key to a deeper-lying layer of meaning in them. The exact sleuthing we did then, we will however not repeat once again in this new book. We have also left out most of the footnotes we previously added in order to support our research. This, however, does not in the least mean that this new book is a mere summary of our major studies concerning Francis and Clare. We have sometimes given our remarks on texts which we did not take into account in *Respectfully Yours*. On the other hand, in this new book, we have left out texts to which we gave much attention in the former – for example A Salutation of Virtues and the central part of the Later Rule. The two Chapters in *Respectfully Yours*, which form an exposition of the texts in which Francis divulges what his vision on Mount La Verna meant to him, we have included in a general way – simplified and rewritten. We have done this in view of the fact that it is in these very writings that Francis presents himself as a seeker of God. This is after all how we wish to present him: a mystic marked by an encounter with his crucified and risen Lord.

---

[15] Blaise Pascal, *Oeuvres Complètes*. Paris, 1963: from 'Pensée Inédité XV; 640. John Henry Newman also employed this method of convergence in connection with pointers towards the credibility of truths of faith.

Insights which we developed after the publication of *Respectful-ly Yours* have also been included. More than in that book, we have now given attention to the question as to how Francis' texts can shed light onto what is of importance in our own times. This is one of the reasons why we have tried to avoid academic language and to argue in an as uncomplicated a manner as possible. Who-ever desires more clarity as to certain issues, can consult the above-mentioned studies.

To take a leap: a thought-experiment

So we wish to listen to Francis' own words. Is it however possible to take the leap from his way of thinking to ours? Of course we cannot avoid giving our own interpretation to his thoughts. Nev-ertheless, if we want to view the challenges of our times in his spirit, the question presents itself as to which of his texts we should especially consider. An experiment in thinking is called for.

Suppose that Francis should walk in on a group of readers. What would he say? One doesn't have to be an expert on Francis to be certain of the fact that his first words would be: 'May the Lord give you peace!' And then? After that he would most proba-bly say: 'Have you gone completely mad wasting so much time on me? I was and still am nothing more than a 'window' onto Jesus Christ. It is all about Him. For mercy's sake listen to Him! I once wrote down very clearly: He is 'all our riches, that is enough' (the Praises of God). And we would then say: 'Yes, brother Francis, but the way in which you and your faith in Jesus Christ reacted to the movements and convolutions in the society of your times has much to offer us here and now. For we are also living in times in which much is slipping away. Your way of dealing with things made you a prophet, not only then, but also now.'

And we – our thought-experiment is now running its own course – can hear Francis say; 'Listen then to my last words: to my Testament, to the Canticle of the Creatures, the Canticle of Exhortation and to my Admonitions. Be quite sure of the fact that I did not give a theoretical vision for a better society in my

Testament, but rather that in it I briefly and forcefully described a very profound encounter. And that in the Admonitions I unmasked many a religious illusion. In the Canticle of the Creatures which you still sing, I sang about what I believe is most important in our lives. And if that were not enough, then I will tell you what it says in the Earlier Rule, namely that the "brothers come together, wherever they want to, to discuss matters concerning God" (Chapter 18,1). That is what it was all about. Or if you want to hear it all in other words, then read my Psalm XIV from the Office of the Passion, written for during the Advent and which renders my dream about the future of mankind. In the middle it says: "Seek God and your soul will live". Isn't that meant for all times? Or did you think that you privileged people in the twenty-first century were an exception? You certainly have a high opinion of yourself! Alright, I admit it. In a certain way your position, anno 2007, is very special. You rich and powerful people live at the centre of a world which has become a village: at the centre and at the top. Just like the rich in Assisi in my times. That is why I have one more piece of advice for you: read my Letter to the Rulers of the Peoples. For that is what you are: rulers of the peoples in your own surroundings.'

You would become very quiet if you were to let such an experiment work on you. It is a pity that it does remain silent and that it only remains a mere experiment. But the clear, melodious voice of Francis still echoes in that charged silence – a silence which, here on earth, you will not very often become aware of.

1. Francis' Gospel-inspired message

Francis had only just begun to radically follow Christ, when he presented himself before the bishop of Assisi, who said to him: 'It seems to me that you lead a very rough and hard life, not having or possessing anything in this world.' The Saint of God replied: 'Lord, if we had any possessions, we would need arms to protect them with because they cause many disputes and lawsuits. And possessions usually impede the love of God and neighbour. Therefore we do not want to possess anything in this world.'[1] The bishop had used the words 'hard and rough' which very literally evoke the idea of unprotected bare skin. Isn't this how we humans are created?! And doesn't Francis' life-style amount to showing that living without possessions is very much like living without protection? Francis' answer takes the form of a disarming counter-question: may we protect ourselves at the cost of the tender skin of others?

The famous meeting to discuss the Rule, which Francis and his eleven brothers of the first hour had with Pope Innocent III, ran along the same lines. The scene has always appealed to the imagination: at the centre stood the pontiff (one of the great mediaeval popes) and opposite him, the ragged little group with their dishevelled appearance. The words they exchanged were once again meant to caution one another against entertaining any illusions: The pope used almost exactly the same words the bishop had: 'Your life is too hard and severe, if you wish to found a congregation possessing nothing in this world.' When Francis pointed out the importance of having faith in Jesus Christ, the pope in his turn pointed out the fragility of the human condition: 'human nature is weak (*fragilis*) and never remains in the same state. Think about that.'[2]

---

[1] From *The Anonymous of Perugia*, 17, in: *Francis of Assisi: Early Documents. Volume II. The Founder*; 41.

[2] *The Anonymous of Perugia*, 34b, in: *Francis of Assisi: Early Documents. Volume II. The Founder*; 50.

The metaphor of the woman in the desert, with which Francis, a day later, managed to convince the pope to give his permission for the Rule, is an example of clever story-telling. This story about a woman who had conceived many sons by a king, but who had nothing with which to keep them alive, makes a surprising point. To begin with, Francis made it clear that the woman should be able to count on the king who had begotten her sons, to care for them. Next, he indicated himself to be the woman concerned. 'My lord', he said, 'I am that little poor woman whom the loving Lord, in His mercy, has adorned, and through whom He has been pleased to give birth to legitimate sons.'[3] In other words: Francis knew very well that his existence was fragile and precarious. However, he assessed the consequences of his vulnerability in a different way to which the pope did so. What usually leads to constraint or even to sealing oneself completely off, led in his case to a daring invocation of God's caring proximity. The recognition of his own need induced led him to take a great leap; a leap of faith in God.

The fact that the pope was convinced also – so the story goes – had to do with a dream he himself had had. In it, he had seen a small man supporting the Basilica of Saint John Lateran in Rom upon his shoulder. He recognised Francis to be the supporting figure.

What happened during this meeting – or if you will, confrontation – with the pope set the tone for what Francis and his brothers set out to undertake. Convincing the pope also meant that they had received permission to preach about what inspired them while travelling the road through town and country-side. Although they had not studied theology, the pope had nevertheless given his blessing for them to go ahead.

How did he preach?

There are only a few textual witnesses concerning Francis' manner of preaching. These demonstrate that he also did this is his very

---

[3] *Legend of Three Companions*, 51, in: *Francis of Assisi: Early Documents. Volume II. The Founder*; 97 f.

own way. Thomas of Split, who listened to him as a young man in Bologna in 1222 tells us:

> 'In the same year (1222) on the feast of the Assumption of the Mother of God, when I was residing at the Studium in Bologna, I saw Saint Francis preaching in the square in front of the town hall, where almost all the inhabitants of the city had assembled. The theme of his sermon was: "Angels, People, Demons." He spoke so well and so clearly about these three kinds of rational creatures that this unlettered man's sermon became the source of not a little amazement for the many educated people who were present. He did not, however, hold to the usual manner of preaching, but spoke like a political orator." The whole tenor of his words concerned itself with abolishing hostilities and renewing agreements of peace. His habit was filthy, his whole appearance contemptible, and his face unattractive; but God gave his words such efficacy that many factions of the nobility, among whom the monstrous madness of long-standing enmities had raged uncontrollably with much bloodshed, were led to negotiate peace. There was such great popular reverence and devotion towards him, that a mob of men and women crowded in upon him, jostling about either to touch the fringe of his habit or even tear off a shred of his ragged clothing.'[4]

It was not in one of Bologna's churches that he addressed the crowd, but rather in the central square of the town. And he did so very frankly. The fact that he, not only then and there, constantly sought to bring peace wherever he was, is very well expressed by the image of him that is kept in Subiaco (a Benedictine abbey in central Italy). On it he can be seen with one hand over his heart and in his other hand he is holding the text 'peace to this house'. It is as if the artist wished to convey that, according to Francis, one can only bring peace if one has peace within oneself. It was as a bringer of peace that he wished to be a disciple of Christ. He requested that the way he desired to greet people be recorded in his Testament: 'The Lord has revealed a greeting to me; we must say: "may the Lord give you peace".'

---

[4] In: *Francis of Assisi: Early Documents. Volume II. The Founder*; 808.

What did he preach?

What did Francis and his brothers have to say? The answer is clearly given in Chapter 21 of the Earlier Rule:

1. Whenever it pleases them, all my brothers can announce this or similar exhortation and praise among all peoples with the blessing of God:
2. Fear and honour, praise and bless, give thanks and adore the Lord God Almighty in Trinity and in Unity, Father, Son, and Holy Spirit, the Creator of all.
3. Do penance, performing worthy fruits of penance because we shall soon die.
4. Give and it will be given to you.
5. Forgive and you shall be forgiven.
6. If you do not forgive people their sins, the Lord will not forgive you yours. Confess all your sins.
7. Blessed are those who die in penance, for they shall be in the kingdom of heaven.
8. Woe to those who do not die in penance, for they shall be children of the devil whose works they do and they shall go into everlasting fire.
9. Beware of and abstain from every evil and persevere in good till the end.[5]

Did throngs of people come to hear Francis tell them *this*: that they should fear God and especially do penance? If the people of his day and age may have done this – that is to say if they did so at all – should we not at least ascertain that this kind of language sounds very strange to us? How do we deal with concepts such as: 'praise' and 'penance'? We have many things on our mind other than exclaiming 'alleluia' in an exalted fashion. And 'to do penance' evokes all sorts of forms of self-chastisement which modern individuals are not waiting for.

---

[5] *Francis of Assisi: Early Documents. Volume I. The Saint.* Edited by Regis J. Armstrong, O.F.M. Cap., J.A. Wayne Hellmann, O.F.M. Conv., William J. Short, O.F.M., New York – London – Manila, 1999;78.

If anywhere, then it is here that we should put aside all sorts of associations we have as far as these concepts are concerned. On the other hand, it may be good to realise that Francis often proclaimed things that put one's hackles up – then as well as now. As popular as he was in his final years – and still is with many – he did not hesitate to speak very frankly on all sorts of issues, agreeable or not; especially about things that mattered greatly to him.

A snapshot?

Was this piece from the Rule perhaps not something rather like a snapshot, taken whilst Francis happened to be chastising his audience? The answer has to be that nowhere does the Rule give us such snapshots. This is already evident from the history of the development of this 'manual' for the communal life of the brothers. The young community had soon felt in need of a communal 'manual' for their way of life. Their shared experiences were extensively discussed during their annual gatherings and were integrated into the Rule, chapter for chapter. This all took place very gradually: once something had been tried out sufficiently or when new issues arose, things were agreed upon. From the very beginning, the Gospels had served as a point of orientation for the inspiration of the community. Here, their initial enthusiasm received a basis which managed to direct their spontaneous way of life. In short: Francis and his followers read the Gospels from the point of view of those who have no possessions. And their life-style of possessing nothing was illuminated by what they read or heard about the life of Jesus and his apostles.

This was also true concerning the brothers' wish to proclaim and bear witness to the Gospel. 'All my brothers' – here Francis himself is clearly speaking – 'may do this whenever they feel it is appropriate.' Clearly more than enough room for spontaneity. Still, at the same time he gives directions for what they should say.

As old-fashioned as this programme for giving sermons – for this is what Chapter 21 from the Earlier Rule must be called – may seem, as far as Francis was concerned it was definitely not a casual summary which could just as well have looked completely different. This is not only evident from the development of the Rule as the condensed experience of the young community, but also from the remarkable fact that it can be demonstrated that this sermon-programme formed the basis for many a text by Francis, for example the Canticle of the Creatures, the well-known song in which he once again summarised what had inspired him during his life. One could therefore also call it a *sermon-in-song*.

A summons to praise God and to repent

It is important to discover what exactly is set out in Francis' sermon-programme, which can be found in Chapter 21 of the Earlier Rule. What did these concepts of 'praise' and 'penance' evoke for Francis. Had he perhaps taken these concepts from Jesus? Only once these questions have been answered, may we pose the question as to the validity of our possible estrangement from and aversion to these two concepts.

Would it not be much stranger if something that was of such importance to someone eight hundred years ago were *not* to cause some degree of estrangement here and now? The deep chasm between his world and his views and ours is evident. During the last three centuries the world has continued to change in an ever increasing tempo. Especially new is the self-conscious intervention by the individual who, aided by the increasingly refined and specialised sciences, actively attunes his life to what he considers to be of value. Have 'praise' and 'penance' therefore become things of the past?

To gain insight into these issues, it is a good idea to investigate the structure of the cited Chapter 21 of the Earlier Rule. It contains:

1) a call *to recognize God*. This recognition fans out into six types of homage (verses 1 and 2);

2) a call *to do penance*. This call is also made concrete in a series of admonitions which are almost all derived from the New Testament (verses 3-9).

The fact that this two-fold division is based on Scripture is obvious. Which texts containing such a division come to mind? There are various possibilities. What about the way in which angels praise God after the birth of Jesus? 'Glory to God in the highest heaven, and on earth peace among those whom he favours!' (Luke 2:14). Or the double commandment: 'Love God and your neighbour as yourself' (compare Matthew 22:37-39).

These two-fold divisions certainly resonate in the sermon-programme. However, we believe that there is a text from the Bible which comes even closer to the critical words found in Francis' programme: Jesus' call – his first words in the Gospel according to Mark: 'Repent, and believe (have faith) in the good news.' The words 'repent' and 'have faith', however, are not to be found in Francis' sermon-programme. How did we then form the idea that this initial call by Jesus lies at the base of his sermon-programme? Taking a look at his Testament would be helpful.

Penance

It is very significant that 'penance' is the word with which Francis begins his Testament. By using it, he is doing nothing else than summarizing his whole life as a man who has converted to Christ. In this Last Will, he wished to leave behind a lasting memento to the original charisma of the brotherhood[6], probably because it was suffering from a certain bourgeois-attitude. Or had the 'trap of success' become an issue? For by now the brotherhood of beggars had become a large and respected order. The beginning of the Testament runs as follows:

1. The Lord gave me, Brother Francis, thus to begin doing penance in this way: for when I was in sin, it seemed too bitter for me to see lepers.
2. And the Lord Himself led me among them, and I showed mercy to them.

[6] Compare Gerard Pieter Freeman and Hans Sevenhoven, 'The Legacy of a Poor Man. Commentary on the Testament of Francis of Assisi. I-V'. In: *Franciscan Digest* 3 (1993); 1-18; 80-98; 4 (1994); 34-63; 63-83; 6 (1996); 1-26.

3. And when I left them, what had seemed bitter to me was turned into sweetness of soul and body. And afterwards I delayed a little and left the world.

4. And the Lord gave me such faith in churches that I would pray with simplicity in this way and say:

5. "We adore You, Lord Jesus Christ, in all Your churches throughout the whole world, and we bless You, because by Your holy cross You have redeemed the world."

6. Afterwards the Lord gave me, and gives me still such great faith in priests, who live according to the rite of the holy Roman Church, because of their orders, that, were they to persecute me, I would still to have recourse to them.

7. And if I had as much wisdom as Solomon and found impoverished priests of this world, I would not preach in their parishes against their will.

8. And I desire to respect, love, and honour them and all others as my lords.

9. And I do not want to consider any sin in them, because I discern the Son of God in them and they are my lords.

10. And I act in this way because, in this world, I see nothing corporally of the most high Son of God except His most holy Body and Blood which they receive and they alone administer to others.

11. I want to have these most holy mysteries honoured and venerated above all things and to reserve them in precious places.

12. Wherever I find our Lord's most holy names and written words in unbecoming places, I want to gather them up, and I beg that they be gathered up and placed in a becoming place.

13. And we must honor all theologians and those who minister the most holy divine words and respect them as those who minister to us spirit and life.

14. And after the Lord gave me some brothers, no one showed me what I had to do, but the Most High Himself revealed to me that I should live according to the pattern of the Holy Gospel.[7]

---

[7] *Francis of Assisi: Early Documents. Volume I. The Saint*; 124-125.

In no way does this retrospection look anything like a 'final statement' in which the basic principles of the new way of life were
theoretically to be set out. 'Theory', in the sense of what is able to
be abstractly stated, was foreign to Francis. Here he is relating primary experiences. To begin with, what the original experience of
his life with God had been: the encounter with lepers. They were
society's outcasts in those days. And suddenly, in the midst of his
search for a meaningful life, Francis had stood face to face with one
of these horribly diseased people who had always repulsed him. He
could no longer run away. His biographer narrates: 'Francis made
himself dismount, and give him a coin, kissing his hand as he did
so. After he accepted a kiss of peace from him, Francis remounted
and continued his way.'[8]

By not running away and by staying with the leper, the merchant's son drastically limited his own options. At the same time
however, this limitation meant an enormous breakthrough: by
embracing the leper, Francis broke through the bonds of how 'one'
should act and what 'one' should think. Through the restriction of
his own freedoms and habits, he grew as a person. From then on
the recognition of the boundaries between people meant for him:
seeing this individual here and now and doing justice to that del-
icate skin, that 'boundary' which above all other boundaries
demands respect – also and especially when that skin is so disfigured.

'Leaving the world behind'

This is how Francis summarized the conclusion he had drawn from
his decisive encounter. He withdrew from the 'world' which up
until then had been the measure and norm for his life. This world,
which put money, power and fame first, he had found to be very
much wanting. His new 'measure' would be his deprived brothers
and sisters. He had discovered a way of mutual interaction, in

---

[8] *The Legend of Three Companions*, 11. In: *Francis of Assisi: Early Documents.
Volume II. The Founder*; 74.

which God's mercy is the supportive power. His yearning for more riches, power and fame had lost the struggle against a different kind of 'interest' (from *inter esse*: Latin for 'to be amongst') – literally, a different kind of 'amongst-ness' – namely to be amongst those on the margins of society.

'Penance' is the word Francis used to denote this profound change of interest. From then on, he and his brothers called themselves 'penitents' (*poenitentes*) from Assisi. This name did not only refer to an inner disposition, but also to a group, recognisable to wider society. Interior and exterior therefore corresponded to one another. They chose this word because, for a long time, it had been used by those wishing to lead a life inspired by the Gospel. The word 'penance' was known from the Latin translation of Mark 1:15. There, the conversion which Jesus called for, is designated by the word *poenitentia* (penance). Penance therefore meant: the rejection of a substandard existence and embracing the space of God-with-us. Apart from 'moderation' and 'abstinence', it also meant the liberation from an oppressive existence. Or in other words, penance also meant 'to repair'.

For Francis and his brothers, doing penance meant nothing else than turning completely inside-out and upside-down. The endless urge to possess more and more made way for the desire to 'return' or 'give back' to God what belongs to Him. They translated this 'giving back' into concrete deeds by doing justice to the victims of the injustice of their times. For them, personal repentance and social engagement – heart and hand – belonged together.

In the shifts that took place in Francis' penance or conversion, we can discern three discoveries having to do with existential limitations or boundaries:

- The recognition of every individual as a restricted and demarcated being as well as the confirmation that this demarcation is part of the very essence of our being, created as we are as 'skin-creatures' – bestown with an outer skin and membranes: a retina and eardrums. This is not a condition which we regretfully have to take into the bargain; on the contrary: this is the way we are able to communicate with others.

- A precondition for respecting the boundaries of the other is that I must learn to lay myself open and to let my own heart be touched. The recognition of the other's vulnerability demands the recognition and experience of my own vulnerability.
- The recognition of the other also demands that I make room for the sensitivity of the other within the sensitivity I have for the maintenance of my own position. This can only take place if I totally and seriously consider the other and myself as able to be touched.

In view of this it becomes clear what Francis and his brothers meant with their call to repent: they indeed meant 'to turn the world upside-down'.[9] For them this involved the *reparation* of whatever has gone wrong or has been purposely bungled; it involved the reparation of the indifference and lack of compassion, the ugly consequences of which they saw around them. One may ask whether such a summons – clearly an echo of Jesus' own call for repentance and vigilance – is not also directed at those who, in our own times, have let themselves be carried away on the flood of boundless individualism.

Having faith

Every word and every cross-reference in the subsequent parts of Francis' Testament also count. To start with: the way to pray in verse 5. This prayer to Christ, who brought salvation through His holy cross, was a matter of 'faith' for him. He states so explicitly: 'such' faith (verse 4); just as further on he also emphatically speaks of the 'great' faith he has received in the church's priests (verse 6). It is as if he wished to emphasize: I realise that it is far from self-evident to have faith in the liberating power which an ignominious death on a cross is supposed to give; just as hard as it is to summon up faith in ministers of the church who aren't really capable. And even so, in both cases Francis wishes to state his own 'even so'.

---

[9] Compare Koo van der Wal, *Die Umkehrung der Welt. Über den Verlust von Umwelt, Gemeinschaft und Sinn.* Würzburg, 2004.

The fact that he subsequently used so many words discussing the church must have had to do with his experience that some brothers did not tend to treat the all too human church with respect. Taking stock of the entire opening of the Testament, it is noticeable that the first part (up to verse 4) is concerned with the theme of penance, and that verses 4 to 14 deal with faith or trust. Why is it, that exactly this word 'faith' has such a prominent place here? For the answer to this, we must once again go back to Mark 1:15 and to the call with which Jesus began his preaching: 'The time is fulfilled, and the kingdom of God has come near; repent, and believe (have faith) in the good news.'

Also in Jesus' words – the initial words of Francis' Testament repeat Him – God's initiative is mentioned before anything else: 'The kingdom of God has come near.' This is followed by his invitation, not only to repent, but to have faith in the Good News as well.

What seems to be a real possibility here, namely that Francis in drawing up his Testament based himself on Jesus' call to do penance and to have faith, becomes a certainty once the fact has been established that these two concepts determine the structure of his great prayer of thanks in Chapter 23 of the Earlier Rule. This is important: as far as Francis was concerned, it was apparently entirely normal to give penance a central place in a prayer of praise and thanks.[10]

Faith as praise

Let us have another look at the sermon-programme from the Earlier Rule. The fact that 'penance' has such a central place in it can be made clear via the Testament. The same goes for the fact that as far as Francis was concerned, 'doing penance' was primarily

---

[10] Leonhard Lehmann, '<Gratias agimus tibi>. Structure and Content of Chapter XXIII of the Regula non Bullata.' In: *Laurentianum* (1982); 312-375. (Also: '<We thank You>: The Structure and Content of Chapter 23 of the *Earler Rule*.' In: *Greyfriars Review* 5:1 (1991); 1-54, compare 'the target sentence'.

expressed in 'doing works of mercy'. However, is it useful to link praise, which is called for by the sermon-programme, to faith, which is given so much attention in the opening of the Testament?

In order to obtain an answer to this, let us listen to the ample intermezzo between the description of Francis' decision to withdraw from society (Testament verse 3) and his statement concerning the coming of the first bothers. How does he raise the subject of faith which he emphasises so much, in these verses 4 to 13 of the Testament? In Chapter 21 of the Earlier Rule it appears that the word 'faith' has sort of been 'translated' into different words, all of which concern the theme 'praise' and 'honour'. Four of these verbs also appear in the summons with which the sermon-programme opens, namely 'to worship, to bless, to fear and to honour' (Earlier Rule, verse 2), translated in the Testament as 'to adore, to bless' (verse 5), 'to respect' (to be in awe of) and 'to honour' (verse 8).

The act of having faith or 'trusting' in God was evidently, according to Francis, especially expressed in acts of praise: for him having faith especially came down to praising and doing homage. In this way he tried to prove his faithfulness to his Lord. It was exactly as a believer (as someone having faith), that he was concerned with acts of respectful recognition and gratitude.[11]

Of the many riches of this way of viewing the act of having faith, we will only mention the following:

• As far as Francis is concerned, having faith is above all the experience of having a personal relationship: a completely dynamic relationship, entirely directed toward the Other, who has touched one's heart and who still remains the Future One. Francis was centuries ahead of the narrow conception of faith being the acceptance of truths on the authority of another. As far as

---

[11] The concurrence of 'faith' and 'praise' (believing and glorifying) makes one think (and sing), especially when considering what the Gospel of Luke says about Jesus' mother. Immediately after Elisabeth tells her she is blessed because of her faith, she sings this faith out in a hymn of praise (the *Magnificat*), compare Luke 1:45 ff.

this is concerned, he stood in the biblical tradition. As a child of his time, he adhered to the self-evident faithfulness and homage of a vassal to his lord.

- His need to express what moved him inwardly can also be seen here. Francis was in this way a 'confessor' who – as is expressed by the Latin *confiteri* – made the confession of guilt and the profession of faith and praise a (public) act of worship.

- Francis was also a talented poet and singer of songs of praise, who at a young age had discovered his vocation to glorify. This is also expressed in his going out, again and again, to rouse to worship and to the service of their brothers and sisters whoever wanted to hear so – which is what the Earlier Rule that we are discussing here is all about. What Augustine repeats as a refrain in one of his greatest sermons, characterizes the way Francis wished to serve: *canta et ambula*, 'sing and walk on'.[12]

As a man of esteem, Francis stands in his manner of having faith far removed from all the endless disputes, in which – in antiquity as well as modernity – knowing and having faith, or having faith and working were seen as placed in contraposition. This does not mean that the awe Francis had for the mystery of God and the other were not marked by darkness and toil. The history of the development of the Canticle of the Creatures demonstrates that 'profession of faith' and 'suffering' were sometimes, for him, made of the same stuff. Every act of genuine faith – also for Francis – must sooner or later be fought for and must overcome the fear which is rooted in our experience of mortality and guilt. And even so: in spite of everything, praise and thanks can also be the 'yes' – the answer – to the Word of faithfulness which God has already given. By virtue of His unmistakable promise, a person may bear witness to the light that he has been touched by and remain searching for the full light. 'Sing and walk on'.

It may be true that perceiving a flash of light gives a special sense of joy, but sometimes this joy must be purified into 'true joy'.

---

[12] Sermo 256; *PL* 38, 1191-1193. In Augustine's *Confessiones*, 'confession of sin', 'profession of faith' and 'crying out in praise' resound in unison.

The story that Francis told about the improbable joy he felt when he was rejected in the cold and dark – by brothers from whom he would have expected otherwise – is one of the texts which characterize him most strongly.[13]

What does praising mean?

For Francis, having faith is expressed by praising. However, what on earth is someone from our times supposed to do with praising? Are we able to empathise with something that was so self-evident in other cultures?

However, firstly the following: the praying Francis addressed God before all as the *Good* God. He was, it is true, certainly touched by what is beautiful – in the Canticle of the Creatures for example, he uses the word 'beautiful' (*bello*) three times and always in connection with light (of the sun, the moon, the stars and fire). However being touched by God's goodness appears to have had the upper hand. This goodness and mercy seem to be at the centre of his will to recognize God through praising Him.

What effect does something which touches us as being very good or very beautiful have on us? We are often at a loss and 'can't find the words to describe it'. Held in awe as we are, we must release the hold which we spontaneously thought we had on the object of our amazement. For a moment it may then seem as if we can make do with the admittance of our inability to speak, but very soon we discover that this silence is – must be – the precursor of that which we cannot keep from saying or singing out loud. Our voice has then received a special timbre, that of the sigh: 'Oh, how beautiful!' Being touched by something very beautiful or good means that in some way we are wounded by this something that is so different from anything else; this something which touches our sensitivity. However, amazing as it seems, the emergence of this wound is simultaneously the release of our praise. The feeling of unworthiness in praising something so beautiful and good is accompanied

---

[13] See Chapter 5: True Joy.

by the realisation that this unworthiness is already in itself the insti-
gation of our praise. And at the same time there is the certainty that
in this case our praise is never really sufficient. Our joy about what
is so ravishing is mixed with the pain of never being able to sing
its praises adequately. We, who at first thought we could sing its
praise, realize that we will never be able to give it pure praise. For
it always remains impossible to really sing out completely and
utterly.

Even so, it is exactly in this poignant deficiency that the possibility of giving the utmost praise lies. Our effort to increase our
recognition to the same level as that which touches us so very much
– this effort we can give up. Our embarrassment towards what
transcends us – the embarrassment concerning our powerlessness
– can become a sacrifice of meekness. And this meekness has the
power to turn our inability to give into a gift itself. Again and again
we can leave behind our efforts to completely do justice to what is
worthy of praise. It is exactly as we are, with all our shortcomings
that we can sing out our praise. The deficiency of our praise and
our unworthiness to sing out our praise is sung away. It is true that
our embarrassment and duality remain, but what also remains is
the beautiful adventure of the passionate recognition of what is
amazingly of a different order. The sigh concerning our powerlessness and the praise of the truly good and beautiful are harmonised. In giving, human inability can become human praise.

Giving back

In some texts Francis summarises the six-fold homage to which
the sermon-programme of the Earlier Rule summons the world, in
two little words: giving back – for example in the conclusion of
Chapter 17 of the Earlier Rule. In it, the giving back of what is
'good to the Lord, the most high and sublime God' proceeds seamlessly into 'giving back all honour and homage, all praise and blessing, all thanks and glory'. The echo of the sermon-programme can
clearly be heard here. After a closer look, it appears that the two
words 'giving back' form one of the keys to Francis' spirituality.

2. The Canticle of the Creatures

Francis' Canticle of the Creatures is the most well-known of his texts. It could be called the musical expression of Francis' attitude towards life: one last time he sang out what had inspired him most profoundly. He let his brothers sing it over and over again as an encouraging 'farewell' during his final days. It has its own special place in world-literature, is still sung to this day and is loved by many.

1. *Altissimu onnipotente bon signore,*
   tue so le laude, la gloria e l'honore et onne benedictione.
   1. Most High, all-powerful, good Lord,
      Yours are the praises, the glory, and the honour, and all blessing,
2. *Ad te solo, altissiomo, se konfano,*
   et nullu homo ene dignu te mentovare.
   2. To You alone, Most High, do they belong,
      and no human is worthy to mention Your name.
3. *Laudato sie, mi signore, cun tucte le tue creature,*
   spetialmente messor lo frate sole,
   lo qual'è iorno, et allumini noi per loi.
   3. Praised be You, my Lord, with all Your creatures,
      especially Sir Brother Sun,
      who is the day and through whom You give us light.
4. *Et ellu è bellu e radiante cun grande splendore,*
   de te, altissimo, porta significatione.
   4. And he is beautiful and radiant with great splendor;
      and bears a likeness of You, Most High One.
5. *Laudato si, mi signore, per sora luna e le stelle,*
   in celu l'ài formate clarite et pretiose et belle.
   5. Praised be You, my Lord, through Sister Moon and the stars,
      in heaven You formed them clear and precious and beautiful.

6. *Laudato si, mi signore, per frate vento,*
    et per aere et nubilo et sereno et onne tempo,
    per lo quale e le tue creature dai sustentamento.

    6.   Praised be You, my Lord, through Brother Wind,
          and through the air, cloudy and serene, and every kind of
          weather,
          through whom You give sustenance to Your creatures.

7. *Laudati si, mi signore, per sor aqua,*
    la quale è multo utile et humile et pretiosa et casta.

    7.   Praised be You, my Lord, through Sister Water,
          who is very useful and humble and precious and chaste.

8. *Laudato si, mi signore, per frate focu,*
    per lo quale enn'allumini la nocte,
    ed ello è bello et iocundo et robustoso et forte.

    8.   Praised be You, my Lord, through Brother Fire,
          through whom You light the night,
          and he is beautiful and playful and robust and strong.

9. *Laudato si, mi signore, per sora nostra matre terra,*
    la quale ne sustena et governa,
    et produce diversi fructi con coloriti flori et herba.

    9.   Praised be You, my Lord, through our Sister Mother Earth,
          who sustains and governs us,
          and who produces various fruit with colored flowers and herbs.

10. *Laudato si, mi signore, per quelli ke perdonano per lo tuo amore,*
    et sostengo infirmitate et tribulatione.

    10.   Praised be You, my Lord, through those who give pardon for
          Your love,
          and bear infirmity and tribulation.

11. *Beati quelli ke 'l sosterrano in pace,*
    ka da te, altissimo, sirano incoronati.

    11.   Blessed are those who endure in peace
          for by You, Most High, shall they be crowned.

12. *Laudato si, mi signore, per sora nostra morte corporale,*
    da la quale nullu homo vivente po' skappare.

    12.   Praised be You, my Lord, through our Sister Bodily Death,
          from whom no one living can escape.

13. *Guai a quelli, ke morrano ne le peccata mortali:*
      beati quelli ke troverà ne le tue sanctissime voluntati,
      ka la morte secunda nol farrà male.

    13. Woe to those who die in mortal sin:
          blessed are those whom death will find in Your most holy will,
          for the second death shall do them no harm.

14. *Laudate et benedicete mi signore,*
      et rengratiate et serviateli cun grande humilitate.

    14. Praise and bless my Lord and give Him thanks
          and serve Him with great humility.[1]

This song of praise dates from the final year of Francis' life. He was 44 years old at the time. One could call it a summary of the life-wisdom he had gradually acquired. Above all it sings of his solidarity with all creation; a solidarity which is also able to bridge the deepest faultlines – oppression, guilt and death. In it, the poet even recognizes the elements wind, water, fire and earth as his brothers and sisters.

The special place Francis therefore has in the Roman-Catholic tradition, was confirmed when he was proclaimed 'patron of ecologists'. A fashionable and perhaps rather ludicrous feather in the cap of this poor little man? Maybe so. But by doing so, attention was drawn to the radical message given by this gospel-inspired man; not a message calling for the subjection of nature, let alone one calling for reckless exploitation. This way of singing praises was unheard of – disturbing even, just as Francis himself was disturbing for his contemporaries. Because of what was deeply hidden in the simplicity of his person, he managed to surprise over and over again: profoundly modest he could also be exuberant; at the same time he was humble as well as frank.

The importance this song has for the understanding of Francis' spirituality cannot be underestimated. Every serious attempt to clarify its basic structure is therefore worth the effort. One such attempt is Rotzetter's study about the influence of Francis' sermon-programme

---

[1] *Francis of Assisi: Early Documents. Volume I. The Saint*; 113 ff.

on his writings, especially on the Canticle of the Creatures. In it he demonstrates that this Canticle is composed along the lines of this programme and that it should therefore be regarded as a sermon-in-song.[2] The song is of course also the expression of an emotion – but a comparison with some modern ideas on poetry goes no further than this.

How was it conceived?

The Canticle acquires an enigmatic dimension when we consider the circumstances under which Francis composed it. We know from *The Assisi Compilation* how badly off he was at that time, both physically and mentally. He was suffering from various diseases. The extremely painful ailment to his eyes, which he had contracted on his trip to the Holy Land six years previously, especially robbed him of his sleep.

Since September 1224, when he had had his vision of the Crucified One, his hands, feet and side were marked with the wounds of the crucifixion. Even so, during the grim winter of 1225 he had again undertaken a journey in order to preach. After that he was no longer capable of doing so. Unable to bear any light, he was housed in a tiny dwelling made of straw mats, where he lay in the dark. It was swarming with mice which made it extra difficult for him to find any rest. Worst of all was the fact that he was much tried mentally and spiritually. We can assume that these afflictions were exacerbated by his wondering whether he hadn't failed as the leader and inspirer of the evangelical movement he had started – and which was now going other ways than he so desired. After going through fifty days of this, he began to feel sorry for himself.

How on earth did Francis, in the midst of this sorrow and on the edge of despair, end up singing – and singing this radiant song at that? Did hope suddenly flame up? Was he able to reconcile himself to his difficult fate because of this? But how could this

---

[2] Anton Rotzetter, 'Gott in der Verkündigung des Franz von Assisi'. In: *Laurentianum*, 23 (1982); 40-76.

happen? How could someone who was so broken start singing such a clear and melodious song of praise? From what perspective did his feelings reverse themselves and did the darkness brighten up into that radiant light?

We do not cherish the illusion that these questions can be answered conclusively. If a psychological reversal was involved, it remains hidden from us. And this holds especially true for any act of grace which he may have received. Even so, one enigmatic fact remains intriguing: the free urge to create, which even in the deepest embarrassment finds the occasion to sing the praise of God. Perhaps it is this creativity which is so fascinating, because the question as to what 'praise' and 'honour' mean at all, forms a problem for us modern-day people and even embarrasses us. More than is nowadays realized, there is an intrinsic connection between the ability to praise God and the ability to recognise the precariousness of our existence. Can what Francis' contemporaries tell us about the development of the Canticle perhaps clarify something of the concurrence of human deficiency and this praise? We will go into this further on, however firstly we will touch on some characteristic facts.

Division into three parts

The poet's attention moves from above to below: from the heavens (verses 1-5) to the earth (verses 6-9). Viewed in this way, the poem is an echo of what the Bible teaches about the bond between heaven and earth. Concerning the world below, the four elements are remarkably enough portrayed in pairs as male and female. Following upon this portrayal of the skies and the earth (macro-cosmos), the third piece of the song gives an account of the human condition (micro-cosmos) (verses 10 and the following).[3] The final

---

[3] Adolfo Oxilia, *Il Cantico di frate Sole*. Firenze 1984; 13 and Chapter XIII; 131-136. Leonhard Lehmann, *Tiefe und Weite. Der universale Grundzug in den Gebeten des Franziskus von Assisi.* (Franziskanische Forschungen, 29. Heft), Werl-Westfalen, 1984; Chapter 11; 279-324; idem in: *Francis Master of Prayer*. Translated by Paul Van Halderen. Dehli, 1999; 302 ff.

words are 'with great humility': Francis sang this song from the
bottom up – from the basis of existence. He, who had discovered
a new form of solidarity with his fellow-creatures, was able to exalt
everything and everyone with a fundamental respect from this position. 'Praised, be you, my Lord' sounds eight times: six times for
and by the heavenly bodies and the elements; twice for and by
those suffering as well as by 'Sister Bodily Death'.

As jubilant as this all sounds, there still remain some pressing
questions – because this jubilation also integrates sickness, guilt
and death. Why did the singer give these difficult moments in our
human existence such a prominent place in his song of praise? And
is it not strange that he did not even mention Jesus Christ who
meant so very much to him?

His sermon-programme in the Canticle

In his comparison of the Canticle with Francis' sermon-programme, Rotzetter established the fact that five of the six verbs
which denote the praise of God in the sermon-programme, also
occur in the Canticle. In the verses framing the song these are: 'the
praises (…), the honour and all blessing' (verse 1) and again 'praise
and bless and give thanks' (verse 14). Verse 2: 'no human is worthy to mention Your name' expresses what in the sermon-programme was denoted with 'fear' or 'awe'. In a nutshell: the first two
parts of the Canticle (verses 1 to 9) can, together with the refrain-
verse (verse 14), be seen as a rendering of the summons to give
praise from the sermon-programme.

Rotzetter has compared the second part of the sermon-programme, the summons to do penance, with the third part of the
Canticle which focuses on man (verses 10-13). The similarity of
these two texts is striking: the last part of the Canticle conforms
verse for verse to the parts concerning the summons to do penance.
It has to be concluded that the Canticle follows the structure of the
sermon-programme; however it is true that the reference to disease
(*infirmitate*, verse 10), which the sick singer included in the Canticle, is missing from the sermon-programme. The admonition

'persevere till the end' (verse 9 of the sermon-programme in Chapter 21 of the Earlier Rule) does however point in the same direction.

A sermon-programme lying at the base of this purest of poems? Doesn't this observation demean this perfect verse? What is however so skilful, is that this underlying structure – like the Christogramme which is woven into the Canticle and which we shall uncover further on – does not detract from the poetic eloquence of the poem. On the contrary – the poem owes its strength to it.

All the same, there still remains an important difficulty. In the Canticle there is no reference whatsoever to the concepts 'penance' or 'penitence' which are central to the second part of the sermon-programme. Does this weaken our exposition of the Canticle being a typically 'Franciscan' sermon? Or should we adhere to our position and rather pose the question as to what it means that exactly in the places where, according to the sermon-programme, one would expect a reference to 'penance', twice the early Italian word for 'to bear' appears (verses 10 and 11)? We believe that Francis did indeed replace the concept 'penance' with 'to bear'.

This verb to bear (in the Canticle *sostengo*; *sosterano*) has its origins in the Latin word *sustinere* (to bear, to take upon oneself, to persevere). The remarkable use of the verb 'to bear' in the Canticle is not a coincidence. Just as with penance, the attitude which is expressed by to bear is of the greatest importance to Francis. This can be seen in a number of places in his writings. Bearing is nothing less than one of the central concepts of his spirituality. We shall go into this in more detail in Chapter 5 of this book. In this Chapter we shall deal with the significance of the Canticle's emphasis on the bearing of life's difficulties.

Penance as patience

To start with, one can consider the history concerning the conception of this song. When Francis sang it for his brothers he was very ill. Tested to his very limits, his life became a question of all or nothing, sink or swim: he chose to swim. The Canticle's basic plan is, as we have seen, that of the sermon-programme: a sum-mons to give praise connected to a summons to do penance. Here however 'penance' is expressed in 'forgiving' and in the 'bearing in peace' of whatever makes life difficult for us. We have already seen that this summons to give praise is the expression of the faith which is man's answer to God.

The word-pair 'faith and penance' (*fides et poenitentia*) is there-fore expressed by 'praise and bearing' in the Canticle. Although Jesus' summons *to repent* was understood by Francis as a summons to do penance, here he translated 'penance' in a new way as *bear-ing*. The verb to bear is (in Latin) related to the noun patience (*patientia*). One could say that Jesus' summons to 'faith and penance' became a summons to 'faith and patience' (*fides et pati-entia*) for Francis.

Seen in this light it is not surprising that his song shows remark-able similarities to Revelation which deals with the extremes of existence for man and mankind. What it says about the 'last things' must have occupied Francis greatly after September 1224, when he had his vision of Christ and received the stigmata on Mount La Verna. Since then, the sight of his suffering Lord, whose wounds he bore as signs in his own body, must have especially nourished his reflection on one's task to bear.

The Canticle does not however only give direct references to Revelation, namely in verses 1, 11 and 13. There is further una-nimity with this final bible-book: the combination of the concepts faith and patience also appears twice in Revelation. In a testing sit-uation, when it comes to the crunch, it says: 'Here is a call for the endurance and faith of the saints' (*Hic est patientia, et fides sancto-rum*, Revelation 13:10). And a little further on: 'Here is a call for the endurance of the saints, those who keep the commandments of God and hold fast to the faith of Jesus' (*Hic patientia sanctorum est, qui custodiunt mandata Dei, et fidem Jesu*, Revelation 14:12). These words reflect the atmosphere of persecution which the young Christian community was faced with. Patience is the answer to an emergency. The third part of the Canticle, where Francis sings of 'enduring in peace', also echoes this.

A sonnet for Clare and her sisters

Francis' Canticle of Exhortation was rediscovered fairly recently.
This song must have been written during the same period in which
the Canticle of the Creatures was written. The brothers with whom
he was closest tell us:

> 'After he [Francis] composed the Praises of the Lord for his crea-
> tures, he also composed some holy words with chant for the greater
> consolation of the Poor Ladies of the Monastery of San Damiano.
> He did this especially because he knew how much his illness trou-
> bled them. And since he was unable to console and visit them
> personally because of that illness, he wanted those words to be pro-
> claimed to them by his companions.'[4]

This song of consolation goes as follows:

1. *Audite, poverelle, dal Signór[e] vocáte,*
2. *ke de multe parte et provincie séte adunáte:*
3. *Vivate sémpre / en-veritáte,*
4. *ke en obediéntia moriäte.*
   1. Listen, little poor ones called by the Lord,
   2. who have come together from many parts and provinces:
   3. live always in truth,
   4. that you may die in obedience.

5. *Non guardate al la vitá de-fóre,*
6. *ka quella dello spírito / è-miglióre.*
7. *Io ve prégo per-grand'amóre,*
8. *k'aiate discreciöne / / de le lemosene ke ve dà-el Segnór[e].*
   5. Do not look at the life without,
   6. for that of the Spirit is better.
   7. I beg you out of great love,
   8. to use with discernment the alms which the Lord gives you.

---

[4] *The Assisi Compilation 85,* in: *Francis of Assisi: Early Documents. Volume II.
The Founder;* 188.

9. Quelle ke sunt adgravate de ínfirmitáte
10. et l'altre ke per lor[o] s[u]ò adfatigáte.
11. tutte quante lo sostengáte en-páce,
  9. Those weighed down by sickness
  10. and the others wearied because of them,
  11. all of you: bear it in peace,

12. ka multo ve[n]deri[te] cara quésta fa[t]íga,
13. ka cascúna serà-regína / /
14. en celo coronata cum la Vérgene María.
  12. for you will sell this fatigue at a very high price.
  13. and each one will be crowned queen,
  14. in heaven with the Virgin Mary.[5]

Francis probably borrowed the sonnet-form – two strophes of four and two strophes of three lines – from certain ballads by the troubadours of his time. We cannot do justice to the rich contents of this sonnet. Just as in the Canticle, in it we can hear the summons 'to bear' the burden of being nursed 'in peace'. In the last verse there is a reference to Revelation, just as in verse 11 of the Canticle of the Creatures.

Clare's fourth Letter to Agnes of Prague, also written during the final days of her life, contains striking references to Revelation as well. In the last phase of her life, words and images from this final bible-book – a book of sadness as well as of consolation – also welled up in her.

The creatures as brothers and sisters

The personification of the elements wind, water, fire and earth as brothers and sisters is food for thought right up to this very

[5] *The Canticle of Exhortation for the Ladies of San Damiano,* in: *Francis of Assisi: Early Documents. Volume I. The Saint*; 115. As for the sonnet-form which we found in the poem, it originated in Italy in the 13th century, (Macmillans' Encyclopedia).

day. In a unique way, Francis expressed the extreme opposite of
what happened during the twentieth century when millions of
brother and sister human-beings were thoroughly humiliated in
concentration-camps and reduced to raw-materials and fuel.[6] For
the converted Francis, a new relationship with his fellow-creatures had opened up: a relationship of belonging, of respect and
admiration and of supportive partnership. It is striking how pos-
itively the singer describes the elements: nothing about the ter-
ror and destruction which wind, water, fire and earthquakes
sometimes bring about. Apparently he did not wish to give an
objective description from all possible angles. He rather expresses
the frame of mind of someone for whom the destructive forces
– first and foremost in himself – no longer have the final say.
This song echoes a thankful recognition of our earthly and material state of being.

The third part of the Canticle, which deals with man, is sometimes rashly ignored. The Canticle is then turned into a naïve glorification of nature and removes it from the frame-work of the history of God-with-us, in which Francis' life played itself out after
his conversion. His experiences on Mount La Verna had confirmed
what Christ meant to him as the One-Who-Lives-and-Suffers-with-
Us. The Canticle can only be understood as Francis' ballad of life
if in it one can discern how he, lying sick in the darkened hovel
near the cloister of San Damiano, had to wrestle with his physical
and spiritual collapse. And how he had to try to get through this
feeling of abandonment while keeping faith in his Fellow Sufferer
from Whom he had received the stigmata a year before.

Exposition of the human condition

In the third part of the Canticle, Francis talks about forgiveness,
about enduring disease and oppression and about the physical

---

[6] Compare Eloi Leclerc, *Le cantique des créatures ou les symboles de l'union. Un
analyse de Saint François d'Assise.* Paris, 1970.

death from which none can escape. In a word: he sings frankly
and openly about the dark or tragic sides of our life. Nowhere however, does he mention people marrying and raising children; creating art and making use of tools; sailing the seas and subduing
nature; enjoying, living and owning. Nothing of this at all. The
modern listener, with his or her overview of all possible existential
relationships and products of civilisation, will probably quickly
conclude: what limitations, at the very most, does this Christian
mystic give us! What a reduction to the narrow edge of 'border-
line-situations' which make up that from which we cannot escape
in our existence. Is the final part of the song perhaps more than
an image of the distress of a brave and sick person trying to change
this distress into a virtue?

However evident these questions may seem, they do not
approach the full significance of what the Canticle says about the
human condition. As we have seen, in recalling the elements, Francis was not averse to a one-sided selection of those characteristics
of water, wind, fire and earth which are beneficial. What could
have prevented him from doing the same when it came to man?
An inborn or cancerous pessimism? Francis was definitely not a
naive believer in the goodness of man. However his happy-go-lucky
nature, both before and after his conversion (although in different
ways), do not make it plausible that he would unexpectedly manifest himself here as a pessimist.

Or should we rather take counsel with ourselves? Perhaps we
should leave aside our well established convictions and pose ourselves the question as to whether the things that are summed up
by Francis are not sombre out-of-the-way issues from his point of
view. Then we can take the 'lessons for the living' which resound
in the Canticle, seriously along with our modern embarrassment
concerning vulnerability and mortality. There is, by the way, a significant resemblance between what the Canticle says about the
human condition and what the concluding lines of the apostolic
creed (the Credo) and the second part of the Our Father say about
this. Francis incorporated what it all comes down to: forgiveness,
reconciliation and hope in ultimate salvation.

Welcome 'Sister Bodily Death'

If Francis' entire life was 'one long poem in action' (Simone Weil), then the way in which he moulded his passing away was also clearly considered. His request to be placed naked upon the ground in his final hours, turned it into a movingly staged death. The annual remembrance of Francis' passing away, also called his *transitus* (transition), is always impressive. Even so, one gets the feeling that his way of dealing with death is far removed from the manner of living and dying that people (also the faithful) eight centuries down the road think they are capable of. 'Welcome, Sister Bodily Death!' Who is able to repeat these words? Doesn't Francis express such a special view of life with these words that the average person will have to relinquish every endeavour to imitate this? How indeed did he dare to speak like this, while Paul wrote about death as 'the last enemy' (1 Corinthians 15:26). Was this 'welcome' perhaps not a kind of *salto vitale* by which he not only somersaulted away from average mortals, but also away from, for example, Clare who was overwhelmed with grief by his passing away?

When Francis sang and had his brothers sing about 'our Sister, Bodily Death' he was really on the brink of death. It is significant that his Canticle, as we have already remarked upon, speaks the language of the final, in a certain sense 'ultimate' or 'eschatological', bible-book of Revelation. From this he borrowed the words concerning 'the second death' which 'shall do no harm' to those whom 'death will find in Your most holy will' (verse 13).

The second death

This 'second death', the definite break with God, which is to be distinguished from the bodily death which gives access to life with God, is also mentioned in the letter to the angel of the Church in Smyrna in Revelation:

> 'And to the angel of the church in Smyrna write: "These are the words of the first and the last, who was dead and came to life: I know your affliction and your poverty, even though you are rich.

I know the slander on the part of those who say that they are Jews and are not, but are a synagogue of Satan. Do not fear what you are about to suffer. Beware, the devil is about to throw some of you into prison so that you may be tested, and for ten days you will have affliction. Be faithful until death, and I will give you the crown of life. Let anyone who has an ear listen to what the Spirit is saying to the churches. Whoever conquers will not be harmed by the second death"' (Revelation 2:8-11).

The fact that Francis in verse 11 of his Canticle also uses the image of the coronation with the 'crown of life', and that he also does this in his Canticle of Exhortation, 'each one will be crowned queen in heaven with the Virgin Mary' (verse 6), suggests that this letter to the Church in Smyrna meant a lot to him. The 'tribulation' (*tribulatio*) which is mentioned twice there, he also uses in verse 10 of the Canticle. And isn't what is said about 'the poverty' of the Church in Smyrna in this letter, also not the tenor of what is said in the central text of the Later Rule? Here 'the most beloved brothers' are also called 'heirs and kings of the Kingdom of Heaven'; 'poor in temporal things but exalted in virtue'. 'Crowned kings', exactly because they were poor: this is the image Francis must have held in 1223. Perhaps he became especially attached to this letter to Smyrna after the Living One appeared to him on Mount La Verna as the Crucified One in 1224. The letter says: 'These are the words of the first and the last, who was dead and came to life.'

As we shall see, the *A* and *O* sounds in the Canticle emphasise his engagement with Christ, 'the first and the last', during the final two years of his life. Through death, Christ entered life. This is how Francis must have viewed his own approaching death, keeping in mind what the same letter to the church in Smyrna states: 'Be faithful until death, and I will give you the crown of life.' Our 'bodily death' can be the door to life. In this way it is our companion and even 'our Sister'. In recognising this at the end of his life Francis, although poorer than ever, was rich. When a brother advised the sick Francis to let himself be read to from the Prophets, he replied:

'It is good to read the testimonies of Scripture, and it is good to seek the Lord our God in them. But I have already taken in so much of Scripture that I have more than enough for meditating and reflecting. I do not need more, son; I know Christ, poor and crucified' (2 Celano 105).

Acceptance

For Francis, Christ signified the sympathy and companionship of God-with-us all the way into the most profound darkness of death. In the Canticle he sang out his answer of faith. Just like Jesus, here he accepted the fact that he was a mortal through and through and made of dust: the acceptance, therefore, of his sick body. He did not sing about 'our Sister *Bodily* Death' just anyhow. Acceptance in the form of a 'returning' song of praise; an acceptance, through which the extreme dependence which he had come to bear, could grow into attachment. The painfully experienced bondage to the earthly elements grew into an attachment to them – and not as a result of superhuman exertion, but rather in the realisation of the fact that we may 'boast in our weaknesses and in carrying each day the holy cross of our Lord Jesus Christ' (Admonition 5,8).

The three statements in the third part of this song: 'for Your love', 'in peace' and 'Your most holy will' are references to the Holy Spirit who is given by Christ as a Partner to his own. For this Spirit *is* God's Love, God's Peace and God's Will. These names illustrate from where the sick songster received the power to thank God together with the whole of creation, even for 'our Sister, Bodily Death'. These illustrations however, may not let us forget that, according to Paul, this same Spirit sighs from the depths. It is not only nature who suffers labour pains and groans: man, waiting for corporeal deliverance also does so. 'Likewise the Spirit of God intercedes on behalf of us with sighs too deep for words' (compare Romans 8:22-26). This profound sighing also lay at the base of this last sonorous song by Francis. It is the song of someone who bodily lived through the ponderousness of our earthly load. The final word 'humility' emphasizes the fact that the song was sung from the depths and that it can always be sung again from down there. Francis' spirituality may therefore be justly called a 'spirituality from below'.[7]

A contemporary of Francis discusses the Canticle

Our amazement was concerned with Francis' will to praise God from the depths of dejection. The question is how this will to praise was awoken in Francis. Can we discover something of this using the biographies? Let us listen to a part of *The Assisi Compilation*:

'Blessed Francis lay there for more than fifty days, and was unable to bear the light of the sun during the day or the light of a fire at night. He stayed in the dark in the house, inside that little cell. In addition, day and night he had great pains in his eyes so that at night he could scarcely rest or sleep. This was very harmful and was a serious aggravation for his eye disease and his other illnesses.

Sometimes he did want to rest and sleep, but there were many mice in the house and in the little cell made of mats where he was lying, in one part of the house. They were running around him, and even over him, and would not let him sleep. They even disturbed him greatly at the time of prayer. They bothered him not only at night, but also during the day, even climbing up on his table when he was eating, so much so that his companions, and he himself, considered it a temptation of the devil, which it was.

One night as blessed Francis was reflecting on all the troubles he was enduring, he was moved by piety for himself. "Lord", he said to himself, "make haste to help me in my illnesses, so that I may be able to bear them patiently." And suddenly he was told in spirit: "Tell me, brother, what if, in exchange for your illnesses and troubles, someone were to give you a treasure? And it would be so great and precious that, even if the whole earth were changed to pure gold, all stones to precious stones, and all water to balsam, you would still judge and hold all these things as nothing, as if they were earth,

[7] Anselm Grün O.S.B. and Meinrad Dufner O.S.B., *Spiritualität von Unten*, Münsterschwarzach, 1994.

stones and water, in comparison to the great and precious treasure which was given you. Wouldn't you greatly rejoice?"

"Lord", blessed Francis answered, "this treasure would indeed be great, worth seeking, very precious, greatly lovable, and desirable." "Then, brother," he was told, "be glad and rejoice in your illnesses and troubles, because as of now, you are as secure as if you were already in my kingdom".'[8]

In this story Francis once again surprises us: now as someone who even in the gravest of difficulties does not belie his mercantile background and who presents (or is presented with) matters in such a way that he is able to strike a special deal using his sufferings. Are these images of self-interest, compensation and barter embarrassing? We cannot be certain whether to attribute them to his biographers, on the assumption that they may not have reached the same spiritual level Francis himself attained.

A step by step approach

Here we encounter a step by step manner of reasoning, which Francis applied a couple of times and which he knew from the Bible. An example is Paul's hymn to love in the First Letter to the Corinthians, 13:1-2:

'If I speak in the tongues of mortals and of angels, but do not have love, I am a noisy gong or a clanging cymbal. And if I have prophetic powers, and understand all mysteries and all knowledge, and if I have all faith, so as to remove mountains, but do not have love, I am nothing. If I give away all my possessions, and if I hand over my body so that I may boast, but do not have love, I gain nothing.'

The ultimate in earthly possessions or human achievements is presented, increasing each time, and linked to the choice between all or nothing. In view of what is ultimately of most importance, this choice is presented as sharply as possible. Then by drawing a com-

---

[8] *The Assisi Compilation* 83, in: *Francis of Assisi: Early Documents. Volume II. The Founder*; 185.

parison to love, the undying quality of true love becomes apparent. The maximum of knowledge and worth presented earlier on, now functions as a trampoline to a totally different perspective and a totally different set of values.

All the same, the story from *The Assisi Compilation* makes the point that God is referred to using the image of the incomparable 'treasure' – just as Scripture does –, in any case for those who wish to take the leap and wish to recognise Him as the ultimate focus of their desire. Knowing God has everything to do then with the faithful understanding of the paradox concerning the importance of pure disinterest. Or with what Francis and Clare call the possession of Poverty, i.e. of complete Generosity. Clare says in her First Letter to Agnes of Prague: 'O holy poverty: to those who hold and long for her the Kingdom of heaven is promised by God.'

Living in an 'as if' (or make-believe) reality

It remains a fact that the leap that Francis took – the leap from dejection through self-pity to the jubilant praise of God's Goodness – is for the greater part lost in the mystery of what happened to him at San Damiano. Or is it possible to suggest – with the necessary diffidence – two moments which perhaps could then have been at issue? In both cases it is not more than an intuition, however one that is supported by the witnesses of Francis' companions.

The first moment lies in the liberating words that Francis heard according to his companions: 'Be glad and rejoice in your illnesses and troubles, because as of now, you are as secure *as if* you were already in my kingdom.' [9]

We emphasize the words 'in the midst of your illnesses and troubles'; 'in my kingdom', and especially 'as if'. Perhaps Francis' visitation or affliction was that in his misery he had struggled with the thought that God, on Whom he had based his life, had forsaken

[9] *The Assisi Compilation* 83, in: *Francis of Assisi: Early Documents. Volume II. The Founder*; 185.

him in his suffering. Had he, in that dark hovel, felt that he would have to live as if God (in Whom he believed) was no longer with him, especially now that he was suffering unbearably? And did he wear himself out even more pondering the question whether God's painful absence wasn't due to his own fault or failure?

His rebound and way out lay in the fact that he still managed to see a certain dimension in his exhaustion and illness – which both still thoroughly remained his part – 'as if' he had already been received into the security of God's Kingdom. Of course in all clear-headedness, nobody would desire to have to live in a make-believe or in an 'as if' world. But isn't it exactly everyday reality that there is nothing else for believers to do – as well as for all the others who are not trapped in the naive conviction that reality is only made up of what is registered by our senses? Believers live in an in between situation. For them the experience of everyday reality, namely the fact that it seems as if God is absent, is not true reality, but rather an 'as if'. The reality in which God has revealed himself to be present is, however, usually not experienced by them. All the same, their faith that God really is present nourishes their hope and desire.

Perhaps we may assume that Francis was allowed to experience the transition from the one type of 'as if' (namely that of God's absence in his suffering) to the second type of 'as if' (namely of his reception into God's Kingdom as one who suffers). And all this based on the deep recognition that it is exactly our impotence and our failings – that painful embarrassment towards ourselves – which can feed the flames of our praise and can therefore assist us in unreluctantly leaping into the mercy of God whom we need so badly.

This is the second moment we wish to put forward. It is the conviction which for example Thérèse of Lisieux expressed and lived out so magnificently. If God revealed himself to such an extreme in Christ's suffering on the Cross, has He not also made our duality and our abandonment his dwelling for good?

Whatever happened in that hovel near the cloister of San Damiano, the tension did not disappear from Francis' life after the jubilation of the Canticle. Every time he went through periods of difficulty and endurance during the last months of his life, he would ask his brothers to sing the Canticle for him. Francis remained someone who was on a journey, a *homo viator* living in an ambiguous reality and in need of consolation. However, since the crisis at San Damiano, the drama had changed. The threatening despair had been broken open for good. The duality was reconciled. The tragedy became a play of consolation.

The modern individual's resistance and repugnance

Listening to the Canticle, many may experience difficulty in the fact that Francis sang the praise of God in such a self-evident manner. Two reasons can be given for this resistance. The first concerns the contrast between divine grandeur and, at least for modern individuals, the excessive emphasis on human smallness. The second is concerned with the frank speaking to and about God, in comparison with the experience of God's concealment nowadays. We will touch on both difficulties.

The contrast between God's grandeur and human smallness cannot easily be reconciled with the notion of liberty and the right to self-determination which were gained after much struggle in the past and which are even now still being fought for. Even after two centuries of having lived and learned to distrust the slogans of the Enlightenment concerning human autonomy and the Progress of civilisation, we cannot and will not return to the subservience which used to characterise society and the church.

As far as the second contrast is concerned: the image of the radiant sun in the Canticle is totally inclusive. Sir Brother Sun is *con grande splendore*, 'with great splendor', the reference to God's presence in His creation. But does this radiant clarity still hold as far as we moderns are concerned? Are we capable of speaking to and about God in this very way? We have forfeited this way of speaking because in our times the experience of God's hiddenness usually surrounds us. God's silence, also in worst-case scenarios, makes it extra difficult to deal with His mystery. Wouldn't it be a good thing to embrace Nietzsche's remarks which criticized the lack of shame and diffidence believers held for the God they so publicly confessed? A challenge to consider a profound reorientation lies in such questions. We will limit ourselves to a few trails which Francis left to us.

God's hiddenness

Concerning God's hiddenness, it would be a mistake to consider this a recent theme. It hearkens back to biblical speaking, for example in Isaiah 45:15: 'Truly, you are a God who hides himself'. There is a long tradition in which great minds and hearts, such as Dionysius, Cusanus, Luther, John of the Cross and Pascal reflected upon the hiddenness of God (or rather: of God who conceals himself).

If we attend more closely to Francis, it becomes evident that this issue is more complicated than we perhaps initially thought. The recognition of God's hiddenness is certainly not absent in his spirituality. His first Admonition revolves around the conviction that 'the Father dwells in inaccessible light' (verse 5). Francis does not hide the fact that in his view God cannot be known in His essence; this also holds true where His manifestation in Jesus is concerned – unless however we are assisted in recognizing Him as He is. This can only take place through the inspiration of the Holy Spirit.

Already in the beginning of the Canticle we can read that no human is worthy to mention God's Name. From then on the entire song is directed to the creatures: one single cry calling them to praise their Creator. God's light cannot be looked at directly – Francis is also not able to do this. He may not have shared in the timidity of many in thanking God and praising him, but he was definitely conscious of the daringness of these acts. Again and again he can do no more in his prayers than stutter variations of the word 'good'. If it is true, as some surmise, that the concluding verse of the Canticle served as a refrain after every strophe, then the repetition of the final word 'humility' would only confirm that there was nothing triumphant, and certainly nothing unabashed, about Francis' praise of God.

Exactly, some will say; that is exactly the whole point: this repetition of the word humility only emphasizes the cancelling out of the individual in regard to the radiant grandeur of God. And then we are back to square one: back to the first contrast which painfully touches on our feelings of self-esteem.

God's grandeur

How did Francis experience this humility which is mentioned at the conclusion of the Canticle? This question must be taken seriously, because in a certain sense this humility has a false bottom: for the singer of the Canticle, the word 'humility' above all signified who God was for him. In a long series of 33 eulogies which he wrote after his vision of Christ on Mount La Verna he says to God himself: 'You are humility'. Just as he says: 'You are wisdom', 'You are patience', 'You are beauty'. God himself *is* Humility, *is* Support, *is* Mercy. Speaking about God's humility, Francis draws upon a special biblical source which still streams on in the tradition of the Church. In recent times this vision has once again hesitatingly been recalled into our consciousness.

In this light, the call to humility which ends the Canticle receives an incomparably rich sonority. It is an incitement for all creatures, especially for people, to actively be the image of what God in his engagement towards us always already was. 'Giving back' to God in praise, – key words from his writings – attain a unique depth here: the praise of God's humility. In his Letter to the Entire Order Francis writes: 'Let everyone be struck with fear, let the whole world tremble, and let the heavens exult when Christ, the Son of the living God, is present on the altar in the hands of a priest!' And he reminds them:

> 'O wonderful loftiness and stupendous dignity! O sublime humility! O humble sublimity! The Lord of the universe, God and the Son of God, so humbles Himself that for our salvation He hides Him-

self under an ordinary piece of bread! Brothers, look at the humility of God, and pour out your hearts before Him! Humble yourselves that you may be exalted by Him! Hold back nothing of yourselves for yourselves that He Who gives Himself totally to you may receive you totally!'(26-29).

The mystery of God's coming near means for Francis: *grandeur* which expresses itself in profound *humility*, and *might* which reveals itself in *self-emptying*. Francis leaves us with the question whether the contrast we ascertained, does not begin to look very different. God's self-expression in the tortured Christ – can this be called belittling and curtailing?

Fear of God

However there is more. One of the answers to the strange mystery of God's hiddenness lies in the special place of man in contrast to God. Francis made himself the interpreter of this understanding of embarrassment and awe: 'no human is worthy to mention Your Name'. Using an old expression: he knew 'the fear of the Lord'. Whoever has heard him concerning God's humility may surmise that the songster's diffidence originated from his understanding of the fact that God's grandeur does not cancel out his humility, but rather underlines it.

The most profound basis for his diffidence was given by Francis where in his writings he speaks about 'the fear of the Lord' in an original manner.[10] Here he does not speak about the awe or diffidence which man must have for God, but conversely about the diffidence God has for the individual who shares in Jesus' vulnerability. 'Diffidence' is therefore, just as for example 'Wisdom' or 'Love', one of the names with which Francis – mostly following the tradition of faith – expresses his understanding of a characteristic proper to one of the Divine Persons. 'Diffidence' therefore refers to the reserve with which God the Father creates space for his

---

[10] Admonitions 27,5; The Earlier Rule, 17,6; see Chapter 7 for a more detailed discussion.

children; leaving them free and respecting them – and in doing so hiding Himself. Where Francis reflected upon the 'fear of God', he must have seen this as a reflection of God's original Diffidence.

In this light, the Canticle may rightly be called a 'praise of embarrassment'. It is after all a song of praise originating from the deep embarrassment in which Francis found himself to be: the embarrassment concerning both his inability as well as *inability to accept* his inability. However it is also the praise which wells up from a feeling of diffidence for God's coming near which embarrasses us. And maybe God's diffidence could also be called God's embarrassment: embarrassment concerning what people do with His creation as well as to each other.

Life-giving distance

The amazing thing about the Canticle – this creation by a sick man, which calls upon the whole of creation to praise and give thanks to God – is the fact that the singer did not grow and blossom in spite of, but exactly due to his humility and embarrassment. Its conception is bathed in the fertile warmth of God's light, as much as in the concealing cloud of His hiddenness. 'Praised be You, my Lord, through Brother Wind, and through the air, cloudy and serene, and every kind of weather, through whom You give sustenance to Your creatures.'

The grandeur of God, the One who is totally the Other – revealing itself as bewildering Humility. The Hiddenness of Him in whose boundless Respect we are able to stand firm and find security. What may be contrasts for us, lie fused together in the one mystery of God. Perhaps this mystery can be somewhat referred to using the word 'Distance'. This word means, on the one hand, the right distance by which people receive space and time to become themselves and, on the other hand, the action of relinquishing by which this right distance becomes possible.

As we shall see, Francis' conversion and his life-style that followed upon this are characterised by three centres of focus: that of 'giving back' (or thankfully relinquishing), that of 'bearing' (or respecting in awe) – and both of these an expression of his will 'to serve'. The human expression of what Francis was given to understand concerning the mystery of Him, whose mystery is a mystery of life-giving Distance, can be found in these central concepts.

Christogramme

Earlier on we posed the question whether it is not rather remarkable that Christ, who meant so much for Francis, is not mentioned in the Canticle. Our answer is that, although it is true that Jesus Christ is not explicitly mentioned, his name is indeed woven into the text of the song. We have already remarked on the fact that the Canticle's train of thought descends from above to below. The two first words 'Most High' and the last word 'humility' mark this fact. The singer then sings his song from below to above. In this way he 'gives back' in praise that which was given to him from above to admire and 'to bear'. After a closer look it appears that not only the first and the last words can be connected to each other. Anton Rotzetter has pointed out that this goes for the whole of the first line and for the whole of the last line of this song.[11] Just as 'great humility' corresponds to 'Most High', 'thanks' and 'serve Him' correspond to 'Good Lord' and 'All-powerful'.

If the lines between the corresponding concepts are connected, a Christogramme appears as a watermark or seal to the entire song. The vertical line together with the cross namely form the initial letters of the name of Jesus Christ: the Greek letters I and X. (From the earliest times of Christendom an abbreviation of Jesus Christ's name.)

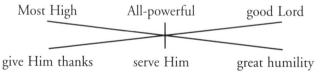

| Most High | All-powerful | good Lord |
| give Him thanks | serve Him | great humility |

[11] Compare A. Rotzetter, 'Der Sonnengesang des hl. Franziskus von Assisi als missionarisches Lied von aktueller Bedeutung'. In: A. Camps und G. Hunold (Hg.), *Erschaffe mir ein neues Volk,* Mettingen 1982; 44-61; 45 and further; Leonhard Lehmann, *Francis Master of Prayer*; 311.

This Christogramme is confirmed by the sounds that dominate in the first, respectively last lines of the early-Italian original. In the first line *O* sounds four times – probably even five times. (The letter 'u' in *Altissimu* was undoubtedly pronounced as *O*). In the final line *A* sounds five times. In Francis' day and age the number five referred to the five wounds of Christ. The *O*- and *A*-sounds refer to Christ in Revelation where He is the 'Alpha' and 'Omega'. Moreover, Leonhard Lehmann has drawn attention to the number of lines of verse making up the Canticle: thirty-three (the traditional number of years of Jesus' life).[12] For Francis, 'Sir Brother Sun' probably also symbolised Jesus Christ: 'the dawn from on high' (Luke 1:78).

This Christogramme which compiles and holds the Canticle together, again makes it clear that this song of praise by the creatures only reveals its true significance if it is listened to within the context of salvation-history, which is made manifest in Christ. Alexander Gerken also remarks on the fact that the third part of the Canticle, concerning humankind (verses 10-14), is the song's supportive basis:

> 'Without this salvation-historical framework, the praise by the creatures would have been problematic and untenable for Francis, who understood the social injustice of his day and the sinfulness of many a minister of the Church very well.'[13]

Francis' conviction that his entire life was placed within the continuing drama of Christ, who lives with and through His Church, had already been woven by him into the texts, in which he dealt with his vision on Mount La Verna, before he sang out his Canticle.

With the final words of the song 'praise and bless my Lord and give Him thanks and serve Him with great humility' Francis gave, as it were, his signature to the interpretation-in-song of his lifestyle. The above-mentioned troika of to thank, to serve and to bear (to praise and bless in humility) reappears in this 'signature'. Three

---

[12] Leonhard Lehmann, *Tiefe und Weite*; 299 and further.
[13] Alexander Gerken, 'The Theological Intuition of St. Francis of Assisi.' In: *GreyFriars Review* 7 (1993); 71-94; 78.

aspects concerning the content of the single word 'respect' are at issue here. What is all too often written at the end of a letter without a second thought portrays Francis – life-artist and poet – totally: *respectfully* yours.

3. Francis' Admonitions: a pathway to learning

The Canticle turned out to be a sermon-in-song based on Francis' sermon-programme. Where, however, according to this programme the word 'penance' would have been expected, the song sings of 'bearing' whatever weakens and dejects us. This probably means that during the period of his life in which he wrote this song of praise, Francis came to understand doing penance as the bearing of whatever happens to us and what cannot be changed.

Is this concept bearing found more often in Francis' writings? Could it then be called one of the central themes of his spirituality? And above all: what attitude towards life is expressed by it? For the answer to these questions we will have a closer look at Francis' Admonitions. To start with, it is important to consider whether this collection is more than just a haphazard assemblage of separate texts.

For whomever wishes to delve into Francis' spirituality, there are many reasons to consider this collection of sayings. It contains the 'marrow' of what Francis wished to pass on. Some therefore even consider the collection of Admonitions to be nothing less than his 'Sermon on the Mount'. One thing is certain: we are dealing here with a vital and central core of Francis' art of living. It remains to be seen whether the word 'Admonitions' covers the complete meaning of these texts. If they are the fruits of a long search for purified wisdom, then a more appropriate description of their content would be 'kernels of wisdom'. We prefer to call this collection a 'pathway to learning': by seriously considering these sayings, the reader can gradually become familiar with Francis' art of living.

That this is easier said than done is confirmed by the special consideration which – in the history of active spirituality – has always been given to the continuous exercise of the virtues or 'attitudes'. In our era of the information super-highway and easily digestible info-bites, the emphasis on this unavoidably time-consuming 'learning by doing' is more appropriate than ever.

Uncovering a ground-plan

Each of the 28 sayings in the Admonitions contains its own message which can be considered separately from the others. However this does not exclude a possible connection between the individual sayings. There are reasons to suppose that they have been grouped according to a certain plan. The consensus that was held until recently, namely that Francis was a freely associating writer who did not arrange his texts in a well thought through manner, has become contested due to fresh work by various researchers. It can be demonstrated that some of his writings are carefully constructed. The possibility that this also holds for the entire collection of Admonitions is well worth researching. A good starting point would be to question whether regularities or irregularities in this collection meet the eye.

Halfway down the pathway of learning

Admonitions 13, 14, 15 and 16 form the exact halfway-mark along this pathway of learning. Characteristic to these four texts is that each of them comments upon a beatitude by Jesus from the Sermon on the Mount (Matthew 5:1-12).

Admonition 13
"Blessed are the peacemakers, for they will be called children of God".
A servant of God cannot know how much patience and humility he has within himself as long as he is content. When the time

comes, however, when those who should make him content do the opposite, he has as much patience and humility as he has at that time and no more.'

Admonition 14

"*Blessed are the poor in spirit for theirs is the kingdom of heaven.*" There are many who, while insisting on prayers and obligations, inflict many abstinences and punishments upon their bodies. But they are immediately offended and disturbed about a single word which seems to be harmful to their bodies or about something which might be taken away from them. These people are not poor in spirit, for some one who is truly poor in spirit hates himself and loves those who strike him on the cheek.'

Admonition 15

"*'Blessed are the peacemakers, for they will be called children of God.*" Those people are truly peacemakers who, regardless of what they suffer in this world, preserve peace of spirit and body out of love of our Lord Jesus Christ.'

Admonition 16

"*Blessed are the clean in heart, for they will see God.*" The truly clean of heart are those who look down upon earthly things, seek those of heaven, and, with a clean heart and spirit, never cease adoring and seeing the Lord God living and true.'

Francis comments twice on Jesus' words 'blessed are the peacemakers' (Admonitions 13 and 15); once on 'blessed are the poor in spirit' (Admonition 14) and once on 'blessed are the clean in heart' (Admonition 16). The reference to poverty (Admonition 14) is therefore positioned between the two reflections upon what bringing peace embraces (Admonitions 13 and 15). This can hardly be coincidental. Admonition 16 concludes this series of four with a call to worship God. The two moments in the sermon-programme, the call to worship God and to do penance, can be recognised here. For here the worship of God is connected to poverty, peace, humility and patience. Our reflections upon Admonitions 13 and 15 can be found at the end of this Chapter. Admonitions 14 and 16 must be left out of consideration here.

Ground-plan of the pathway to learning

Jesus' words that open the first Admonition – 'I am the Way, the Truth and the Life' – determine the structure of the entire collection. The TRUTH (the dogmatic section) and the LIFE (the spiritual section) together form the WAY along the Admonitions. This WAY has its origin and destination in the hiddenness of God. This is as much a way of aversion from the self-seeking attitude of the old Adam (Admonition 2), as it is of conversion to Christ, the new Adam, who is referred to in a veiled manner in Admonition 27. At the centre of the collection, Francis makes Jesus' beatitudes his own, in order to point out that a life lived in peace can paradoxically coincide with hardship and suffering – and that this peace blossoms into the worship of the living and true God for the 'clean in heart'.

The long series of Admonitions does indeed look much like a WAY along all sorts of moments of instruction (dogmatic section) and of a life which makes blessed (spiritual section).[1] Viewed in this manner, the collection may somewhat rightfully be called a pathway to learning. This pathway to learning enables the message of each and every saying to be better understood in the light of its place within the whole. However an exposition of this kind falls outside the scope of this book. As we go along, we shall give special attention to some of the Admonitions.

---

[1] For the connection see: Pierre Brunette, *Essai d'analyse symbolique des Admonitions de François d'Assise. Une herméneutique de son expérience spirituelle à travers ses écrits.* Montréal, 1989; 52; *Respectfully Yours,* Chapter 2; 57-75.

Scheme of the path to learning:

Admonition 1: God's hidden mystery (verse 3): Lord, *show* us the Father and it will be enough for us; (verse 14): how long will you be hard of *heart?*

Admonition 2: the old Adam, commentary on a word from the Old Testament: *dixit* [he said].

THE TRUTH   (the dogmatic section)
Admonitions   3   4   5   6   7   8   9   10   11   12
ten Admonitions commenting on words from the New Testament: *dicit / ait* [he says].

four commentaries on beatitudes of Jesus: *beatus* [blessed].

Admonition 13
Admonition 14
Admonition 15
Admonition 16

17   18   19   20   21   22   23   24   25   26

THE LIFE   (the spiritual section)
Admonitions   26   25   24   23   22   21   20   19   18   17
ten Admonitions also beginning with *beatus* [blessed].

Admonition 27: the new Adam

Admonition 28: exhortation to keep God's gifts hidden. Verse 1: the good things which the Lord *shows* to him; verse 3: who safeguards the secrets of the Lord in his *heart*.

THE WAY

Beginning and end of the pathway to learning

The beginning and end of the pathway to learning are concluded by the mystical theme of God's veiled presence. For the greater part, Admonition 1 revolves around God's hiddenness: 'The Father dwells in inaccessible light'. 'Show us the Father, and we will be satisfied'

(John 14:8). This request by the apostle Philip of Jesus expresses man's desire for the hidden God. Francis then says that God can only be seen 'in Spirit'. This also goes for the Son, in whom the Father both reveals and conceals himself. In Jesus Christ's humanity and in the Eucharist, God comes to us in a concealed way. This presence is only revealed to those who contemplate in Jesus' humanity his divinity with 'spiritual eyes'.

Admonition 1

Essential moments of Francis' spirituality are contained in this introduction to the collection of Admonitions: the incarnation of God's Son, his eucharistic self-revelation and God's hiddenness. He states here that these are only able to be approached through the faithful understanding of the inscrutable and – for him at least – all-determining fact that God is humility and that he withdraws from all interest that is not nourished by the loving *Inter-esse* (Interest = being amongst) which is the Holy Spirit, Who imparts these things. Further on in this Chapter we shall give a more ample reflection upon this Admonition.

Admonition 28

The fact that a certain hiddenness is also required of people – especially when this concerns a profound relationship with God – can be found in the final, the 28th Admonition:

> 'Blessed is the servant who stores up in heaven the good things which the Lord shows to him and does not wish to reveal them to people under the guise of a reward, because the Most High Himself will reveal His deeds to whomever He wishes. Blessed is the servant who safeguards the secrets of the Lord in his heart.'

This conclusion to the collection of Admonitions is a conclusion in the sense of 'ending' as well as in the sense of 'screening' or 'cordoning off' in order to respect the intimacy of this contemplation. It is no coincidence that the final words of this last Admonition implicitly refer to Jesus' mother, the contemplative believer. While

Admonition 1 opened with Jesus, the Way to the Father, the final
Admonition conjures up the person of Mary: image of and example for the Church, who contemplates the mysteries of the Lord in
her heart (compare Luke 2:19 and 51).

The second and one-but-last Admonition

These two sayings are also clearly connected to each other, however not as each other's mirror-image, but rather as each other's
opposite.

Admonition 2

> 'The Lord said to Adam: Eat of every tree; you may not eat, how-
> ever, of the tree of the knowledge of good and evil. He was able to
> eat of every tree of paradise, because he did not sin as long as he did
> not go against obedience. For that person eats of the tree of the
> knowledge of good who makes his will his own and, in this way,
> exalts himself over the good things the Lord says and does in him.
> And so, through the suggestion of the devil and the transgression of
> the command, it became the apple of the knowledge of evil. There-
> fore it is fitting that he suffer punishment.'

This relatively short text is the only one that exclusively comments
upon words from the Old Testament, namely from Genesis 2:6-17.
The insights that Francis offers here in a condensed form are vital
cores of his spirituality. They shall be seen to be of a determining
quality for the structure of the entire collection. The positioning
of this text about the fall of Adam immediately after the first
Admonition can therefore hardly be called a coincidence.

While Admonition 2 deals with the old Adam who lost his place
in paradise, the one-but-last Admonition 27 confronts us with the
new Adam – as we hope to make plausible in Chapter 7. This new
Adam bound himself to the new tree of life (the cross) and in doing
so won back paradise. In the light of this interpretation, the place
of this description of Christ within the collection of Admonitions
is especially significant. This Admonition marks a break in the

series of Admonitions (13-28) all beginning with 'blessed are'. Its form is also unique.

Two series of ten Admonitions

Within the group of 24 Admonitions surrounding the four Admonitions commenting on Jesus' beatitudes, Admonition 1 and Admonition 28 are connected to each other as we have already seen. Admonitions 2 and 27 are also connected. The remaining Admonitions form two series of TEN sayings each: Admonitions 3 to 12 and Admonitions 17 to 26.

First series: Admonitions 3 to 12

These sayings all have an dogmatic character. They impress upon us moments of teaching found in the New Testament – from Jesus himself or from Paul's letters.

Second series: Admonitions 17 to 26

This dogmatic aspect is not missing from the series of Admonitions 17 to 26. Here however, a spiritual life is presented. These Admonitions namely have in common that each of them begins with 'blessed'. One could call them ten of Francis' own beatitudes. However he only formulates these after having reflected upon four of Jesus' own beatitudes (Admonitions 13 to 16). Jesus' centrally placed words open the way for what Francis wishes to present in the second half of the collection. This second series can be characterised as the spiritual part of the collection.

The symbolism of a church

The pathway to learning can somewhat rightly also be presented as a guided-tour of a church. It has often been remarked upon that Francis' thinking was spatial. In the Canticle of the Creatures he says for example: 'Blessed are those whom death will find *in* Your most holy will'. At crucial points in his writings he says: 'in the love which is God'. In the same way he considers obedience to be the space in which the brothers are to be found, or from which some have unfortunately left.

Efforts to memorise things by heart are made considerably easier if one imagines a building with many chambers and then places in them one by one the individual objects or themes which one wants to remember. In mnemotechnique, the art of memorising, imagining a building has served well through the ages. In this way, the 'building' of the Admonitions can serve as a tool in aid of memory.[2]

The fact that there are 28 Admonitions is a decisive factor for us. Already before Francis' times, this number was deemed to be a symbolic reference to the Church. We shall return to the symbolic value of the number 28 in Chapter 7.[3]

We do not postulate more than a certain plausibility as to the use of a church-building metaphor for the collection of Admonitions. This metaphor can however come to our aid in visualising its pleasing overall structure.

If we imagine the pathway to learning as a tour of a church, then the four commentaries on Jesus' beatitudes (Admonitions 13-16) are oriented towards the East and form the apse: the holy of holies. In the current symbolism of the church-building – a reference to the Body of Christ – the apse denotes Christ as Head of the Church.

Admonitions 1 and 28 are situated on the West side, the entrance to and exit from the church. Together with Admonitions 2 and 27 these texts mark the hall or atrium. During the Middle Ages, a tympanum, on which Christ was depicted as the *Maiestas Domini* holding a book on which were inscribed the words 'I am

---

[2] Compare Mary Carruthers, *The Book of Memory. A Study of Memory in Medieval Culture* (Cambridge, 1990), 91f.; Marianne Schlosser, "Bonaventura. De perfectione vitae." in *Wissenschaft und Weisheit*, 57 (1994); 21-71; 29.

[3] See: *Respectfully Yours,* 'Appendix. The Symbolism of Numbers', The Number 28; 403.

the Way, the Truth and the Life', was often erected above the entrance to a church.[4] The first sentence of the Admonitions is: 'The Lord Jesus says to his disciples: 'I am the way, the truth and the life; no one comes to the Father except through me.'

The two series of ten, Admonitions 3 to 12 on the one hand and Admonitions 17 to 26 on the other, can be seen as delineating the ship of the church. In church-building symbolism, this space in which the faithful are gathered refers pre-eminently to the Body of Christ.

The arrangement of the frescos in the Upper Church in Assisi

However desirable it may be, research into the origins of and the historical context surrounding text-patterns in Francis' writings only partly fall within the scope of this book. All the same, we wish to emphasise a couple of similarities between the 'church-building' of the Admonitions and the arrangement of the frescos in the Upper Church of the San Francesco in Assisi. The frescos in the ship of the church, painted between 1277 and 1300, just as the subtitles were, are based on the biography of Francis written by Bonaventure in 1261. If a comparison is drawn between the arrangement of the collection of Admonitions and the arrangement of the frescos in the Upper Church, three things meet the eye:

• The Upper Church has 28 paintings concerned with Francis. (Twenty of these are about his life and death. The other images deal with events which took place after his death.) This number tallies with the number of Admonitions.
• The fall of Adam is depicted on the right hand side of the apse. On the left, Jesus Christ, the new Adam can be seen. Just as Admonitions 2 and 27 were opposite each other in the 'church-building' of the Admonitions, here the old and the new Adam are also placed opposite each other.

---

[4] Georges Duby. *Le temps des cathédrales. L'art et la société 980-1420.* Paris, 1976; 346; compare; 336f.

• Certain images in the Upper Church appear to have purposely
  been related to other images. These mutual 'mirrors' result in
  cross-connections. Likewise, a number of remarkable connecting lines (or if you wish 'cross-bows') can be determined within
  the collection of Admonitions.[5]

The arrangement of the frescos

Old Testament: Creation and fall
Old Adam

1	2	3	4	5	6	7	8	9	10	11	12	
												13 14
Apse												Entrance
												15 16
28	27	26	25	24	23	22	21	20	19	18	17	

New Adam
New Testament: Christ's Passion

Especially the number 28 and the positions of the 'old and new
Adams' can hardly be a coincidence. The question therefore arises
whether the architects of the Upper Church had the structure of
the collection of Admonitions in mind when drawing up the blue-
print for their church. We view this as highly improbable. The way
in which Francis structured his collection is not immediately clear.
We also do not have any witnesses, either contemporary or from a
later period, which describe the structure of the Admonitions as has
been laid bare by us – let alone the similarities with the Upper
Church we have established. Francis, as well as the architects of
the Upper Church were probably dependant on ideas or examples
which already existed before Francis' time. We are unfortunately
not competent enough to research this.

---

[5] See: *Respectfully Yours*; 68-74.

Francis' vision on Mount La Verna

What could have been the intention of the compiler of the Admonitions in carefully structuring and bringing together these sayings, which probably already existed in part? Why would he have desired to sketch the image of a church using these sayings? And supposing – which we do – that Francis himself was the compiler and that he indeed, like some researchers believe, arranged the collection towards the end of his life – what could have then motivated him to do so in exactly this way? These questions cannot be definitely answered. However we do think it is possible to connect the underlying structure with an event of tantamount importance in Francis' life.

We have in mind the vision he had on Mount La Verna, the memories of which he physically carried around with him during the last two years of his life in the form of Christ's wounds in his body; Christ, the Crucified One who as the Eternal Living One is Head of the Church, his Body. Francis had seen him depicted in this way on the image in the church of San Damiano, where he received his task: 'Go forth and restore My house' (2 Celano 10). As we shall see in Chapters 6 and 7, he also saw him, although in an incomparably more painful and joyful way, in the vision he had on Mount La Verna.

'Seeing with spiritual eyes': a reflection upon Admonition 1

Admonition 1

1. The Lord Jesus says to his disciples: 'I am the way, the truth and the life; no one comes to the Father except through me.
2. If you knew me, you would also know my Father; and from now on, you do know him and have seen him.'
3. Philip says to him: 'Lord show us the Father and it will be enough for us.'
4. Jesus says to him: 'Have I been with you for so long a time and you have not known me? Philip, whoever sees me sees my Father as well.'
5. The Father dwells in inaccessible light, and God is spirit, and no one has ever seen God.

6. Therefore He cannot be seen except in the Spirit because it is the Spirit that gives life; the flesh has nothing to offer.

7. But because He is equal to the Father, the Son is not seen by anyone other than the Father or other than the Holy Spirit.

8. All those who saw the Lord Jesus according to the humanity, therefore, and did not see and believe according to the Spirit and the Divinity that He is the true Son of God were condemned.

9. Now in the same way, all those who see the sacrament sanctified by the words of the Lord upon the altar at the hands of the priest in the form of bread and wine, and who do not see and believe according to the Spirit and the Divinity that it is truly the Body and Blood of our Lord Jesus Christ, are condemned.

10. [This] is affirmed by the Most High Himself Who says: 'This is my Body and the Blood of my new covenant [which will be shed for many];

11. and Whoever eats my flesh and drinks my blood has eternal life.'

12. It is the Spirit of the Lord, therefore, That lives in Its faithful, That receives the Body and Blood of the Lord.

13. All others who do not share in this same Spirit and presume to receive Him eat and drink judgement on themselves.

14. Therefore: children, how long will you be hard of heart?

15. Why do you not know the truth and believe in the Son of God?

16. Behold, each day He humbles Himself as when He came from the royal throne into the Virgin's womb;

17. each day He Himself comes to us, appearing humbly:

18. each day He comes down from the bosom of the Father upon the altar in the hands of a priest.

19. As He revealed Himself to the holy apostles in true flesh, so He reveals Himself to us now in sacred bread.

20. And as they saw only His flesh by an insight of their flesh, yet believed that He was God as they contemplated Him with their spiritual eyes,

21. let us, as we see bread and wine with our bodily eyes, see and firmly believe that they are His most holy Body and Blood living and true.
22. And in this way the Lord is always with His faithful, as He Himself says: Behold I am with you until the end of the age.

It is evident from the above how carefully Francis often composed his texts. Lord and Jesus appears eight times, Father eight times and Spirit eight times as well. The symbolism of the number 8 goes back to the Bible: it refers to a new beginning between God and humanity. Likewise, in his Testament, Francis also mentions God's initiative eight times and in the Canticle – after his moving experience of the newness given him by God in all his misery – 'praised be you my Lord' sounds eight times as well.

The fact that the number 8 plays a role in this first Admonition is explained by the Admonition's central theme: that one can only come to realise who Jesus Christ really is through God's initiative and inspiration.

God, hidden and near

Here Francis indeed concentrates on the question as to how the incarnation of God's Son can become accessible for us: which manner of looking enables us to see this mystery? God's hiddenness, prominent in the first five verses, is no less pregnant with mystery when God reveals himself in Jesus. When the One who is not able to be seen revealed Himself in Jesus, who is the One not deemed worthy to be seen, God's hiddenness was not suspended. On the contrary rather. Exactly in this very notion of coming closer, in this disconcerting nearness, God's presence is withdrawn from our grasp. In more human terms: God is less able to be understood in the humanity of his Son than in his inaccessible grandeur. Doesn't the fact that God is the Most High, answer to our all too human expectations, conscious as we are of our own finite limitations? And the fact that the Son, God from God, identifies himself with the lowest and reveals himself in the breaking of the eucharistic

Bread – isn't it exactly this which exceeds all our knowledge and understanding?

This mystery of God's self-revelation, which at the same time is his concealment, can perhaps be approached in this way: when God revealed himself step by step in the Old Testament and even more so in the New Testament, then he became more and more the One who makes space and gives place. The self-emptying and humiliation about which the Letter to the Philippians speaks in such a charged manner, is the proof that God has definitely come close to us in Christ. For He approaches us as He is: as the One who gives himself while remaining who He is; as the One who sets us free by letting us be free; as self-giving Love who identifies with those who have become estranged and have fallen.

In a certain way one could say that God's revelation in our tattered reality is also a 'retreat'. The eminent Dutch theologian Noordmans put it this way: 'God's grandeur and richness are in retreat.' The One who appeared and shared our life is defenceless and insignificant. Certainly, this Son of Man is also majestic even in his suffering and dying. As such he has his own beauty. But how different is this radiance from what we are able to comprehend using our own human concepts of power, wisdom and grandness. This is why it is urgent that we must learn to see and think differently.

It is concerning this different way of seeing and knowing the Lord that Francis speaks. This shift in our breadth of outlook is all-important to him. For if the Lord Jesus is the Way to the Father (verse 1), what is then the right way to Jesus? Francis' question is: *with what type of eyes* are we able to see Him in his true self: He who descended from the lap of the Father and who made manifest God's humility to such a degree. It is remarkable that Francis decided to introduce the Admonitions, his pathway to learning, with this very question. How does Jesus Christ let himself be known in his humanity as the One in whom we may see the Father? The question as to how we can avoid pseudo-knowledge and pseudo-piety runs right through many of Francis' Admonitions. To start with however, the question concerning knowledge of the Son of Man is the most important.

Seeing in the Spirit

The key sentence can be found in verse 6 of Admonition 1: 'God cannot be seen except in the Spirit because it is the Spirit that gives life'. This is a key sentence in the literal sense of the word, for only in the Spirit can we gain access to the knowledge of God's gift of Himself in Jesus Christ.

What do these words 'seeing in the Spirit' point to? We would not be on the right track if we were to immediately think about the spirit as immaterial or incorporeal. By adding a word quoted from the Gospel according to John and from the Creed, Francis points us in the right direction: the Spirit is the Life Giver. The true life given us by the Holy Spirit is expressed in being inspired by God's love. This is another name for the Holy Spirit who is the Ardour and Interest (the Being Amongst) of God. Francis points out that God's humility can only be known in this Spirit of disinterested and humble love.

Whether physically seeing the man Jesus then and there in Galilee, or in seeing the bread and wine of the Eucharist, this one fact is all-determining: seeing in the Spirit. Negatively speaking, this means that God does not reveal himself to an unloving gaze directed at the eucharistic elements as if they were just any objects. Because the Holy Spirit is the Loving Bond and Loving Gaze between the Father and the Son, He is the only one who can show us who the Son essentially is in his self-sacrifice.

There is no other access to the truth – the truth who is the Son himself. Augustine expressed this insight in saying: 'The only access to the truth is through love'. Real truth only reveals itself to eyes which have been given life by God's Interest. And this fragile truth remains inaccessible to the lifeless gaze of self-interest – 'an insight of the flesh', as Francis puts it in verse 20.

Francis' viewpoint can be recognised in the contemporary acknowledgement of the fact that our understanding of things is usually led by our own interests. Our selfish desires are often the fathers of our seemingly unselfish thoughts and observations. Not that Francis actually theorises about this influence of our self-interest (or interest) which often pre-forms or perverts our observations.

No, he simply points out the only Interest as well as the only Meaning which are truly of importance to us. He points out the desire of the Holy Spirit. Paradoxically enough this means that he focuses on the interest (importance) of disinterested (unselfish) Love. It is *this* interest which gives access to true knowledge. And this not only goes for our relationship with God, but also for our mutual human relationships – as is evident in a number of other sayings from Francis' pathway to learning.

With the eyes of the Spirit who lives in us

Further on in Admonition 1, Francis again points out the Holy Spirit as the One who inspires our faithful understanding of matters. It comes down to 'seeing and believing according to the Spirit' (verse 9). And in verse 12: 'It is the Spirit of the Lord, therefore, That lives in Its faithful, That receives the Body and Blood of the Lord.' The Holy Spirit is therefore the true Receiver. The word 'receive' has a dual significance here. On the one hand it concerns the receiving of the Lord in the act of faithfully 'seeing' as inspired by the Holy Spirit, and on the other hand as the literal consumption of the eucharistic Bread and Wine: 'The Spirit of the Lord, That lives in Its faithful' (verse 12). To Francis, the 'dwelling in' of the Holy Spirit is a dear and precious thing. In his Letter to the Faithful, the fact that 'the Spirit of the Lord will rest upon all those who have served, and will make a home and dwelling place in them' (verse 48), is the inspiration for one of the most intimate texts Francis has left us concerning the relationship with the Triune God. Here in Admonition 1, this understanding of the indwelling of the Holy Spirit 'in the faithful' is connected in an interesting way to what is given prominence in verse 6, namely that God can only be seen in the Spirit. The connection to what is proclaimed in the Gospel according to John can be seen. It concerns a mutual indwelling: of the Spirit in the faithful, and of the faithful in the Spirit. It is only *in* this mutual 'presence', in this intimate relationship with the Spirit, so says Francis, in which the Son is able to be recognised – and seen 'with spiritual eyes' (verse 20).

This 'seeing with spiritual eyes' (which is what the whole of Admonition 1 is all about) can perhaps be clarified by referring to the name given to the Holy Spirit by Francis in Admonition 27, namely *discretio* (discretion). The verb *discernere* means 'to perceive' or 'to discern'. It is used by Francis when he speaks about recognising God's presence in priests, even if they are sinful people (Testament 9). The word *discretio* also has a meaning which can be heard in the English 'discreet'. It alludes to a sensitivity which combines 'recognition' with 'reserve', and 'discernment' with 'respect'. As the One who is Sensitivity itself, the Spirit 'sees' and helps the faithful to see in this way as well.

Seeing and believing

Faith is mentioned for good reasons. For these two words, 'seeing and believing', are repeatedly emphasised by Francis. Physical seeing is, as it were, permeated by faith. And seeing with our physical eyes embodies our living faith in God's presence, also and exactly where He reveals himself and becomes humble in the man Jesus. This mystery is so fragile that it cannot be mastered by an uninterested or indifferent gaze or by an interest which is nourished by the desire to possess. The Lord withdraws from this type of gaze and, in doing so, becomes more than ever the One who cannot be seen.

'Seeing and believing': at issue here is a seeing that has come into motion; a dynamic type of seeing that results in a broader outlook. The everyday aspects that we can observe in the man Jesus and in his eucharistic gifts of bread and wine, come into true perspective. Our normal experience (but what is normal?) sometimes gives rise to this more profound type of seeing. Sometimes the simplicity of a flower standing upright can suddenly move us – and then we can see the flower 'with different eyes'. That all too familiar sunflower we now see afresh, in a totally different perspective. Suddenly it shows itself, standing upright through the power of the Sun – a symbol of the human being who is able to turn and face God. Usually however, our vision is not touched by such grace.

More often than not, the question arises as to why it is simply not sufficient just to see. Why bother with believing? Why must we, when it comes down to what is most important, make do with *believing*? Is it however a question of 'making do with'? If we stop and take stock of what Scripture says about the act of believing, then we can learn that 'believing' is not a kind of surrogate for 'seeing'. It is not a comfort-blanket; nor is it a Cinderella to physical seeing; nor is it a consolation for not really being able to see. In the act of believing, a possibility opens up which reaches further than a mere cognitive kind of seeing. The possibility to entrust and abandon oneself to God – in short: to start moving, venturing out towards God.

A moved heart

This movement of our innermost being (our heart) is a movement instigated by God's Spirit – indeed, it *is* the Holy Spirit itself. Following Scripture, Francis speaks with acumen about man's heart which is 'hardened' (verse 14). But our heart was created to venture out. And if the Spirit's breath of life moves us, our heart can indeed venture out towards Christ and draw our gaze – our seeing – along with it into the depths of God's presence in the self-revelation of his Beloved.

Our faithful understanding of God's coming close to us in Jesus and in the Eucharist is a matter of the heart, inspired by the Holy Spirit. If not so, then we grope around in the dark. But could it be otherwise, seeing that God's self-revelation is also a matter of *his* heart? Doesn't the fact that God's revelation of himself in his near hiddenness and in his hidden nearness, above all demonstrate His loving respect for us? In respecting our capacity to affirm Him and to submit to Him in all freedom, He 'tempers' his radiance, so that he will only be 'seen' by those, who in the Holy Spirit, desire to see Him with all their heart.

All this having been said and done, the fact remains that Francis speaks about seeing and believing. The physical seeing remains intact – it keeps fulfilling its task. But however material this physical seeing is and remains, the believer has at the same time the sense of being engaged into a new relationship of giving and receiving life. Only within this relationship can the Eucharist be truly understood. The Eucharist is taken up into our physical existence in order that we, as corporeal as we are, are then taken up into the Body of the Risen Lord: into the 'House of Bread', which is inspired by the Holy Spirit.

Affective seeing

'Seeing with spiritual eyes': this is, one could say, the 'contemplative life'. However, this does not only hold for those of the faithful who have purposely chosen to be 'contemplatively religious'. All those who confess the Triune God are only able to know Him if they have become 'contemplatives' in the Spirit. But as far as this goes, instead of using the word 'contemplatives', couldn't we just as well or even rather use the word 'affectives'? For this all amounts to people who have been touched in their hearts by God's infectious Love. This Spirit of love forms and permeates faithful contemplation. Whatever word is chosen, most important of all is that in becoming aware of the mystery of God's self-revelation, any desire to master it does not have a chance. God's Spirit is generosity and respect and our answer to this loving respect can only be respect and gratitude. In the realisation of our unworthiness, we can only respectfully search for His nearness.

Letting oneself be 'brought home' by the Spirit

Francis' First Admonition is very relevant to the issues we are dealing with here. In addition to all that has been said about the connection between understanding and interest, we would like to remark upon the following.

Francis explicitly deals with our manner of seeing: with which eyes and within what sort of solidarity are we truly able to know the Lord? This question as to possible ways of interpretation has priority within contemporary thought. In addition, Francis connects the question concerning our ways of understanding and comprehending to a fact that also intrigues many these days: the hiddenness of God – while also revealing Himself in Jesus. This added reference to Christ's humanity is however less often heard nowadays. Of course this does not detract from what Francis has to say.

If we try to understand what something means, then we try to place it *within* a context in which we feel at ease in our heart of hearts. The important question then is: within which 'home' – meaning within which context of our life, observations and thinking – do we place that which we desire to understand? This boils down to the question whether we are capable of describing our original context of existence. This is the 'home' in which we already live, prior to forming all possible theories: and this in various contexts (social, economic, linguistic etc.).

We will of course discover no such reflections with Francis. However the radical turn that Francis gives in all simplicity, does shine a light on this. To be able to understand Jesus in his humanity and in the Eucharist, a radical conversion is necessary. Prior to being able to interpret, to 'bring home' who He is, we must first of all change 'homes' ourselves, that is: we must first be 'brought home' in and through God's Spirit. Only once we are in the Spirit and only once the Spirit has moved us from within, are we able to recognise the Lord's hidden truth. In other words: we need to 'move house': from a self-directed 'bringing home' (interpretation) to a complying 'being brought home'.

This 'moving house' is called 'learning to have faith'. This amounts to crossing the usual line dividing what we up until then had considered to be meaningful or unmeaningful. To be capable of 'moving house' we moderns need to wean ourselves off much of what we have come to regard as self-evident and normal. If we are to live as believers, we must constantly be weaned in order to discover who Jesus truly is. The more we have got used to seeing and valuing the way things are usually done nowadays, the more we will have to go through the 'habit-kicking programme' offered by the Spirit as Helper. This 'rehabilitation programme' is not easy –

certainly not if we have been spoiled. Our situation can then be compared to that of the Magi on their long trip to the Child as described by the poet T.S. Eliot: 'A cold coming we had of it (…) with the voices singing in our ears, saying that this was all folly.'[6] The departure from home-base and the trek to Bethlehem turned out to be 'a little like dying'. Where addicts are concerned, could it have been anything else? And especially: in the end the One who lets himself be found compensates everything. Or, the extremely reserved way Eliot describes the arrival of the Magi: 'it was (you may say) satisfactory.'

The 'home' that is awaiting us upon arrival at the Lord is described concisely in the marked simplicity of an old Dutch Christmas carol: 'neither windows, nor doors could be closed there'. Here again it is simplicity that marks truth. And this truth is that our new 'home' will be an 'open home'. In this aspect it is also different from the well-known rooms and gates in and behind which we tend to lock up so much. But this simplicity also marks what is good. This goodness is the fact that this new home will also be open to shepherds and to all those who live on the edge of our selfish society. And this dwelling of the Son of Man is neither temporary nor fleeting, but permanent as is confirmed by the concluding line of the first Admonition: 'Behold I am with you until the end of the age.'

'Bringing Peace': a reflection on Admonitions 13 and 15

The popular image of Francis being a man of peace is no contemporary discovery: his actions as a bringer of peace made a great impression on his own contemporaries. In his writings, he himself let it be known that he saw bringing peace as his special vocation. And looking back on his life shortly before his death, he stated that God had revealed to him that he should use the following greeting: 'May the Lord give you peace.' (Testament 23). He felt

---

[6] *The Complete Poems and Plays of T.S. Eliot*, 'Journey of the Magi', 1927; 103.

that *this* was his mission; that this is what he wished to convey to his disciples. The fact that he wanted there to be no misunderstandings concerning the place that the bringing of peace had in his spirituality is also apparent from the following: right in the middle of his Admonitions – his pathway to learning – he twice comments on Jesus' beatitudes about the bringers of peace.

Admonition 13
"*'Blessed are the peacemakers, for they will be called children of God.'*" A servant of God cannot know how much patience and humility he has within himself as long as he is content. When the time comes, however, when those who should make him content do the opposite, he has as much patience and humility as he has at that time and no more.'

Admonition 15
"*'Blessed are the peacemakers, for they will be called children of God.'*" Those people are truly peacemakers who, regardless of what they suffer in this world, preserve peace of spirit and body out of love of our Lord Jesus Christ.'

What Francis says about peace here, we wish to clarify with other statements from his writings. Only by doing this can we fathom the deep life-giving source from which the meditating Francis drew for his far-reaching choices. This radicalism explains the conviction which his words still hold today.

Before going on however, the following: major social issues are not explicitly dealt with in the quoted Admonitions. Francis gauges the attitudes through which the reformation of social relations is able to take place. Here the master focuses on the testing of motivation and orientation – both of which are determining factors when it comes to the extent to which someone will endeavour to better society. The concrete reformation of social relations was indeed also important to him. His Rules and letters show that he – from a religious point of view – recognised the importance of this. These references – focussed as they are on the social context of Francis' times – are especially important to us because they illuminate his Gospel-based inspiration: an inspiration which should once again gain expression in our own situation and times.

Testing the authenticity of peace

Characteristic for Francis' spiritual leadership is the emphasis he places on the authenticity of behaviour. In his Admonitions we hear again and again the question whether the attitude people appear to show in their pious behaviour is authentic or not. Does it correspond to their inner reality? Most of his Admonitions turn out to be sayings which test this authenticity. Confronted with religious behaviour, he unmasks whatever is nothing more than veneer, fake or front. His critical stance and desire for honesty have something very modern about them. However, Francis stands aside from this modern mentality as far as this critical stance results in a wish to wilfully unmask and depreciate people. Just like Jesus, he wanted to above all wake people up and help them out of their day-dreaming. Most of his Admonitions therefore function as a sort of litmus-test to help discern whether the inner attitude corresponds to what may seem attractive from the outside.

Admonition 13 also offers a way to test whatever presents itself as 'patient and humble' – for Francis a test, a probe into that which presents itself as evangelically virtuous. But, one may ask, isn't attention shifted away from Jesus' words about the peacemakers through this? For what exactly do patience and humility have to do with peace? It is indeed remarkable that the word *peace* is only mentioned in the citation of Jesus' beatitude. After that, Francis concentrates on the question whether or not wishes and desires have to be fulfilled.

Is it fair to regard his way of commenting as rather strange? The word which twice over receives an important place in Francis' commentary, namely *satisfacere*, means to satisfy or to sate cherished desires. If Francis fixes his attention on this satisfaction, then this is because he views man in his essence as desire. *The* question for him is therefore: which desire or which wish drives us? And up until what point are we capable of tolerating the fact that we are frustrated in the fulfilment of these wishes and desires? Can we bear not possessing?

Francis' sober conclusion is: the patience and humility a person is capable of mustering reveals the extent to which he or she is really at peace with the situation – and therefore whether capable of passing on true peace to others. The real test concerning the question whether one is a peacemaker in the style of Jesus, is if one is able to accept with God's help whatever is essentially strange to one's innermost being; to swallow what is bitter.

Even if, while holding Jesus' Gethsemane experience and the introduction to Francis' Testament in mind, we try to understand this point of view concerning the value of 'swallowing what is bit-ter', the question remains what the intrinsic connection is between patience and humility on the one hand and peace on the other. What does Francis mean by peace at its most profound level? Before dealing with this question we will first try and understand what making peace means according to Francis.

Truly following Jesus

Action or activity can be perceived in the word 'peacemakers': lit-erally 'those who make peace'. Only once we have become con-scious of this, does the meaning of Admonition 15 become clear. After once again citing Jesus' beatitude, Francis continues: 'Those people are truly peacemakers who, regardless of what they suffer in this world, preserve peace of spirit and body out of love of our Lord Jesus Christ.'

The two verbs which form the basis of this Admonition are to suffer (or to stand) and to keep peace with. Passive as they are, both create a tension with what is evoked by the word peacemak-ers. We believe that Francis was aware of this tension and wished, through his choice of words, to bring our attention to the power that lies behind the seemingly so passive suffer and keep. The ten-sion between actively bringing-peace and passively suffering is not a pure contradiction when looked at more closely. Whatever you cannot do anything about and have to submit to, can at the same time be something with which you can certainly achieve results. One can accept one's situation and bear it. Francis adds that a person is able to do this because of the love of our Lord Jesus Christ. If someone is motivated by this, then suffering can attain the significance of consciously bearing. Or, as Etty Hillesum puts it: 'to take in pain under one's roof'; to 'bear' it.[7]

As we shall see in Chapter 4, Francis makes it very clear that the act of bearing has a central position in his view of a Christian's vocation. One's capacity for action is often apparent from one's capacity to bear. He speaks about the bearing of the other in all his or her fragility (Admonition 18); about the bearing of sickness and oppression (Canticle of the Creatures) and about the bearing of Christ's cross (Admonition 5). Again and again, the act of acceptance of or resilience to reality in its entirety is concerned – also when this is bitter and provokes resistance. For only then can people fully become helpers of the Holy Spirit who is working at the restoration and re-creation of what has been damaged in God's good Creation. Only as co-healers will we become peacemakers.

A superhuman task?

It is difficult to avoid asking whether we are able to bear and 'experience' this notion of suffering. Isn't Francis recommending us superhuman patience? Something no one is capable of mustering up? In speaking of people who 'regardless of what they suffer in this world, preserve peace', he seemingly leaves no room for exceptions. From the fact that elsewhere in his writings he also radically expresses this conviction, it is apparent that this is not a pious slip of the tongue. His Letter to a Minister reads: 'You must consider as grace all that impedes you from loving the Lord God and

---

[7] Ester "Etty" Hillesum (b. January 14, 1914 in Hilversum, The Netherlands – d. November 30, 1943 in Auschwitz) was a young Jewish woman who kept a diary during World War II. See: *Etty. A Dairy. 1941-1943,* (translated by A.J. Pomerans). London 1983.

whoever has become an impediment to you, whether brothers or others, even if they lay hands on you. And may you want it to be this way and not otherwise' (verses 2-3).

It may be true that this text confirms the fact that Francis' spirituality is characterised by a tendency towards universality, but is the universal criterion he wields in Admonition 15 all the same no less human? Who is able to attain this?

Where Francis is concerned it is advisable to be very careful in using the word 'superhuman'. Not because it would be extra difficult to determine what achievements people are capable of in comparison to this exceptional man – but rather because Francis, in dealing with what people are capable of, does not in the least have in mind what we humans can do. For him the fact that people would be able to achieve things of worth on their own merit without God's assistance, is out of the question. Moreover, his outlook on people and their possible growth and development was from the very start determined by the dynamics which captivated him in the person of Jesus Christ: the descending and relinquishing dynamics of God's Love who became flesh of our flesh in His Son. Because Jesus Christ, the Word of the Father 'received the flesh of our humanity and frailty', humankind – fragile as it is and remains – received its divinity from God.[8] Therefore man, amongst the other creatures, is indeed 'the image of His beloved Son according to the body and to His likeness according to the Spirit' (Admonition 5,1). With the nobility of being made in this image, comes the task to love in the same descending and relinquishing manner as expressed in Jesus' humility and patience. If, in following Jesus, people appear to be able to accomplish something (and all the more if they are able to do so to a high degree), then it is always because it pleases the Spirit of the Father and Son to work in and with them. How is this insight applied regarding the call to bring peace?

---

[8] *Francis of Assisi: Early Documents. Volume I. The Saint,* 'Later Admonition and Exhortation to the Brothers and Sisters of Penance' (= Second Version of the Letter to the Faithful); 4; 46.

Peace: God's gift

Seeing that the standard set by Francis by far exceeds the usual human capacity, we suspect he was not thinking of a purely human peace when speaking of keeping the peace. And didn't this hold true for his Lord's utterances as well? When Jesus promised his peace to his disciples: 'Peace I leave with you; my peace I give to you', he added 'I do not give to you as the world gives.' (John 14:27). What did Jesus mean when he spoke of 'my peace'? These words from his Final Discourse only receive their full meaning by relating them to the way in which the risen Lord greeted His disciples three times with the words 'Peace be with you' followed by 'Receive the Holy Spirit' (John 20:22). In promising his peace, he apparently did not give them an idea or ideal, but rather the Holy Spirit itself. This is the concrete power of God which inspires and which is able to heal the deepest chasms and schisms (the words quoted are immediately followed by 'If you forgive the sins of any, they are forgiven them' (John 20:23). The risen Lord offers the Holy Spirit as his gift: 'receive the Holy Spirit'. This Gift is the Life-force that will help bring reconciliation and peace in us and through us. Seen in this light, the words 'my peace' as spoken by Jesus, are a veiled reference to the Holy Spirit whom elsewhere in John's Gospel is called the Helper (Succour) as well as 'the Gift of God' in his conversation with the woman at the well (John 4:10).

In imitating Jesus, could Francis also have understood peace to be a Gift from God? This would mean that when we truly are at peace, the Holy Spirit is working in and through us. We could then consider peace to be one of the pseudonyms for the Holy Spirit.

The virtues 'patience and humility' which appear twice in Admonition 13, help us discover what Francis had learned about the biblical concept 'peace'. How much 'patience and humility' someone has, we can read there, will only become clear when his wishes and desires are frustrated. Being satisfied or not plays a central role in this Admonition, in which the word peace itself, as we have seen already, does not appear. All attention is focussed on the way in which a servant of God deals with discord and dissatisfaction. In Admonition

27 we also come across the word-pair 'patience and humility' as well as how to deal with frustration.

A challenge to patience and humility

In Admonition 27 Francis contrasts the combinations 'patience and humility' and 'anger and disturbance': 'Where there is patience and humility, there is neither anger nor disturbance' (Admonition 27, verse 2). A somewhat enigmatic saying which fits into the series of contrasting pairs of virtues and pairs of vices and weaknesses. In the inner struggle between the forces exerting their influence within us, 'anger and disturbance' (aggression and disquiet) form a threat to our serene 'humility and patience'. Did Francis have this in mind when in Admonition 13 he realistically reminded us about the profound dissatisfaction which can be a result of the frustration of our desires?

The dissatisfaction which in Admonition 13 evidently forms a challenge to 'patience and humility', and with this a temptation to excitement and anger (and therefore to lovelessness), is portrayed in Francis' famous story about true Joy. This story is essentially about having patience in an extreme situation in which a legitimate desire for the relief of primary needs is nevertheless frustrated in a malicious way. The dénouement comes at the very end: 'I tell you this: If I had patience and did not become upset, true joy, as well as true virtue and the salvation of my soul, would consist in this'.[9] 'True joy' is the authentic satisfaction expressed in not reciprocating the icy lovelessness of others.

Touchstone

Admonition 13, a test for true peace, implies the following question: are you capable of bearing in patience and humility being frustrated by others in your legitimate desire for recognition?

---

[9] *Francis of Assisi: Early Documents. Volume I. The Saint,* 'True and Perfect Joy'; 167.

Strongly worded: can you remain at peace while an essential desire of yours is frustrated? Only once you have passed this test, can you be called a true peacemaker as meant by Jesus in his Beatitudes.

Admonition 15 clarifies this notion of peace and making peace by explicitly repeating aspects mentioned in Admonition 13. What was described in Admonition 13 as 'who bear in patience and humility' is summarized and elucidated in Admonition 15 with 'regardless of what they suffer in this world'. And the positive quality of the peaceful bearing of essential frustrations is expressed in this Admonition by 'preserve peace of spirit and body out of love of our Lord Jesus Christ.'

These last words are important. The combination of peace and love (in combination with patience and humility) is repeatedly mentioned in Francis' writings. The way Francis sees it, this combination apparently springs from the action of the Holy Spirit who is divine Love itself. In light of this, the full significance of the seemingly worn-out phrase in Admonition 15, namely 'out of love of our Lord Jesus Christ', becomes clear. The love of our Lord Jesus Christ is the Holy Spirit who can inspire us in such a way that we can stay at peace while suffering anything.

At this very core of his pathway to learning, Francis appears to have been influenced by Paul's testimony in Romans 8:28 and 35: 'Who will separate us from the love of Christ? Will hardship, or distress, or persecution, or famine, or nakedness, or peril, or sword? (…) For I am convinced that neither death, nor life, nor angels, nor rulers, nor things present, nor things to come, nor powers, nor height, nor depth, nor anything else in all creation, will be able to separate us from the love of God in Christ Jesus our Lord.'

Peace springs from the heart

Francis' usual greeting was: 'May the Lord give you peace!' The Lord had revealed this to him. As we have already seen, this greeting therefore had an incomparably more powerful significance for Francis, than what we usually suppose can be discerned in a greeting. In the eyes of the man from Assisi, true peacemakers are nothing less than bearers and bringers of the Holy Spirit: passing on the Spirit they themselves have received for nothing, totally free. This is especially true where Jesus is concerned. His words 'Blessed are the peacemakers, for they will be called children of God', apply primarily and especially to Himself, who as the relayer of the Spirit is of course *the* Peacemaker and *the* Child of God. But also those who try to follow Jesus and in whom 'the Spirit of the Lord rests and dwells' shall be – and Francis is quite sure about this – 'the children of the heavenly Father, Whose works they do.'[10] To be able to gauge the full depth of what Francis says in Admonition 15 – 'preserve peace of spirit and body out of love of our Lord Jesus Christ' – it is important to gain insight into the connection between the different relationships with Christ. If we relate the words spirit and body to Francis' bold statement about the faithful who carry Christ in their heart and body, it turns out that Francis is concerned with the harmonisation of the exterior and interior, of the body and the soul when it comes to peace. More pregnantly expressed: he is concerned with the expression of an interior attitude by exterior behaviour; the movement from inside to outside – in short, the motherly phenomenon of pregnancy and giving birth.

Anything done for the sake of appearance without echoing an interior attitude, was always suspicious in the eyes of Francis, disciple of Jesus. We have already seen how his critical stance was focussed on the testing of exterior behaviour in order to discover if it is authentic; that is in order to see whether it is based on an attitude of the heart. It is totally clear to him that it all comes down to the actual realisation of interior movements by those who have been touched by God's Spirit. If we are moved by somebody else, then we must do what has to be done. Not with the illusion of our own power, but in the clear realisation that the Holy Spirit who moves us, wishes us to bear fruit in this way. Later on, the 14th century mystic Ruusbrouc put it this way: the Holy Spirit works 'from within to without'. In his Rule, Francis expresses this insight

[10] Second Version of the Letter to the Faithful, 48; 49.

as follows: 'Let them pay attention to what they must desire above all else: to have the Spirit of the Lord and Its holy activity.'[11] 'The Holy Spirit' and its 'activity' belong to each other. This is also absolutely true for those who have come to know the Spirit as Peace itself. This Peace insists on 'working through' – insists on the outward manifestation of what the heart has received from God. Only through this 'working through' can the authenticity of interior attitudes be gauged. And this manifestation holds for the body of every individual as well as for the Body of the Church.

Francis' commentary on Jesus' Beatitudes could not have been more concise: true bringers of peace 'are those who, regardless of what they suffer in this world, preserve peace of spirit and body out of love of our Lord Jesus Christ.' This confluence of bringing and preserving is remarkable: whoever preserves this Spirit of peace (this fire, this pure life), shall also pass it on to others. And whoever passes this fire on by means of their 'infectious' behaviour, keeps and preserves it as well. There is only true life where life is generated. True peace is preserved by passing on this peace. Francis' understanding of what real peace entails, is narrowly connected to one of the core convictions of his spirituality, namely that in a certain way all people are called to motherhood – men and women alike. Only in the bearing and nourishing of the other who is our neighbour, shall authentic life in community and therefore true peace arise. The patience and humility of the real peacemakers are strikingly mirrored in the capacity to bear, which as we shall see, is dealt with in Admonition 18: 'Blessed is the person who supports his neighbour in his weakness as he would want to be supported were he in a similar situation.'

Durable peace?

Was Francis' work as a peacemaker a success in the long run? If we can depend on what historians tell us of the durability of what he

[11] *Francis of Assisi: Early Documents. Volume I. The Saint,* 'The Later Rule, Chapter X: 8; 105

was able to achieve with his efforts, then we have to be sceptical. During his life, or soon after it, a lot of his work seems to have been undone. But does this fact detract in any way from what Admonitions 13 and 15 have to say? Does it plead against these Admonitions that Francis' peacemaking efforts were often frustrated – and eventually ended up in failure? Or is this fact of life exactly a confirmation of the spiritual dimension of these two texts on making peace?

We believe the last to be the case. If we take into consideration that the Admonitions received their definite form during the final period of Francis' life, a period in which the seriously ill man physically experienced how difficult it is to muster patience in such a situation, then the two Admonitions become even more valuable.[12] They bear the watermark of purification won through true experience. Francis was probably able to conclude that his peace- and reconciliation efforts were less durable than he had hoped for. His recognition of the absolute necessity of God's 'Succour' – if our human efforts are to have any chance of taking root and sticking – will only have become stronger through this. Admonitions 13 and 15 bear testimony to this recognition of the Breath which, through humility and patience, enables us to make steadfast our desire in spite of everything. It is this same understanding and this same enthusiasm which, till his final hour, enabled him to radiate the peace and joy which still captivate and challenge us today.

[12] Regis J. Armstrong, 'Prophetic Implications of the <Admonitions>'. In: *Laurentianum* 26 (1985); 398-464; 407 ff.

4. Thanking, serving, bearing

The way in which Francis understood Jesus' call to conversion and faith, made us in Chapter 1 aware of how he saw faith as praise and repentance as bearing. The concept bearing turned out to hold a special place in his writings, especially in his Canticle of the Creatures.

Reading through the places in Francis' writings where he speaks about the praise of God, a surprising fact comes to light. The act of praising – which according to his sermon-programme also includes being in awe of, respecting, blessing, thanking and worshipping – is repeatedly summarised by him using the words giving back. For Francis, these words apparently contain all that can be summarised as praising recognition of God.

It is also remarkable that bearing appears predominantly in the pathway to learning of the Admonitions. In them, giving back is also to be found in certain key positions. And last but not least, the attitude of serving forms the thread that runs throughout the entire pathway to learning. Whoever wishes to understand the content of these apparently key concepts for Francis, will therefore have to consult the Admonitions.

Whoever considers the fact that thanking is one of the strongest expressions of what Francis meant with giving back, may find it handy to denote the central concepts mentioned by using the trio: thanking-serving-bearing. It is interesting that the three ways people can ruin their lives can also be memorised using a – very contrasting – trio: claiming-controlling-climbing; just as these three c's can in turn be recognised in their counterparts expressed in the rhyme-sequence sharing-caring-bearing.

First we shall deal with some texts by Francis in which he not only comments upon the concepts to bear and to give back, but also on their counterparts. Next, we shall go into the significance of serving for him. In Chapter 5 we shall deal more thoroughly with the content of giving back and bearing – both being expressions of fundamental serving.

'Bearing' and 'giving back': Admonition 18

In the 'church-building of the Admonitions', Admonitions 11, 12, 17 and 18 form the cornerstones surrounding the centrally positioned commentaries on Jesus' beatitudes. Common to these texts is the fact that they, word for word or in the form of descriptions, form a contrast to Admonition 2 which deals with the central aspect of sin.[1] This Admonition deals severely with two aspects concerning the old Adam 'who exalts himself over the good things the Lord says and does in him' and 'makes his will his own'.

1. The Lord said to Adam: Eat of every tree; you may not eat, however, of the tree of the knowledge of good and evil.
2. He was able to eat of every tree of paradise, because he did not sin as long as he did not go against obedience.
3. For that person eats of the tree of the knowledge of good who makes his will his own and, in this way, exalts himself over the good things the Lord says and does in him.
4. And so, through the suggestion of the devil and the transgression of the commandment, it became the apple of the knowledge of evil.
5. Therefore it is fitting that he suffer punishment (Admonition 2).

In strong contrast to this, Admonition 17 states:
1. 'Blessed is that servant who no more exalts himself over the good the Lord says or does through him than over what He says or does through another.
2. A person sins who wishes to receive more from his neighbour than what he wishes to give of himself to the Lord God.

---

[1] *Respectfully Yours,* Chapter 2; 80 ff.

Admonition 18 formulates this contrast using the two positive concepts 'bearing' and 'giving back'.

1. 'Blessed is the person who bears his neighbour in his weakness as he would want to be borne were he in a similar situation.

2. Blessed is the servant who gives back every good to the Lord God because whoever holds onto something for himself hides the money of his Lord God within himself, and what he thinks he has will be taken away from him.'

In this single saying, Admonition 18 concisely gives the opposites to 'exalting oneself' and 'making something one's own' using the concepts bearing and giving back. Elsewhere these two concepts also hold a significant place for Francis and this raises some questions:

1. Why exactly are these two key concepts, or if you will key values, emphasised? What is concealed behind these concepts?

2. What is the significance of the fact that he combines these two attitudes of 'bearing' and 'giving back' in one and the same Admonition, namely Admonition 18?

These questions can be clarified by initially concentrating on the contrasting Admonition 2.

The testing of good and evil: Admonition 2

This saying forms a striking moment in the pathway to learning of the Admonitions. For immediately after having opened the collection with a meditation on God's hiddenness, Francis deals here with man's hidden centre, namely man's will and the possible deliverance from it. Sharply formulated, one could say that here he is endeavouring to delve into the origins of moral evil. With the help of an image from Genesis he tries to get at the very core of sin.

The prohibition to eat of the fruit of a single certain tree raises one's eyebrows. Why permission to 'eat of every tree' but *not* to 'eat of the tree of knowledge of good'? If this is just a matter of 'obedience', why is this then expressed using the image of not eating? Where exactly does the 'transgression of the commandment' begin? This would amount to something like 'how far am I still allowed to go?', were Francis not to make a remarkable move in verse 3 – a move inwards:

> 'For that person eats of the tree of the knowledge of good who makes his will his own and, in this way, exalts himself over the good things the Lord says and does in him' (Admonition 2).

The good which is recognised or which is on the other hand disregarded is, as Francis sees it, a matter of the *will* and does not belong to the order of concrete things. The will is expressed in words and deeds. The goodness of someone's good deeds and words has its deepest roots not in one's own will, but in God's. This notion is based on the belief that God is the One who is good and the Source of man's life (compare Philippians 2:13).

This belief raises the question regarding the relationship between dependence on God's goodness and the fact that man has been endowed with a free will. The answer is that this mystery is precisely hidden in God's goodness and in His self-revelation to man. The Creator gives people space and time to be His co-workers and fellow-creators, inspired by Him. As is written in the first story of creation: 'Let us make humankind in our image, according to our likeness' (Genesis 1:26). Called to be 'image and likeness': herein lies the inviolable dignity of humankind and its calling to share in the 'freedom of the children of God' (Romans 8:21). Psalm 8 also expresses this in such an impressive way:

> 'Yet you have made them a little lower than God, and crowned them with glory and honour. You have given them dominion over the works of your hands' (Psalm 8:5-6a).

Meditating upon this, Francis wrote in Admonition 5:

> 'Consider, O human being, in what great excellence the Lord God has placed you, for He created and formed you to the image of His beloved Son according to the body and to His likeness according to the Spirit' (verse 1).

God's goodness: source of all good will

God is good and is only good. Francis proclaims this again and again. And He gives all that is good its concrete existence. Whenever someone wants good things, says or does something good, this is also the fruit of God's inspiration. Nothing is bad in itself. Evil only comes into being when, through sin, someone corrupts reality which in itself is good. This corruption originates in the will to affirm oneself by negating the fact that God is the source of goodness. Because God is 'closer to us than our innermost being' (Augustine), He is the source of our will to do good. Perhaps we can refer here to what Jesus paradoxically said: 'My teaching is not mine but his who sent me' (John 7:16). Emphatically '*my* teaching', yet first and foremost that of his Father. Francis says the same: my intuitions and inclinations which are expressed in my good words and deeds do not in the end belong to myself. If I do not recognise this, then I overstep a limit and trespass upon my innermost being.

Seen in this way, the core of sin is therefore the negation of a difference, namely the difference between mine and Yours, between my will and God's will. It is true that people are permitted to take of whatever is growing around them as they see fit. This 'seeing fit' is however only truly good if it does not get in the way of doing good, something to which others have a right. In other words: whatever the other has a right to, forms the limit of what I can and may 'eat'.

The eating of the fruit of paradise is, as Francis sees it, an image of the unlawful seizing of possessions. 'Making one's will one's own' amounts to acts of absorbing, annexing and enlisting into a lifestyle that is focused on the augmentation of one's own honour and glory. In this scenario one appoints oneself to be the final norm concerning good and bad and in actual fact wants to play at being a god. The image of 'eating' – symbolising the unlawful appropriation of the good fruit – not only denotes being infected by evil but also the realisation of this fact. The good fruit has become the 'fruit of the knowledge of evil'. 'Sin' means nothing less than the denial of God's ownership. This is the same thing as disregarding His bestowing generosity. On the other hand, 'the knowledge of good' means the recognition of the One who is good: of the goodness of God's Spirit who lives in and works with us.

Self-appropriation: a kind of plagiarism

Whenever someone consciously disregards God by attributing whatever good that he, thanks to Him, has been able to do or say, he does not only become guilty of great ingratitude, but also of a form of theft which is similar to plagiarism: he makes a show of things by using what rightly belongs to another.

This swelling of the inflated self which 'appropriates' and 'exalts itself' actually amounts to an appalling shrinkage of one's 'humanity'. By becoming fatally engrossed in the narrow world of 'my-me-mine', the sinner isolates himself from the other and constricts his own life. In doing so, he strangles himself by robbing himself of his complete development as a human being. In order to once again be able to live up to God's gifts, he will therefore have to restrict his false claims. He will have to bear his 'punishment' for disregarding God. This punishment means that he voluntarily give up his self-glorification and self-enrichment – of which others have also become the victims – and step down from his self-made throne. Of course this means a painful restriction of claims to power that have run wild, but at the same time it heralds the end of the shrinkage of his true self. 'Punishment' (*poena*) just like 'penance' (*poenitentia*) means relief and deliverance: by doing justice to others and to the Other.

God as the One who is first

By heartily recognising God as the Bestower of all that is good, one lets God really be God and 'gives back to God what belongs to God' (Admonition 11,4). This recognition which is characterised by giving back is accompanied by the following: honouring Him who deserves honour, doing justice to Him, recognising Him by professing gratitude and thanking Him.

Is God recognised as the sole owner by doing this? Yes: in the sense that man himself cannot assert property-rights and that he recognises that all things good originate from God. However in a more profound sense 'no': for in His self-revelation in Israel and in Christ, God did not reveal himself as a self-complacent owner, but as the pre-eminent Giver. Precisely as the 'image of God', man can be someone who gives back freely: man as the 're-presentation' (image) of Him and man 'presenting' (giving back) together with Him. Man as the image of the Giver who has already revealed himself to us, and who was the first to recognise our dignity in being able to become generous givers ourselves. In this way, man as giver-of-respect becomes the image of Him who is the First Giver and utmost Source of respect.

Seen in this light, what does 'knowledge of good' mean in Admonition 2? Here knowledge means the recognition of God who is the source of our life. He is the non-manipulable 'Other'. He is closer to us than we are to ourselves. This recognition includes our assenting to God's generous will. As Francis states elsewhere, by 'laying one's will in the will of the Father', a person can enter into the vastness of God's love. In this he is no longer the prisoner of a narrow-minded arbitrariness. Being in-the-will-of-the-Father means incomparable security for man, however mortal he may be. In comparison to this, the cramped struggle for self-maintenance – which others must pay the price for – is extremely desolate.

Paul's hymn about Jesus Christ

Is there an explanation for the fact that Francis gives such a prominent place to precisely these two biblical concepts 'bearing' and 'giving back'? The combination of these two key values in Admonition 18 especially requires clarification. If it is not a coincidence that they were brought together in a single saying, then what is their relationship? Their opposites pose the same question: what do 'exalting oneself' and 'self-appropriation' have in common?

For those who are looking for the biblical basis of Admonitions 2, 11, 12, 17 and 18, Paul's hymn about Jesus Christ (Philippians 2:6-8) stands out. The key words from Admonition 2 answer 'negatively' to the central words of this hymn, just as the key words from the other Admonitions mentioned do so in a 'positive' way.

Philippians 2, 6-8:	*Admonitions 2 and 11; 12; 17; 18:*	
He who was in the form of God did not regard equality with God as something to be exploited,	he who makes his will his own	negative
	giving back	positive
but he emptied himself taking the form of a slave being born in human likeness.	he who makes his will his own	negative
	giving back	positive
And being found in human form he humbled himself	exalting oneself	negative
	not exalting oneself / bearing	positive
and became obedient to the point of death – even death on a cross.	to go against obedience	negative

Because of his voluntary self-emptying, humiliation and servile obedience, Jesus – as the hymn expresses it – became the highly Exalted One and received the name 'that is above every name: Jesus Christ is Lord'. In typifying Adam's original sin, Francis undoubtedly had Paul's typification of the New Adam in mind – the New Adam about Whom he had heard sung every Holy Week. For Francis, the moments in this hymn laid out, as it were, the co-ordinates for the life of faith of Christ's disciples. Seen in this light, 'conversion' is the continual co-operation with the voluntary self-humiliation and self-emptying which Jesus, obedient unto death, accomplished for all of us. In doing so, Jesus radically reversed the lives of those whose craving for independence and self-expansion comes at the cost to others. It is on this revolution ('upside-down' and 'inside-out') that Francis' and Clare's choice in life-style was based.

Francis' traits of character

Francis' traits may be mentioned as lying behind this choice. The radical break with his father does not only tell us something of Peter Bernadone's hot temper; his son must have been a lot like his father as far as this goes: he could become very angry. The fact that Francis was not always at ease with his own temper could be concluded from how relatively often he uses the word-pair 'patience and humility' in his writings; and this several times as a counterpart to 'anger and excitement'. He must have viewed the exercise of patience and humility as his special task. Bearing is the verb which expresses this exercise.

He only realised what this task entailed after having made his radical choice for a 'downhill' career and for solidarity with the poorest of the poor. He then physically experienced what it meant to maintain oneself in the struggle for a minimal means of subsistence – and to apparently not be able to do so without the help of others. His experience of long-term captivity and illness which as a youth had helped him face reality, was reconfirmed: without the support of others, one cannot survive. Only once one starts giving support oneself, can true happiness blossom. During his final years, his illnesses only intensified his understanding of the fragility of human existence. The fate of the sick is all too often being confined to two square-metres in isolation. Experiencing the support of others will then result in deep joy. Whoever wishes to be free of illusions soon realises that this is the human condition. If people nevertheless rouse themselves to climb the social ladder at the cost of all and sundry, then in doing so they only confirm this precarious instability: this self-induced isolation can also only be terminated through the mutual solidarity of bearing.

The special accent that giving back has for Francis is also a consequence of his personal character and circumstances. Witnesses to the behaviour of the rich merchant's son show that he was a 'bon vivant' in his youth – also in the sense that he was a 'big spender'. Through this generosity he 'made it' with his peers and gained their respect. The self-appropriation which he was later on to so radically reject, had as far as he was concerned not so much to do with lust for money; the real danger lay in the self-appropriation of one's will (Admonition 2).

This does not detract from the experiences he had as a merchant (and later on as a mendicant friar). Due to the falling away of the social demarcations which had existed up until then, the hunt for possessions had run rampant. Even before his conversion he had seen that possessions isolate people. After his conversion he discovered that the poor are continually forced into isolation due to their daily struggle for a minimal means of subsistence. This oppressive situation clamours for the recognition of the right to a life of dignity; for others it demands the recognition of the duty to share with the poor what has been received from God – to thus 'give it back' to God.

Unsteady and vulnerable

In Paul's hymn about Christ as well as in Francis' experiences in life, two 'co-ordinates' of the human condition can be discerned. Whenever people endeavour to maintain themselves by elevating themselves above others, the fundamental unsteadiness or instability of their existence is at issue. And whenever they try to make themselves secure at the cost of others, it is their existential vulnerability that actually rules their life. In choosing for 'bearing' and 'giving back', Francis makes it clear that he has learned from Jesus how to deal in a different fashion with the unavoidable instability and vulnerability of human existence. The pivot on which everything hinges is the priority he confers upon the other: by no longer seeing the other as a competitor but rather as someone who is just as fragile and vulnerable as himself; and seeing the other as someone who liberates him from his stifling isolation because of that person's appeal for recognition and respect.

The fundamental attitudes 'serving', 'bearing' and 'giving back' which characterise the entire pathway to learning of the Admonitions, indeed distinguish themselves by attributing a privileged position to others. Whoever is bent on prestige and possessions is called to order. That is: called into the 'area of living' for and with others, as well as with and for the Other. This area is the occasion for a renewed living together before the face of the Father, which is all that Jesus was concerned with in his life and preaching. This radical reversal in attitudes, necessary for this way of living together, becomes clear as we have seen when Admonition 2 is compared to Admonitions 17 and 18. Whenever the urge to exalt oneself and to self-appropriate is resisted, this pattern of reversal is reproduced. This dynamics, which Francis lays out, as it were along a vertical and horizontal axis, is that of:

- moving from self-exaltation to submissiveness in 'suffering punishment' (Admonition 2), resulting in 'bearing one's neighbour in his weakness' (Admonition 18);
- moving from 'making one's will one's own' (Admonition 2) to 'letting go', which is fulfilled in 'giving back' to the Lord and by recognising 'the rights of the poor'.

Briefly summarised: through 'bearing' and 'giving back', which Francis learned from the incarnate Son of God, a person becomes truly human by doing justice to others. He blossoms by giving space to the other/Other. In this way, the community which Jesus envisioned comes into being.

Serving: a walk along the pathway of learning

Up until now we have not given sufficient attention to two remarkable aspects found in the pathway to learning of the Admonitions. Namely to the high frequency of the word 'servant' as well as to the special role given to 'obedience' after Francis unmasks the true character of original sin as 'disobedience' in Admonition 2. With this, he sets the tone for the Admonitions which follow. What living in obedience means is impressively explained in Admonition 3. However, soon afterwards this 'obedience' takes the shape of 'serving'. Admonition 4 is based on the saying which so typifies Jesus: 'For the Son of Man came not to be served but to serve' (Mark 10:45).

Viewing the pathway to learning of the Admonitions in its entirety, one saying stands out. From Admonition 10 onwards Francis writes again and again 'blessed is the servant'. Especially after the commentaries on Jesus' beatitudes (Admonitions 13 up to and including 16) these words can be found in practically every Admonition – with the exception of Admonitions 20 and 27. Admonition 27 anyhow holds a unique place in the pathway to learning as we shall see.

'Blessed the servant'

It seems as if Francis already knew the answer the old Dutch Catechism would give to the first question it posed: 'Why are we on earth?' 'We are on earth to serve God and to be happy here and in the hereafter.' In the pathway to learning, serving is apparently the conversion by the failing and sinful person (Admonition 2), to Christ who lives in and with His Body, the Church (Admonition 27). This way someone can lead his life in the service of others. For the first brothers this serving took shape in their care for the most disadvantaged, for example lepers, as well as by working as subordinates in tenure and certainly by participating in worship.

The special place given to 'service' and 'obedience' in the carefully constructed pathway to learning says much about Francis' spirituality. At the basis of these attitudes lies the 'will', which already received such a prominent place in Admonition 2. Here 'self-appropriation' and 'self-exaltation' are the subject under discussion. A *self* is dealt with, a willing *I* which shields and elevates itself at the cost of others. This will is nevertheless not presumed to a lesser extent where the basic attitudes of obedience and service are concerned. In this case it is the will which wishes to recognise the other's dignity.

'Serving', 'bearing' and 'giving back' therefore express the will-ingness of the liberated person to henceforth 'obey' his Lord. Several times Francis showed in a descriptive way what this meant. About Jesus he says that 'He placed His will in the will of the Father' saying 'Father, let Your will be done; not as I will, but as You will' (Second Version of the Letter to the Faithful 10). How-ever Francis not only depicted the events in Gethsemane, but also the resurrection of the Crucified One using the same image: 'Holy Father, you held my right hand, led me into your will and have taken me up with glory' (Office of the Passion – Psalm VI, by Francis). Whoever follows Jesus in his surrender, gives his own will space *in* God's will. In doing so he follows the Obedient One and can live as a frank and free person: set free in order to liberate others.

Obedience and service are apparently only genuine if the own free will is in control. Everything that Francis and Clare have to say about this is based on the will that is free. Whoever lives like this, consciously and proudly takes responsibility for the recognition of God and of his neighbours. For, being the image of God, the other also manifests His grandeur. Therefore the will to serve amounts to having the courage to take one's place at the bottom – in order to exalt the other and not to fall into a kind of service which takes on a superior attitude towards those who require support.

Service: is this still applicable?

Can this kind of spirituality in which the willingness to serve has such a central position still have a significance for our society? In our society words like 'servant' or 'maid' have practically disap-peared from daily usage. Apparently, such words clash with broadly held notions and feelings concerning life. Self-determination is deemed important. Service especially appears to detract from the ideal of equality and equivalence which has been won with such great difficulty.

However this does not mean that the service-sector has not at the same time acquired an ever more prominent place in our society.

Besides production, a huge amount of sectors based on social service now form an area in which very many are employed. One only has to recall the care-professions which are receiving so much attention at the moment or the demand everywhere for better security – better service by servants of the law. However regarding all this, the equality of each and every member of society is not considered in the discussion.

In view of this irreversible dam-burst of emancipation directed at equality and equivalence, the question is whether the notion of humble service, as Francis advocates it, amounts to putting the clock back: an impossible and undesirable reversion to feudal times when serfdom was the norm. The evident relationship between the words 'serve' and 'humility' seems to needlessly confirm that Francis cannot be a partner in a discussion concerning the requirements of our day and age. This is exactly because concepts such as 'humility' or 'humbleness' evoke for many the image of the social relations of bygone times that have disappeared once and for all. The conclusion that Francis' notions about 'serving' are inspired by Christian sources, also appears to give reason to fear for the viability of the biblical concept of 'service'. This would therefore also hold true for Jesus' words: 'Learn from me; for I am gentle and humble in heart' (Matthew 11:29) and 'For the Son of Man came not to be served but to serve' (Mark 10:45).

In order to get out of this apparent mess, two steps can be of service. The first step concerns a closer look at what 'service' means in the service-sector these days. The second requires a clarification of what is concealed behind Francis' notion of 'service'. Broadly speaking, the tension between two forms of mobility is at issue here: that of the greatly increased social mobilisation as well as that of the possibility to be, as a neighbour, moved by the fate of the other even while fulfilling our commercial duties.

Service in commercial relationships

The danger of an ever expanding bureaucracy has increased due to the tightening of the professional grip on a number of organisational aspects of society. As a consequence, the relationship between the commercial (that which has been institutionalised and can be organised) and the personal (the direct relationships between people in the domain of their daily lives) has grown askew. In addition, service is often considered to be a 'product' (which says a lot about how production-paradigms and consumption-paradigms have come to dominate our thinking). This can be determined without doubting the necessity of commercial structures in our society. The indirect relationships which are organised for example through legal relationships clearly form the basis upon which direct relationships can thrive and be protected.

Hardening

In trying to discover the specific nature of much of management and planning, the question arises as to in whose service so much organisational and administrative effort is given. Who or what is exactly in charge of all this hum-drum activity?

A single value has gained dominance in affluent societies: that of stocks, securities and economic expansion. The economic sector has come to 'colonise' the political and cultural sectors more and more. The general acceleration or 'speeding up' of communications and trade is often accompanied by a hardening of human attitudes and relationships. Strangely enough, the domination by hardened commercialism is apparently augmented by an increased flexibility on the labour-market. Whoever stands up for the right to protection of the other's vulnerable life, is quickly labelled as 'soft' or 'soft-boiled'.

This kind of hardening amounts to a perilous curtailment of life itself. The hard truth is that it is exactly what is vulnerable and fragile in our life (that tender skin, those membranes with which we are able to pick up light and sound), which cannot be missed in communicating with others and with which we are therefore able to hear their requests and able to be touched by them. Our mobility – literally speaking our moving about and figuratively speaking our empathy with others – is precisely due to our instability and to our sensitivity to what moves us. The amazing power we have to mentally and emotionally empathise with others – the basis for all great literature as well as for so many other art-forms – does not automatically amount to a great humanity: the example of the person who delights in the suffering of others goes to show that true service is a manner of seeing as well as of having respect.

But is it not an unavoidable fact that service – active or not – makes the other painfully aware of the fact that he is the lesser? Considering this, could all forms of service be suspected of being patronising? The fact remains that present day social-service puts equality before everything else. However, in the case of equality being taken into account, empathy with the pain or worries of the other will not always be able to lead to better help or legal assistance. Personal service will have to extend beyond what is possible in the domain of professional help. It is a fact of life that there is much that cannot be helped by right. Here lies a challenge for the willingness to serve personally. We also have in mind all those volunteers who assist without personal gain where structural help is lacking.

In the commercial sector, service does not also have to automatically be something that can be quantified, let alone be something out of the ordinary. The whittling down of 'doing deeds' into 'work-place achievements' has already done enough damage. In commercial activity a smile, a simple gesture, a single well-meant word can also be heart-warming expressions of personal engagement.

Who is my neighbour?

Is Francis' notion of service hopelessly outdated because he lived in a society which, as far as organisation is concerned, cannot in the least compete with ours? And which, besides this, was not ready by far for the emancipation leading to equality and equivalence which has now become more and more common?

It seems an incontestable fact to us that in his emphasis on the importance of humble service – undoubtedly a pleonasm for him!

– he did indeed have in mind an inequality expressed in terms of higher or lower. The decisive question then is as to what sort of inequality he had in mind. Three things may be considered here:

- As we have already stated, it is essential for Francis and Clare that people voluntarily place themselves on a lower level in order to be able to highly respect and therefore exalt the other, whose distress they have come to learn about. For them, as we shall see, the concept 'bearing' circles around elementary, freely assenting respect.

- There is an inequality between people which clearly forms a stage which precedes the equality which must still be won. Modern times has brought about the breakthrough of this striving for emancipation. But there is also an 'inequality' which is greater than equality. Just as there is also, for example, the recognition of the grandeur and precedence of the other (heteronomy). As Levinas remarks, this kind of 'heteronomy' is more than autonomy, although it is important to remember that the generally accepted idea of autonomy is the happy result of the struggle against dehumanising forms of heteronomy.

Jesus' parable about the disgruntled workers in the vineyard (Matthew 20:1-16) assumes equality before the law – which the master of the vineyard upholds. At the same time however, the parable demonstrates that the owner wishes to offer more than he owes his workers by law. The result of his goodness is a positive inequality which is greater than the equality and fairness which is assumed a priori.

What we see here amounts to the recognition of what characterises a person who makes himself a neighbour; especially in comparison to the commercial relationships which people of course also maintain. The Samaritan (compare Luke 10:25-37) did not humble himself when he took the distress of the robbed stranger upon himself and lifted him up onto his own mule. And can one seriously say that Jesus humbled himself when he knelt down to wash the feet of his disciples? In a certain way one can, however it is exactly through this voluntary inequality that he honoured his disciples in a way which would never have been possible were the equality-norm to have been maintained. Everyone understands that a mother who picks up her child and holds it up high is literally in a lower position, but that in doing so she does not manoeuvre herself into a position of inequality which could be called dehumanising. In examples like these it always comes down to the statute (if it can be called this) of the person who recognises the other as his neighbour by making himself the neighbour of the other: something which in a certain way implies the recognition of the honour which the other's grandeur demands.

Making-oneself-a-neighbour: again this always assumes an approach which results in a respectful closeness. Regarding the visiting of lonely elderly people, the Dutch bishops have used the remarkable expression 'sacrament of closeness'.[2] It is true: the attention given by the visitor is in itself a reference to the presence of the pre-eminent Comforter.

- Closely connected to our efforts to discern a benign inequality which is greater than the essential equality between people, is the clarification of the meaning of the concepts brother and sister for Francis and Clare. For both of them, enriching these concepts with what they saw as essential in the nature of motherhood seemed a valuable thing to do:

> 'Wherever the brothers may be or meet one another, let them show that they are members of the same family. And let each one confidently make known his need to the other, for if a mother nourishes and loves her son according to the flesh, how much more diligently must someone love and nourish his brother according to the Spirit! When any brother falls sick, the other brothers must serve him as they would wish to be served themselves' (Later Rule, Chapter 6: 7-9).

In the next Chapter we shall deal with the fact that the idea of spiritual motherhood – also being a task for men – was important for Francis. We mention it here however, in order to emphasise

[2] 'Op zoek naar een zinvolle levensavond. Bisschoppelijk Woord over oud worden'. In: *1-2-1, Katern,* 27 (7 mei 1999); 10.

the concept of a positive inequality and therefore of an attitude of freely chosen humility.

In connection to this, it remains important to remember that of the high ideals held by the French Revolution, 'freedom' and 'equality' received all the attention, whereas the ideal of brotherhood came off very badly indeed. The sociologist E.W. Hofstee once wrote about 'freedom, equality and loneliness'. In doing so, he characterised the situation in our society during the seventies. The increase in individualisation since then has not remedied the situation. This could be a result of the incapacity or unwillingness to imagine the benign inequality of being a brother or sister in the spirit of Francis and Clare: an inequality which is greater than the rightly assumed original equality.

Up until now we have mostly ordered the three key values of Francis' spirituality along side each other: three attitudes which each express an important moment in his following of Christ. It is, however, very much the question whether these three concepts can be lined up in this way. Now that we have learned more about the central place which serving has in the pathway to learning of the Admonitions, the mutual relationship between the three key values begins to look different. The basic value is the willingness to serve in humility. This will sometimes takes the shape of giving back or of bearing. These last two can therefore be considered to be expressions of Francis' willingness to serve. In the next Chapter we will first deal extensively with the art of 'giving back'. Then we will look into the art of 'bearing'.

5. The art of 'giving back' and of 'bearing'

Giving back

These two words appear to mean two things for Francis. Firstly there is the giving back of things received. One can think of: 'paying (back)', 'giving to someone what they have a right to' or 'bringing something back to where it belongs'. And then there is the giving back of praise and honour to God. As has already been noted, Francis summarises the different nuances of the praising of God using these two words. In Admonition 18,2 we clearly have to do with the first meaning:

> 'Blessed is the servant who gives back every good to the Lord God because whoever holds onto something for himself hides the money of his Lord God within himself, and what he thinks he has will be taken away from him.'

Admonitions 18 and 11: the language of money

In Admonition 18 Francis explains 'giving back to the Lord God' with the aid of citations from Jesus' parable of the talents. What is given back, or held back, he describes by using money as a symbol of property. The same is done in a different way in the pendant to Admonition 18, namely in Admonition 11:[1]

1. 'Nothing should displease a servant of God except sin.
2. And no matter how another person may sin, if a servant of God becomes disturbed and angry because of this and not because of charity, he is storing up guilt for himself.

---

[1] Also one of the cornerstones supporting the church-building of the Admonitions. See: *Respectfully Yours,* Chapter 2; 71.

3. That servant of God who does not become angry or disturbed at anyone lives correctly without anything of his own.
4. Blessed is the one for whom nothing remains except for him to return to Caesar what is Caesar's and to God what is God's.'

By quoting from Jesus' story about the imperial taxes, Francis likewise uses the symbol of money to describe both a life without possessions and one in which one clings to them. We shall dwell shortly on the following points:

• the symbolic value that money undoubtedly had for the ex-merchant from Assisi;
• the meaning of 'hides the money within himself' (Admonition 18,2);
• the expressive power of the effigy on the coin used for taxes (Matthew 22:21) as a reference to the commandment to 'give back to God' (Admonition 11).

By doing so, it should become clear what 'giving back' meant for Francis. This also goes for the relationship between 'giving back' to God and the 'right of the poor'.

Francis and money

Money, in any form whatsoever, is the concentration of property. Through it, property can be taken in hand and traded. Money increases mobility: it must circulate. Whoever has a grip on his property in the form of money possesses a means of power that can be wielded with speed. The fact that having money entails having power can be seen for example in the word 'buying-power': power to become independent of others as well as to make others dependent.

Francis was fiercely against his brothers using money, except in case of emergency for the sick (Earlier Rule of 1221, Chapter 8,3). The Later Rule of 1223 is even stricter regarding this (compare Chapter 4 of this Rule). This prohibition must have had to do with his sensitivity to the negative effects incurred by an expanding economy based on money. The desire to increase one's possessions increased the gap between rich and poor and between the powerful and powerless. He had seen how people became possessed by their possessions. Possessions tend to disturb everything that leads to closer ties between God and man and between people themselves. Whoever does not acknowledge God as the Giver of all things runs the risk of becoming cramped in his efforts to maintain his independence.

Interest and returns

In light of the parable of the talents (Matthew 25:14-30) which is cited in Admonition 18, 'giving back' (Latin *reddere*) also acquires the meaning of 'yielding interest' and 'giving returns'. In choosing 'giving back' as his attitude towards life, Francis reminds us of the role of the estate-steward from the Gospels. And in using the words 'giving back', he must also have had in mind the mediaeval practise of rampant usury, which was so controversial. In our present-day economy which is largely based on 'interest rates', the task of stewardship in the biblical sense is still a very up-to-date topic – certainly where a responsible attitude towards the environment and poverty are concerned. Man as steward remains accountable to God. This is certainly echoed in Francis' emphasis on 'giving back to God', who has credited us with so much.

That he eventually gave up the 'mastership'-side or management-aspect of his stewardship, is more characteristic to his way of life: he rather became a partner, a brother to his fellow-creatures and was prepared to learn from them. Admonition 5 which assumes the exalted position of man is illustrative of this. Here he writes: 'And all creatures under heaven serve, know, and obey their Creator, each according to its own nature, better than you' (Admonition 5,2).

The embezzlement of money

'Whoever holds onto something for himself hides the money of his Lord God within himself' (Admonition 18,2). Francis borrowed these words largely from the above-mentioned parable of the talents. In the first place this 'hiding' means that the servant did not creatively make use of the talent entrusted to him and took no risks. Francis however, adds the words 'for himself' and 'within himself'. This demonstrates that here he also had in mind the self-appropriation which he criticised in Admonition 2. 'Hiding' therefore also has the meaning of embezzlement here. This hiding or embezzlement elucidates the fact that not recognising God's generous goodness amounts to defamation. This is because His own disinterested radiance is deposited by men in the darkness of their own covetous self-interest.

Francis realised that every creature is a 'mirror' of God's bestowing goodness (2 Celano 165), as well as how man may freely choose to be such a mirror: 're-presenting' what he is and what he has received. The fact that this 'giving back' to God amounts to the 'reflection' of His light is beautifully depicted by Clare in her figurative use of the word 'mirror'. As we shall see, 'giving back' or 're-presenting' also amounted to 're-flecting' for her.

Respecting by reflecting

The free act of 'giving back to God' is comprised of different moments:
- the recognition of the original Giver;
- recognition which is expressed as gratitude: in the willingness not to despise, not to forget, but to thank;
- gratitude which is expressed in thanking, as well as in concrete service: amongst other things, in doing justice to the poor.

The fact that 'giving back' also probably meant 'reflecting' for Francis, can be presumed from the similarities between Admonitions 18 and 11 (which, as has already been pointed out, are each other's pendants in the pathway to learning). Both deal with 'living without possessions' and with money as the concentration of property; explicitly so in Admonition 18 and in Admonition 11 by referring to what Jesus had to say about the coin used for paying the emperor's tax.

Admonition 11 deals with the realisation that a sinner does not coincide with his sins. By recognising the sinner in his dignity as a creation of God (Admonition 11, 4), we avoid pinning him down to his sinfulness. At the same time, this prevents the person who judges the other from robbing himself of his own freedom by inflexibly clinging to his judgement. Happy is he who manages to keep himself free from hard-heartedness, because he gives the authority to judge to the only One who has the right to do this. In recognising the sinner as an effigy of God, the one who does not pass judgement becomes in his own turn an effigy of the Generous One.

It only becomes apparent that someone can be a reflection of God, if he 'gives back' to God in this way: we are created in the image and likeness – not of a stingy Owner, but of Generosity itself. This reflection, if it is a fully-fledged human act, is not an automatic reflection, like that of a mirror which must necessarily break and reflect incoming light. It is man's honour to give honour in freedom and through his own creativity. By honouring God and his fellow-men in this way he becomes a reflection of God's respect (compare Ephesians 5:1-2).

The art of letting go

'Thanking' had a lot to do with 'letting go' for Francis. This is something that definitely characterises his way of life. A Dutch book about Francis bears the title *The Art of Letting Go*. Now 'letting go' is certainly not something that only holds a special place for this saintly friar minor. Every mother or father knows that it is both unavoidable and painful, however also an extremely good thing, when the moment arrives to let go of their children. It is one of the laws of life. They must leave home and lead their own lives. And everyone will also sooner or later realise that he himself will also have to let go of much more. 'The shroud has no pockets', as popular wisdom puts it so well. This unavoidable maxim, the fact that everything will have to be let go of, makes itself clear in the end. And eventually this maxim will assert itself whether we like it or not.

All the same, there are good reasons to especially associate 'the art of letting go' with Francis. If there is anyone who learned to understand this art better and better as time progressed, then it must be him. Now that these days 'spirituality' is also referred to as 'the art of life', then Francis, regarding this 'letting go', may definitely be called an 'artist of life'.

Is this art of letting go connected to the poverty which is always mentioned where Francis is concerned? Yes, but only if this poverty is not understood as being an ascetic manoeuvre by which he wished to make things difficult for himself and for others. By and by, he learned that the protection which people are in need of to survive can quickly degenerate into a shield which puts others at a disadvantage. For him, poverty amounted to letting go of the cramped efforts to maintain one's independence and to letting go of the covetous self-appropriation of ever more things...... Especially the 'ever more'! It amounted to a radical solidarity with the poorest and to being capable of living as a generous child of God: letting go of all greed and opening up one's grasping hand. In the end it amounted to letting go and leaving things up to God, or to the other. Letting-go-and-leaving-up-to: in a word this comes down to what we call faith, or rather: trust. Trust is: letting go and leaving up to.

Trapeze-artists' work

An experience that Henri Nouwen once had, may assist in clarifying what 'letting-go-and-leaving-up-to' means. During a visit to a circus Nouwen became fascinated with the trapeze-artists. He was so enthusiastic that he decided to accompany the acrobats for a period. In his eyes they appeared to be true masters of theology because they painted a picture of the risky venture that life is: *letting go*. The leader of the troupe, who repeatedly glided through the air, told Nouwen during a conversation they had:

> 'Like most of the audience you probably think that I am the big star of the trapeze-show. But the real star is Joe who catches me. He has to pluck me out of the air at exactly the right moment when I make my great leap towards him. The secret is that I leave the catching completely up to Joe and do nothing myself. (…) The worst thing

a jumper can do, is to try and catch the catcher. (…) If I were to grasp Joe's wrists, I could maybe break them, or he could break mine. That would mean the end for us both. A jumper must jump and a catcher must catch, and with arms outstretched and hands opened wide, the jumper must have faith in his catcher being there.'[2]

The wisdom of the Gospels can be discerned here: you must let go and leave it up to the Catcher to catch you. This means entrusting oneself over and over again.

For Francis, 'faith' and 'trust' are not derived from 'seeing' or 'knowing'. As explained earlier on, he translates 'trust' or 'faith' by using, amongst others, the words respecting, thanking and worshipping. Thanking: recognising that everything you are or have is a gift from God. Recognition and gratitude turn out to be each other's siblings. Everything these words express: respect, honour, praise and thanks – all this 'letting go' of the grasping grip and all this 'leaving up to' – he summarises with the words giving back.

What is this 'giving back' in practise? It takes shape in the concrete recognition of the right of the poor to a life of dignity. It is namely in the poor that one meets Him who said: 'Just as you did it to one of the least of these who are members of my family, you did it to me.' (Matthew 25:40b) Giving back to God: and in doing so becoming a reflection, an image of Him who as the pure Giver lets his sun shine on both the good and the bad: child of the reckless Giver. Man has been *given* the blessing to *give* along with the richly giving God who, before all else, is himself the One who lets go and the One who leaves up to. We believe God takes the risk of leaving very much up to us out of respect for man's freedom. For without freedom there can be no love. When God, as is stated in the Gospels, 'gave us his only begotten Son', this giving is so great

---

[2] Henri J.M. Nouwen, 'Circus Diary I, Finding theTrapeze Artist in the Priest. In: *New Oxford Review* (June 1993); 8-14; idem: 'Circus Diary II, Finding a New Way to Get a Glimpse of God. In: *New Oxford Review, (July / August 1993)*; 6-13. Jurjen Beumer, *Onrustig zoeken naar God. De spiritualiteit van Henri Nouwen.* Tielt, Lannoo, 1999; 86; Michael Ford, *Wounded Prophet. A Portrait of Henri J. M. Nouwen.* New York (Doubleday) 2002[2], Chapter I, 3; 33-40.

that it is like the sun which cannot be looked at directly. What we can do is to place ourselves with open hands and an open heart in this light. Just as Clare writes in her Third Letter to St. Agnes of Prague: 'Place your soul in the splendour of glory'. What we receive is however the light of an *amour fou*. When we are dealing with the most precious thing there is – true Love – we must also loosen the grip of our searching understanding and leave the fulfilment of our desire for insight up to Him. We are just not capable of gazing directly into the Sun.

Francis makes us realise that the art of 'letting go' and 'leaving up to' is decided in the end by the relationship someone may have with God and, in Him, with others. Put in other words: detach-ment leads to the necessary room for attachment to God and to others. For Francis, the notion of giving back goods essentially includes this personal relationship. In his eyes it expresses the very opposite of 'making one's will one's own' (Admonition 2), which must be called sinful because it excludes the rightful recognition of the Other and in doing so, cuts man off from his source of life.

The right of the poor

For Francis, giving back to the Lord God is not just an act of the will. It is also not something that can be done without relating to our fellow-men. In his eyes, this amounted in concrete to passing on to others what had been entrusted to him by God. His life's praxis amounted to the recognition of the right of the poor: 'Alms are a legacy and a justice due to the poor that Our Lord Jesus Christ acquired for us.' (Earlier Rule 1221, Chapter 9,8).

It all comes down to giving back to the poor what they have a right to: namely, the elementary things that are required to live a life in dignity. His biographers tell us how radically he desired to understand this. The 'we desired nothing more' of the Testament (17) is echoed in his words quoted by Celano: 'I do not want to be a thief.' Francis said this to his companion, when they hap-pened upon a pauper who possessed even less than they did. Celano writes:

'Another time when he was coming back from Siena he met a poor man, and the saint said to his companion: "Brother, we must give back to this poor man the mantle that is his. We accepted it on loan until we should happen to find someone poorer than we are." The companion, seeing the need of his pious father, stubbornly objected that he should not provide for someone else by neglecting himself. But the saint said to him: "I do not want to be a thief; we will be accused of theft if we do not give to someone in greater need." So his companion gave in, and he gave up the mantle' (2 Celano 87).

His recognition of the rights of the poor apparently did not take shape in his striving after more income in order to be able to give away more. On the contrary – he chose the way of voluntary *solidarity* with the poor; being poor with the poor in order to stand up for their dignity and rights.

Giving back gratuitously

Giving God back the talents he has entrusted to us, is the acknowledgement of the fact that our existence is a gratuitous gift demanding a reciprocal gratuitous gift. It is important that this giving back is just as gratuitous. To be able to speak of true love and true faith, a minimum of disinterest is required. This validates the words of Jesus' missionary discourse, which was cherished by Francis: 'You received without payment; give without payment' (Matthew 10:8). Negatively stated: just as 'the person who bears his neighbour in his weakness' runs the risk of exalting himself due to his act of bearing, so the person giving back can also lay all sorts of self-exalting claims to his act. If he forgets that the act of giving back is due to God's grace, he lapses into self-satisfaction which no longer has anything to do with God's generosity. For the grasping left-hand knows all too well what the releasing right-hand is doing (compare Matthew 6:3).

Seen in this light, it is significant that Francis concretises his giving back to God by giving back to the poor, who are 'the least of those who are members of his family' (compare Matthew 25:40b). For they themselves are not in the position to give back.

In their inability to reciprocate they resist our will, hidden or not, to better ourselves. But even if we give to the poor in concrete, then the crystal words of John of the Cross 'love is only repaid with love' remain just as clear as they are hard. It is a continuing exercise and certainly not an act which can quasi-piously be attributed to oneself.

Francis experienced this gift and task as an exodus: as a pilgrim in foreign lands; as a descendent of Abraham on the way to 'the land of the living' (Later Rule 1223, Chapter 6,5). His intense relationship to the Eucharist was an expression of his thanks for the nourishment received on his journey (*viaticum*), and a testimony of his willingness to honour the loving Humility, of which, as a brother of the poor, he hoped to become an ever clearer image.

Francis and Luther on 'bringing home'

The words 'giving back' are a translation of the Latin word *reddere* used by Francis. This can mean amongst others: 'bringing home to where it belongs'. The idea of this bringing home of what fills us with wonderment and gratitude is shared by both Francis and Luther. A saying by Luther goes: 'Praise is nothing other than recognising the good things we have received from God, and attributing them not to ourselves but to Him alone and bringing them home (*wider heymtragen*).[3] This shared, biblical emphasis on recognition which is expressed in gratitude (also understood as bringing home to where it belongs) is striking. Both men undoubtedly situated the act of bringing home in a view of the human condition based on faith: before everything, we need to be brought home to where we belong.

This recognition of our life's mission as being 'a bringing home to God' is especially relevant for modern man for two reasons. We are living in an era in which hermeneutics, or the science of interpretation, has acquired a very important role in philosophy and

---

[3] *Kirchenpostille 1522, WA* 10 I, 715; 1-3; cited by J. Happee, *Mediteren met Luther.* Deventer, 1983; 65.

theology (actually this has long since been the case regarding theology). Overly conscious of his own importance as the almost sovereign interpreter or 'placer' of everything he sees, modern man is continuously 'bringing home'. The question as to where he brings home becomes undeniably urgent when the same person admits that he is a home-grown (in the sense of originally being) something or other. How often don't we hear these days: 'I was a home-grown Baptist'; 'I was a home-grown Catholic' (meaning originally I was a Baptist or a Catholic) and the like. And then it is usually left unsaid, where this person has found his *new* spiritual home – if this is at all the case. This is usually unclear for the person concerned. Modern man doesn't feel at home in the old institutions. On the other hand, many also realise that they cannot completely do without the security of their comforting rituals. Every living creature – man included – is in search of security because of its vulnerability: a vulnerability and frailty which cannot be denied with impunity and which exactly as sensitivity both form the invaluable basis of all our contact and communication. Recognised as such, our vulnerability and frailty will time and again together form the starting point for the expression of our gratitude.

Nowadays Christians are all more displaced ('homeless') than they used to be. Their situation may in some ways be compared to the situation of the Jewish people during their stay in the desert and during the exile. Eloi Leclerc, a French Franciscan brother, remarked upon this.[4] The symbolism of the hut erected on the Jewish Feast of Tabernacles – an 'open house' – has much to say to present-day believers. The joy of the Law is celebrated in this 'open house' no matter what. Subjected as we are to the endless impressions with which the modern media bombard us, an open dwelling like this can be a 'home' where, drawing from the sources of faith, we can be guided to a much needed reorientation by introspection and communication.

[4] Eloi Leclerc, *Le peuple de Dieu dans la nuit,* Ed. franciscaines / Desclée de Brouwer, Paris, 2003; idem, *Le chant des sources,* Ed. franciscaines, coll. «Espace franciscain», Paris, 2003.

The deep desire for a home must be taken seriously in our day and age, although only on the condition that the paradoxical connection of this desire to the challenge 'to go and bear fruit' (John 15:16b), is no less earnestly considered. Francis followed the biblical call to lead his life as a pilgrim and stranger so literally, that he radically spurned having a fixed place of residence. However in doing so he in no way forswore his desire for a 'home'. As a 'pilgrim and stranger' he wished to search for this 'home' together with the brothers he had been given, as well as with all his sister and brother fellow-creatures, as the Canticle of the Creatures shows us. For his home-coming in the circle of his brothers was played out in the wider House of Creation: like proudly stated in a mystery-play that was written perhaps not long after Francis' death:

> 'After enjoying a very quiet and healthy sleep, she (Lady Poverty) quickly arose and asked to be shown the enclosure. Taking her to a certain hill, they (namely the friars who had received her) showed her all the world they could see and said: "This, Lady, is our enclosure".'[5]

In this spirit of solidarity he hoped to be able to lead a fruitful life by giving shape to this brotherly bond in a spirit of motherhood (compare 1 Thessalonians 2:7). According to Francis, sisterly and brotherly equality can, as we shall see, only take shape when someone bears the other in his or her fragility – like a mother who bears and lifts up her child.

Modern man, who is conscious of his acquired freedoms and who at the same time is uncertain regarding the question as to for what he is actually free, can find an answer in Chapter 15 of the Gospel according to John. When the Dutch pastor and writer Henri Nouwen wrote 'our most personal desire: finding a fruitful home', he must have been aware of the fact that in doing so he was combining John's text about 'going and bearing fruit' (John 15:16b) with Jesus' words in the ninth verse of that same Chapter: 'Abide

---

[5] *Francis of Assisi: Early Documents. Volume I. The Saint:* 'The Sacred Exchange between Saint Francis and Lady Poverty'; 552, no. 63.

in my love'.[6] The Spirit of love Who inspires the whole of Creation is the 'abiding home' of those who see themselves as being pilgrims at the same time.

Bearing

The Latin word that Francis uses for 'bearing' (*sustinere*), can be retraced to a biblical concept (*hypomenein*) that can mean 'waiting', 'expecting', 'enduring' and 'hoping'. In the New Testament the predominant meaning is 'patiently enduring tribulations'. A vivid example of this is Paul's hymn about love: 'It bears all things, believes all things, hopes all things, endures (*sustinet*) all things' (1 Corinthians 13:7).

The enduring individual is the person who bears what is inflicted upon him, or what he has inflicted upon himself through his own fault. 'Bearing' expresses the attitude of someone who readily adapts as well as of someone who really undergoes, endures and perseveres. Strength is the issue here: the strength to bear and, for the person who can bring himself to remain vigilantly hoping, the strength to endure.

For Francis, the various meanings of 'bearing' circle around the task to accept the unavoidable. He uses the concept 'bearing' for:
• Jesus Christ's endurance of his suffering;
• bearing fear, defamation and persecution;
• suffering punishment for culpability which one has brought upon oneself;
• supporting or lifting up (exalting) one's fellow-man in his frailty.
Among the above-mentioned, the word lifting up (Latin: *sustentare*) requires special attention. In the Canticle of the Creatures it appears twice: in the verses about Brother Wind and Sister Mother Earth. There it has the meaning of 'supporting' in the sense of 'nourishing' or 'giving life'. Seen in this way, the word marks the

---

[6] Henri Nouwen, 'Foreword'. In: Jean Vanier, *Man and Woman He made Them* (London, 1985), X; *Respectfully Yours,* Chapter 2; 195.

transition to the special meaning which 'bearing' has for Francis in two of his writings: namely the 'bearing of one's neighbour'. This is the case in the Second Letter to the Faithful and in Admonition 18. The letter deals with how a brother must act who, as superior, is allowed to be the servant of the others: 'Let him not become angry at the fault of a brother but, with all patience and humility, let him admonish and support him' (44). Just like in Admonition 18, the context shows that here Francis had Jesus' golden rule in mind: 'do as you would have others do unto you'.

Affirmation of the fragile neighbour following the 'golden rule'

The golden rule has a special function in Admonition 18, which praises as blessed 'the person who bears his neighbour in his weakness' (verse 1). Our fragility reminds us of our material state. As children of Adam we are 'earthenware'. And if not massive and heavy, then all the same frail and therefore no less fragile. Because man is in need of assistance and affirmation, the one person is a living appeal to the support of the other – and vice versa. What the psychiatrist Anna Terruwe has written in a number of studies about the necessity of 'affirmation' of and by our fellow-men, undoubtedly subscribes to what Francis concisely expressed in his own way with 'bearing'. This 'vice versa' is important, because there remains the possibility that in bearing all that is difficult, the bearing figure could, in turn, paradoxically exalt himself – by showing off his respectable achievement. Our task is to bear the other without making a song and dance about it.

In the first place, the accepted 'burden' is the neighbour who, as wavering as his existence may be, is one total request for support – all this regardless of whether praise will be garnered or not. But the helper especially begins to realise that he is just as fragile as his neighbour. Any feelings of superiority which may occur to the helper are extremely dubious right from the very beginning. The helper may not forget this for an instant, because the very next moment he may be the one in need of the same assistance. This can happen, and sooner or later this will happen. In other words: 'bearing' and 'being borne' are as relative as they are temporary. This fact remains, also when the helper is in the position to know that the person being helped will never be able to reciprocate.

Bearing on one's own and bearing together

A follower of Francis must also learn to 'bear' his or her own fragility. And we must also learn to bear the fact that our ability to bear will diminish. Sooner or later we will not be able to escape the fact that we will have to bear our own deterioration – just as we cannot avoid bearing our own sinfulness. Besides this, everyone finds it very difficult to bear the fact that he is not as patient as he would like to be or should be. And this especially holds true for those who bear the burden of their own melancholy.

But also for those who are spared this tribulation, there is the task to bear responsibility for one's own life. For it is everyone's dignity as well as burden to have to live their lives themselves. In our modern world however, a fatal misunderstanding threatens. Independence and self-maintenance have acquired unheard of possibilities in our culture. People are now more than ever in the position to save themselves. Self-government seen as independence is automatically viewed as an important good, also in our personal life – until the realisation dawns that no-one can manage without the concrete help and support of others. Everyone has to learn that leading one's *own* life cannot and may not be identified with living alone; and that there is also a good dependence which realises itself in affection for others. All this is very relevant in discerning the full scope which the theme 'bearing' has for Francis. This is not limited to unmasking the identification of doing by oneself with doing alone, for the strong emphasis nowadays on doing can also in itself be questioned. In our times, self-determination seen as management over one's own life is characterised by planning, control and direction. The 'makeable-ness' or 'manufacture' of our own lives still has a certain prestige. The realisation that much cannot be planned or made – and accompanying this, the realisation of a

certain impotence inherent to our lives – summons us to acknowledge whatever must therefore be borne, without by the way meaning that we must bear this alone.

Regarding this, it may perhaps do well to be reminded of our
right to a more contemplative kind of life-style – and not only for
those who have been eliminated from participating in the work-
process by ill-health or old-age. As a matter of fact, ill-health is
often due to overwork demanded by the same increasingly accelerated work-process. A spirituality which recognises its own limits
is characterised by its acceptance of the task to bear – this of course
understood as the task to bear together.

The demonstrable increase in the use of the words 'bearing' and
'patience' by Francis during the final years of his life, can be traced
back to the fact that he then had to endure more and more ill-
health and setbacks. By relinquishing all sorts of privileges and liberated from the illusions of status and standing, he had learned
through experience to what extent life is precarious. His experience
of not having much say in matters as a patient helped him to lay
open the full scope of the golden rule: namely applying it to the
relationship with those who were not in the position to reciprocate:

> 'Blessed is the servant who loves his brother as much when he is sick
> and cannot repay him as when he is well and can repay him' (Admo-
> nition 24).

True Joy

In the story about 'True Joy' which has already been mentioned,
Francis gives us the fullest scope of what 'bearing' means for him.
It is probably taken from his later years. It relates that the greatest
possible successes the brothers could possibly achieve in the eyes of
top-scholars and authorities, or whilst giving their sermons or
doing wonders, apparently do not give true joy. The anticlimax of
this story is:

> 'Then what is true joy? I return from Perugia and arrive here in the
> dead of night. It's winter time, muddy, and so cold that icicles

have formed on the edges of my habit and keep striking my legs and blood flows from such wounds. Freezing, covered with mud and ice, I come to the gate and, after I've knocked and called for some time, a brother comes and asks: 'Who are you?' 'Brother Francis,' I answer. 'Go away!' he says. 'This is not a decent hour to be wandering about! You may not come in!' When I insist, he replies: 'Go away! You are simple and stupid! Don't come back to us again! There are many of us here like you – we don't need you!' I stand again at the door and say: 'For the love of God, take me in tonight!' And he replies: 'I will not! Go to the Crosiers' place and ask there!' I tell you this: If I had patience and did not become upset, true joy, as well as true virtue and the salvation of my soul, would consist in this.'[7]

For Francis, there is apparently only true joy if he manages to keep his patience when, after having endured cold and darkness, he is refused shelter by his brothers. Instead of lovingly receiving him, they leave him outside in the cold and refer him to what was then the 'Salvation Army'. Only he who receives the grace to bear not being borne by his unwilling brothers and does not lose his inner peace because of this, can be said to have true joy.

Here the golden rule, applied to the bearing of the other, also opens up a perspective which reaches much further than the usual assumptions about reciprocal action. Just as the golden rule in Francis' eyes also applies in the case of the other being unable to reciprocate (Admonition 24), it also applies to the same degree when the other is unwilling to offer any support whatsoever and in actual fact abandons his fellow-man who is requesting help. In this case 'enduring' amounts to 'resisting' the temptation to curse the one refusing help.

The fact that this parable forces us to view *joy* from an unexpected angle is what makes it so disturbing. If there is any state of mind which appears to be incompatible with bearing what is difficult and burdensome, then it must be joy. But all the same, in

---

[7] *Francis of Assisi: Early Documents. Volume I. The Saint,* 'True and Perfect Joy'; 166.

referring to joy, Francis, the singing troubadour, lets us hear his own 'but all the same….'!

Bearing: a charged word

What Francis has to say about 'being patient' and 'bearing', reveals much about the way he dealt with the suffering that befell him and with the suffering of others which evoked his pity. Not that he anywhere formulates the proverbial question about 'the meaning of suffering'. He was not a theorist. He 'only' offers us his wisdom of experience, marked by his reflection upon God's word. But the place that the concept 'bearing' holds in his later writings, demonstrates that he, no less than any other, could ignore the question as to how someone should handle the suffering which is his fate and the fate of others.

Whatever 'resignation' may mean to others, for Francis it never meant a passive enduring and this is worth considering. For many, 'bearing' is still (and perhaps more than ever) a charged word. Especially for women. 'Don't complain, but bear it': imposed upon or put to them again and again. By giving 'bearing' such a central place, isn't Francis just adding insult to injury for the women of his times as well as our own? The emphasis he places on the mutual act of bearing and being borne makes it clear that this is not the case. He uncouples the automatic identification of the bearing of difficulties with back-straining work. Or if it does indeed become so, then he understands 'bearing' first and foremost as the strength to bear the unavoidable. And in the case of the burdened fellow-man requesting help, then he will come to his assistance and affirm him. As has been said, for Francis patience means above all the strength to bear, and strength to endure and persevere until better times arrive.

Where is the burdened person to get this strength from? The story about 'true joy' ends by pointing out 'true strength' and 'the salvation of the soul' – therefore an inner strength. Recalling what Francis has passed on to us about the character and origins of the peace he desired to bring, then it becomes clear Who he considered to be

the source of this strength which results in true joy. As we saw in
Chapter 3, he viewed this peace, not as something one can achieve
oneself, but as a gift of the Holy Spirit.

The connection between 'bearing' and 'motherhood'

Did Francis also hear the echo of 'being pregnant' in his use of the
word 'bearing'? Did he know that one of the Hebrew words for mercy
is related to the word for womb in that language? We do not know
if he did. We do know for a fact that the themes of mercy – the opening of his Testament deals with this – as well as that of a motherly
attitude and that of bearing all hold a fundamental place in his spirituality. 'Bearing' may therefore also allude to spiritual motherhood,
which was important to him. In the case of someone 'bearing the
other in his fragility' or exalting the other, Francis would have seen
this as an act of 'giving life'. We cannot however be certain of this.

What he did have in mind regarding 'motherhood' can be
derived from some of his writings. Here he speaks of:
- the growth of the fruit in the mother's womb (Second Letter to
  the Faithful 4);
- carrying in the heart and body; giving birth (Second Letter to
  the Faithful 53);
- loving and feeding the child (Earlier Rule, Chapter 9,11; Later
  Rule, Chapter 6,8);
- feeding, protecting and bearing (Canticle of the Creatures 9);
- giving advice and comforting (A Letter to Brother Leo);
- caring and protecting like Martha (A Rule for Hermitages 2).

These aspects of motherhood conform to what was considered
essential to the role of a mother in Francis' time. A comparison of
Francis' writings shows that the connection between 'bearing' and
'being pregnant' cannot be rejected *a priori*.

> 'The most high Father made known from heaven through His holy
> angel Gabriel this Word of the Father – so worthy, so holy and glo-
> rious – in the womb of the holy and glorious Virgin Mary, from
> whose womb He received the flesh of our humanity and frailty' (Sec-
> ond Letter to the Faithful 4).

Jesus, fruit of the womb of Mary, is portrayed here as the one who totally shared the frailty of our humanity. What this spiritual motherhood meant for every believer, is pregnantly expressed in a mystical passage in the Second Letter to the Faithful. Speaking about God's indwelling in the faithful, he says:

> 'We are mothers when we carry Him in our heart and body through love and a pure and sincere conscience; and give birth to Him through a holy activity, which must shine before others by example' (53).

In the Canticle of the Creatures he portrays 'Sister Earth, our Mother' who is motherly in her feeding, protecting and bearing of us. The things she bears (flowers and herbs), beautiful and good as they may be, are however biblically speaking of a fleeting nature. As earthly as these fruits are, they remain fragile:

> 'Praised be You, my Lord, through our Sister Mother Earth, who sustains and governs us, and who produces various fruits with coloured flowers and herbs' (Canticle of the Creatures 9).

In his Letter to Brother Leo, Francis writes:

> 'Brother Leo, your brother Francis, health and peace. I am speaking to you, my son, in this way as a mother – because all the words that we spoke on the road I place and advise briefly in this message and afterwards, it is not necessary to come to me for counsel. Because I advise you thus: in whatever way it seems better to you to please the Lord God and to follow in His footsteps and poverty, you may do it with the blessing of the Lord and my obedience. And if it is necessary for you for your soul for some consolation to you, and you want to come back to me, come.'[8]

The role-play he sketches in which brothers are 'mother' and 'son' in turn, is also characteristic to Francis' Rule for Hermitages. Apparently Francis was strongly convinced about spiritual motherhood.

---

[8] *Francis of Assisi: Early Documents. Volume I. The Saint*, 'A Letter to Brother Leo'; 123.

In the parable about the poor woman in the desert which Francis told to Pope Innocent III, the words 'I am that poor woman' form the surprising point of this story (Legend of the Three Companions 51). He apparently viewed himself as someone who passed on life, indeed, as a mother, right from the very beginnings of the brotherhood. And it seems he also was addressed as such by his brothers now and again. The fact that Clare also perceived a motherly attitude in Francis is expressed in a special dream, which she related to her sisters:

> 'Sister Philippa, daughter of the late Lord Leonardo of Gislerio, and a nun of the convent of San Damiano, said under oath: (…) Lady Clare also related how once, in a vision, it seemed to her she brought a bowl of hot water to Saint Francis along with a towel for drying his hands. She was climbing a very high stairway, but was going very quickly, almost as though she were going on level ground. When she reached Saint Francis, the saint bared his breast and said to the Lady Clare: "Come, take and drink." After she had sucked from it, the saint admonished her to imbibe once again. After she did so what she had tasted was so sweet and delightful she in no way could describe it. After she had imbibed, that nipple or opening of the breast from which the milk comes remained between the lips of blessed Clare. After she took what remained in her mouth in her hands, it seemed to her it was gold so clear and bright that everything was seen in it as in a mirror.'[9]

We can perhaps conclude that the combination of the concepts 'bearing' and 'fragility' in Admonition 18 also evoked the idea of motherhood for Francis. In the texts regarding the motherly love which the brothers were to show each other according to his Rules, this love is moreover also directed to the sick and needy.

In Francis' time, a number of these motherly tasks were also ascribed to those who gave spiritual direction.[10] The theme of

---

[9] 'The Act of the Process', III, 29 in: *Clare of Assisi. Early Documents.* (Ed. and trans. Regis J. Armstrong O.F.M. Cap). Revised and expanded. St. Bonaventure, NY, 1993; 152.

[10] Compare 2 Celano 49: 'one of his (Francis) companions was yearning with great desire to have something encouraging from the words of our Lord'.

motherhood was often discussed by the Cistercians during the twelfth century. They knew that Anselm of Canterbury had typified Jesus and Paul as 'mother'. The Cistercians typified the role of the abbot in his relationship to the community in this way as well: the 'masculine' nature of his authority was, as it were, supplemented by motherly characteristics.[11]

Biblical sources

How strange these ideas may perhaps appear to modern minds, these spiritual writers, including Francis, took up a theme that has biblical origins. In Numbers 11:11-17, during one of the low points of the journey through the desert, Moses asks the Lord:

> 'Why have you treated your servant so badly? Why have I not found favour in your sight, that you lay the burden of all this people on me? Did I conceive all this people? Did I give birth to them, that you should say to me, 'Carry them in your bosom, as a nurse carries a sucking child', to the land that you promised on oath to their ancestors? (…) I am not able to carry all this people alone, for they are too heavy for me.'

The Lord then orders Moses, fed up as he is, to appoint seventy elders who, together with him, will carry the burden of the people. In Isaiah, the prophet lets God himself speak to his people as a mother:

> 'Listen to me, O house of Jacob, all the remnant of the house of Israel, who have been borne by me from your birth, carried from the womb; even to your old age I am he, even when you turn grey I will carry you. I have made, and I will bear; I will carry and will save. (…) Can a woman forget her nursing-child, or show no compassion for the child of her womb? Even these may forget, yet I will not forget you' (Isaiah 46:3-4 and 49:15).

---

[11] Caroline Walker Bynum, *Jesus as Mother. Studies in the Spirituality of the High Middle Ages.* Berkeley, 1982; 110-169; idem, *Holy Feast and Holy Fast. A Study of the Religious Significance of Food to Medieval Women.* Berkeley, 1986; 30; 73-122.

The image that Jesus gave of himself, turning towards Jerusalem, must have especially made an impression on Francis:

> 'Jerusalem, (…)! How often have I desired to gather your children together as a hen gathers her brood under her wings, and you were not willing!' (Matthew 23:37).

There is namely a report concerning a dream of his in which he also saw himself as a hen, who could not possibly give all her brood a place under her wings. He considered this to be a sign of his incapacity to protect his brothers sufficiently on his own:

> 'Blessed Francis proposed to ask the Lord Pope Honorius, therefore, that one of the cardinals of the Roman Church be a sort of pope (*papa*) of his Order, that is, the Lord of Ostia, to whom the brothers could have recourse in their dealings.
>
> For blessed Francis had had a vision which led him to ask for the cardinal, and to entrust the Order to the Roman Church. He saw a hen that was small and black, with feathered legs and the feet of a domestic dove. It had so many chicks that it was unable to gather them all under its wings, and so they wandered all around her in circles.
>
> Waking from sleep, he began to think about this vision and, immediately, he perceived by means of the Holy Spirit that that hen symbolized him. "I am that hen," he said, "short in stature, and dark by nature. I must be simple like a dove, flying up to heaven with the feathered strokes of virtue. The Lord in his mercy has given, and will give me, many sons whom I will be unable to protect (*protegere*) with my own strength. I must, therefore, commend them to the holy Church who will protect and guide (*protegat et gubernet*) them under the shadow of her wings."
>
> Afterwards blessed Francis told the Supreme Pontiff: "I humbly and resolutely beg your Holiness to give us the Lord of Ostia as pope (*papa*)."… The Lord Pope was pleased with the petition, and he granted blessed Francis that Lord of Ostia, appointing him a most fitting protector (*protector*) of his religion.'[12]

[12] *Francis of Assisi: Early Documents. Volume II. The Founder,* 'The Legend of Three Companions', 63 and 65; 105-106; Théophile Desbonnets, *Legenda Trium Sociorum. Edition critique. AFH* 67, (1974), 38-137; 144; the "Lord of Ostia" is Cardinal Hugolinus who also played a significant role in Clare's life. He became Pope Gregory IX in 1227, succeeding Pope Honorius III. His pontificate lasted till 1241. 'The Three Companions' refers to these facts in no. 67.

The opposite of 'bearing': grousing and speaking ill of

Francis repeatedly criticised the disparaging and speaking ill of others – saying behind someone's back what cannot be said with love in the presence of that person. He must have experienced how gossip and stirring up can ruin the atmosphere in a community. In Admonition 25 he severely rejects this:

> 'Blessed is the servant who loves and respects his brother as much when he is far away from him as when he is with him, and who would not say anything behind his back that he would not say with charity in his presence.'

Slander, disparagement and complaining have of course always existed. The stories about the journey of the Jewish people through the desert contain much 'murmuring'. And the Rule of Benedict unequivocally rejects this murmuring (*murmuratio*). It sees this as the result of not listening well enough.

The word that Francis uses in his own Rule regarding this literally means 'bringing down' or 'demolishing' (*detractio et murmuratio*): activities which are all too recognisable in our day and age. The damaging of a public figure or the smearing of someone's good name – we have enough words to describe this: slurring, maligning, defaming, slandering, branding and so forth. What we see happening here is the 'negative' of 'bearing the other in his frailty'. It amounts to the opposite of what Francis meant with 'bearing': supporting, building up, exalting and affirming. Or to use a word no longer very often used, but which has a place in the Bible: edification.

'Giving back' (re-presenting) and 'mirroring' (reflecting): explanation by Clare

Francis' trio of 'giving back', 'bearing' and 'serving' is mirrored in three key words in Clare's spirituality.[13] She let her recognition of

---

[13] See: Edith A. Van den Goorbergh and Theodore H. Zweerman, *Light Shining Through a Veil. On Saint Clare's Letters to Saint Agnes of Prague*. Leuven, 2000; 279 and 283 ff.

God's mystery speak above all through the words 'poverty', 'humility' and 'love'. Regarding the significance of *giving back* (re-presenting) for Francis, her metaphor of the *mirror* is of central importance. The term 'giving back' is only used by her when expressing what her vocation meant to her. She understood her vocation as a giving back of her live to God. For example she writes to Agnes of Prague: 'Believe nothing, agree to nothing which would make you want to revoke this resolution or which would place a stumbling-block on your way. In that case you would not be giving back (*redderes*) your vows to the Most High in that perfection to which the Spirit of the Lord has called you' (Second Letter 14). In her Testament she writes: 'With what eagerness and fervour of mind and body, therefore, must we keep the commandments of our God and Father, so that, with the help of the Lord, we may return to Him an increase of His talent!'[14] It is true however that after having said this, she explains this 'giving back' by using the metaphor of a mirror three times.[15] Evidently she felt more at home with this metaphor. And even so, in her Testament she doesn't associate it directly with Christ as she does in her Third and Fourth Letters.

In using the metaphor of the 'mirror', Clare throws light on the significance of the 'giving back' which appealed to Francis in such a great way. Our understanding of this is greatly deepened if we become aware of the fact that Francis was concerned with finding a new identity, just as Clare was when she wished to mirror herself in Christ. Oriented towards Christ, he also desired, by 'giving back', to be gradually transformed into someone who was no longer covetous but giving. For Francis, just as it was for Clare, 'giving back' means that one makes the very best of one's talents and by doing so starts to blossom. The focal point of this sister's spirituality illuminated that of her brother's.

[14] *Clare of Assisi. Early Documents.* (Ed. and trans. Regis J. Armstrong O.F.M. Cap). Revised and expanded. St. Bonaventure, NY, 1993, 'The Testament' 18; 57. For the metaphor of the mirror, see: *Light Shining Through a Veil*; 217-220.

[15] Compare *Clare of Assisi. Early Documents*, Clare's Testament, nos. 19, 20 and 21; 57.

We have already seen that for Francis 'giving back' could only be properly understood from the viewpoint of its opposite, namely 'self-appropriation'. To him, 'giving back' also apparently meant 'disowning oneself'. Acknowledging that disowning oneself was necessary, as well as in applying himself to gratitude and respect, he could in his turn greatly enrich what Clare wished to convey with her metaphor of the 'mirror'.

'Bearing like a mother' in Clare's writings

Francis' central concept 'bearing' (*sustinere*), does not appear as frequently in Clare's writings and then only in connection to the suffering of Christ. All the same, also in regard to this aspect, this sister can enrich our understanding of her brother's spirituality. When in her Third Letter she calls Agnes of Prague 'a co-worker' and 'one who holds up the members of His ineffable Body who are giving way', she deepens the concept of 'bearing'. For Francis, this mostly forms a contrast to the 'self-exaltation' and 'self-maintenance' of the person who has no desire to give God a place in his life. Clare builds on this insight. Moreover, she broadens it by calling Agnes a 'support' (literally 'one holding up') of His ineffable Body. Clare associates the task to support one another more explicitly with the Mystical Body of Christ.

In connection to this, it is remarkable how much attention she also gives to the theme of pride 'which will fall'. In her Third Letter to Agnes, the task of 'bearing' receives its absolute opposite in the vain showing-off by those who, as competitors, desire to climb above others. It is significant that in regard to this she uses the figure of Mary. The reference to her exemplary motherhood, confirms our surmise that Clare, probably even to a greater extent than Francis, heard motherly echoes in the invitation by the Gospels to 'bear'.[16]

---

[16] *Light Shining Through a Veil.* Compare 195-199.

And the new generation?

The disqualification as 'softies' of those who use the 'softer powers', as well as the increasing emphasis on a hard or cool mentality are both rife at the moment. Can the new generation still be
bothered with the call to 'serving' and 'bearing'? Or is it possible
that precisely these two attitudes can be used to accommodate a
healthy appetite for expansion and the use of youthful energy?

It is important to realise that 'bearing' often amounts to having-
to-do with others and consequently to doing-something. This has
everything to do with the power of action being expressed as the
power to bear. Why should the strength required to stand up for
someone in distress be no match for the strength required to pin
someone down – let alone for beating him up. Such a show of
power is so much more cowardly and easy. Taking care of someone
else is everything but an admission of powerlessness. It is an expression of the power which is awoken by true sympathy. It is all about
daring to escape the bewitchment of self-interest. Sticking out your
neck by helping your fellow human-beings is much more attractive
than remaining imprisoned in the cage of selfishness.

Essential to sympathetic bearing is the acknowledgement that I
am just as fragile and sensitive as the other who addresses me in
need. This has everything to do with honesty, humility and the
willingness to see who I am in reality, even if this is not very flat-
tering to the ego. But can we still use this word humility? Initially
not usually without resistance. But what if the humility found in
the very best role-models of the past and present were to be accompanied by an aura of steady power and high-spirited courage, without giving a damn for the models of brute-force which are forced
upon us? Why follow the 'rage' which states that humility amounts
to weakness or cringing servility?

Regarding all this, much depends on the ironic unmasking of
macho behaviour and quasi-manliness with all their monotonous
glorification of hardness. This all too often amounts to adolescent
behaviour that can also be found in adults who should long have
outgrown this developmental phase. Remaining stuck at this point
is a form of retardation which is no less ludicrous, even though it

is common. Recognising the ridiculousness of this kind of stagnation in the highly-valued process of dynamic self-realisation will do the rest of the job. If all goes well, this should result in 'works of charity'. Another hopelessly out-dated term? It should once again stand for what really characterises adulthood: the capacity to bear someone and, if necessary, to actually and concretely do this as well. In brief: to support the other, just as you yourself would wish to be supported.

Respectfully yours: Francis

Francis' understanding of ' bearing' in Admonition 18 can be expressed with 'raising high' or 'carrying upon one's shoulders': both are expressions of the concrete recognition of the other who, fragile as he is, is a living call for help. Nothing implies that for Francis this recognition depended upon the good qualities the person in distress might have had. The only thing that mattered to him was that the one in need was his fellow human-being.

The above-mentioned variations on 'bearing' are very descriptive in showing how someone who has fallen is helped to get up again. One could say that these variations both impart esteem or regard. Honour and respect have long been expressed in deeds and words denoting elevation or height. This symbolism of 'high' and 'low' is significant. The respect which is given to dignitaries or to a Royal Highness is an exaggerated form of what is conveyed with the every-day bow or supporting arm. The fact that arrogant behaviour is insufferable and that true humility is pleasurable, only confirms how much the showing of respect characterises genuine humanity.

Respect is also conveyed through the act of 'giving back'. As we have seen, Francis repeatedly used the words 'giving back' in summarising the six-fold expressions of gratitude to which his earliest brothers called all people to give. The giving back of all things good echoes this explicit praise. For it is led by the willingness to recognise God as the Giver of all things good and, in doing so, to pay Him the respect that He is due. As we have seen, it is of a

capital order that this respect for the All Highest becomes concrete
in the recognition of the right of the lowest of the low to a humane
existence. In respecting the lepers and the poor, Francis paid his due
respects to his crucified Master, who lives on in His Church.

Three focal points of Francis' spirituality: always applicable

Francis' spirituality revolves around the way in which he dealt with
the vulnerability, the unavoidable dependency and the instability
of human existence. Thanking or giving back is the expression of
Francis' choice not to let the other become the victim of his own
need to protect his vulnerability. Jesus' self-emptying formed the
model for this. Bearing expresses Francis' wish to above all respect
his equally fragile neighbour in his dignity, in spite of the support
which he himself also felt in need of. The model for this was Jesus'
self-humbling. Giving back and bearing together express his Master's obedient service. In view of this, the three key words of Francis' spirituality can apparently be associated with three basic facts
of human existence: vulnerability, connected to instability as well
as the possibility to be, in all dependency, so free as to be able to
attune this precarious threesome as a whole to God and one's
neighbour.

Why exactly these three central values which, initially perhaps,
seem to be rather arbitrary? Many other very different values can
also be found in his thoughts and deeds – and in the light of Paul's
hymn in his letter to the Philippians they all have a strong biblical basis. This becomes even more clear if the trio of thanking,
serving and bearing is compared to the three temptations Jesus
experienced in the desert (compare Luke 4:1-13).

A certain concurrence meets the eye. The three temptations lie in:
giving priority to the need for bread (an image of property needed
in order to sustain life); the arrogance of power; and the com-
manding of respect and prestige (which in the Gospel are expressed
in images of height). This concurrence may also be deemed striking
because the three temptations which Jesus experienced were probably the model for the three passions in the anthropology of

Immanuel Kant (1724-1804) which are considered to be distortions: greed, lust of power and ambition. In turn, these three played a key role in the efforts by the French philosopher Paul Ricoeur to discern three essential levels in that entire motley diversity we call 'society'. 'Having' (*avoir*) is the catchword for the area we call economy. 'Being able to' (*pouvoir*) refers to the domain of *politics*. 'Being worthy' (*valoir*) pre-eminently characterises the dimension of *culture* and cult.[17]

In Francis' steps towards a life as a penitent, the above-mentioned tripartite was already present in the 'professions' he chose one after the other. Beginning as a merchant, he next tried to making a living as a knight. Eventually he could only muster the fervour for life as a friar minor: a life in the service of his Lord Jesus Christ while dedicating himself to the poorest of the poor.

We do not know if the initiators of the international 'Conciliary Process for Justice, Peace and the Integrity of Creation' were aware of the above-mentioned tripartites. Nevertheless, without forcing the matter, a relationship can be established between the issue of property and the mission to do justice; between the issue of power and the striving towards true peace; and between the issues concerning respect and recognition and that which regarding the ravishment of our earth, cries out for deeds of preservation and the care for creation.

In the light of these parallel fundamental connections, this means that Francis' three key values are still recognisable in our day and age – also concerning global issues surrounding property, the sharing of power and life-styles. Their common source in the Bible is clearly fruitful for our own times.

The basic tone of the Canticle of the Creatures

The *poverello* who summarised this wisdom of life in his Admonitions, is none other than the poet who sang out his joy in the

---

[17] Compare Paul Ricoeur, *Finitude et Culpabilité. Tome I. L'homme faillible.* Paris, 1960; 127 ff. Idem: 'L'Image de Dieu et l'épopée humaine.' In: Paul Ricoeur, *Histoire et vérité.* Paris, 1964²; 112-131;116 ff.

Canticle of the Creatures – and this 'with great humility' from the bottom up. The heartbeat of his life is beautifully rendered in the last verse of this song: 'Praise and bless my Lord and give Him thanks and serve Him with great humility.' This was how he as it were, put his signature to the ballad celebrating his life. This signature of 'thanking', 'serving' and 'exalting in humility' corresponds strikingly to the three key words in the pathway to learning of the Admonitions: 'giving back', 'serving in obedience' and 'bearing'. Attitudes that, as has already been said, may be summarised in the single word 'respecting'.

6. Francis' vision on Mount La Verna

During the last two years of his life, Francis carried the stigmata of Christ's wounds in his hands, feet and side. These appeared some time around the feast of the Exaltation of the Holy Cross on September 14th, 1224. During that period, Francis was in retreat on Mount La Verna between the feast of the Assumption of the Blessed Virgin Mary (August 15th) and the feast of the Archangel Michael (September 29th). His being marked with the wounds from then on only became known to a few of his brothers during his lifetime – and then only by accident. From his deathbed on however, this became a public fact. More often than not, it made a deep impression on his contemporaries. The amazement and admiration surrounding this inexplicable fact, which up until then had never been observed have since been expressed in countless works of art.

At the time, as well as later on, so much attention was given to the stigmatisation itself that Francis' vision which had preceded it, was usually overshadowed. Unjustly so. For much of what had inspired the man of Assisi most profoundly for years on end, can be found in this vision in which the risen Crucified One showed himself to Francis in the shape of a Seraph with six wings. In fact so much can be found in it, that we will devote many pages in this book to the two texts in which he expressed how this vision had touched him.

Two texts? Yes, we are indeed convinced that – besides the 'The Praises of God' which he soon after the vision entrusted to a piece of parchment with his own hand – there is a second text in which Francis, in a concealed fashion, passed on the message of his vision: Admonition 27. Both texts share common traits, and are together of invaluable importance for obtaining an answer to the question concerning who Jesus Christ was for Francis – especially in his consideration of Him in connection to the Church and how he saw Him in His relationship within the mystery of the Triune God. In a word: whoever wishes to understand Francis the mystic, will have to consult not only the Canticle of the Creatures, but also these two texts.

In this Chapter we shall deal with 'The Praises of God' and in the next Chapter with Admonition 27. Before looking into the above-mentioned song of praise, we shall consider how it was conceived. Besides this, we shall also include the report that Thomas of Celano, a contemporary of Francis, left us regarding his vision of Christ.

What happened on Mount La Verna?

In the quiet seclusion of Mount La Verna where the brothers had had a hermitage since 1213, Francis planned to meditate on how he could best fulfil God's will. At the time he was 42 years old. His physical condition had greatly diminished over the previous years, he was tormented by a disease of the eyes and suffered from the arguments about the life-style of the brothers. Sometimes he must have wondered whether his life's mission was not doomed to failure.

He had secluded himself in a small spot which was in shouting distance of the hermitage where his brothers were staying. Leo, his confidant, brought him something to eat everyday. Francis could therefore devote himself to prayer without being disturbed. As is related in The Assisi Compilation (nr. 118), a flock of birds suddenly flew in while he was at prayer one morning. One by one they flew chirping towards him. Amazed, he asked himself what these heavenly messengers could want to tell him. The answer came from within: 'This is a sign that the Lord will do good for you in this cell and give you many consolations.'

As Celano relates, Francis re-entered his cell full of desire to know God's will. He took the Book of Gospels and laid it on the altar inside the cell. He made the sign of the cross emulating the saints, about whom he had heard were wont to ask advice of the Lord in this manner.[1] He then threw himself onto the ground and begged for light in the darkness of his heart. Next he opened the book three times and every time was confronted with a passage concerning the Lord's suffering. His interpretation of this was that during the years left to him, he would have to let himself be transformed into an image of Christ. In the meantime he kept his vigil, fasted and prayed. Then, as Celano tells us, the following happened:

1. While he was staying in that hermitage called La Verna, after the place where it is located,
2. two years prior to the time that he returned his soul to heaven, he saw in a vision of God a (*unum*) man, having six wings like a Seraph, standing over him, arms extended and feet joined, affixed to a cross.
3. Two of his wings were raised up above his head, two were stretched out to fly, and two covered his whole body.
4. When the blessed servant of the Most High saw these things, he was filled with the highest conceivable amazement, but he did not know what this vision wanted to show him.
5. Moreover, he greatly rejoiced and was much delighted by the kind and gracious look with which, as he saw, he was gazed upon by the Seraph. The Seraph's beauty was beyond 'imagination'.
6. But the fact that the Seraph was fixed to the cross and the bitter suffering of that passion thoroughly frightened him.
7. Consequently, he got up, so to say, both sad and glad and joy and sorrow took their turns in his heart.
8. Concerned over the matter, he kept thinking about what this vision could mean and his spirit was extremely anxious to discern a sensible meaning from the vision.

---

[1] Searching for God's will by means of the *sortes biblicae* (bible oracle) was commonly used in the Middle Ages. See Pierre Courcelle's study, 'L'Enfant et les 'sorts bibliques.' In: *Vigiliae Christianae*, VII (1953); 194-220; 211, note 61. *The Life of Saint Francis by Thomas of Celano* (= 1 Celano); 1 Celano 92-93 quotes the distinction between the *sortes sanctorum* (or *sortes apostolorum*) and the *sortes biblicae*; Bertulf (Peter) van Leeuwen et Cornelis P. Voorvelt, 'La Perfection Evangélique Révélée à Saint François.' In: *Franzischkanischen Studien*, 72 (1990); 30-46.

9. While he was unable to perceive anything clearly understandable from the vision, its newness very much pressed upon his heart. Signs of the nails began to appear on his hands and feet, just as he had seen them a little while earlier on the crucified man hovering over him.[2]

This report was written down less than four years after the event. Celano says that he had let himself be informed on matters by Francis' closest companions. They must have in turn heard the details from Francis himself. The author of The Legend of the Three Companions and his biographer Bonaventure both report that the events took place sometime close to the feast of the Exaltation of the Holy Cross (September 14th). By doing so, they presumably wished to draw attention to the connection between the vision and this feast.

The vision was therefore of a crucified man with the wings of a Seraph. Characteristic to this biblical mythical creature are the six wings which are mentioned in pairs. Francis was completely at a loss. Four times we are told that he did not know what to make of this vision. His confusion is expressed by his simultaneous experience of deep joy and intense consternation. The Seraph who is both extremely beautiful as well as frightening, gazes upon Francis. His own 'seeing' (verse 4) is transformed into 'being seen' (verse 5). Bewilderment and fascination characterise this eye to eye encounter.

After the vision had disappeared, the enormous question as to what it all meant remained: 'When the blessed servant of the most High saw these things, he was filled with the highest conceivable amazement, but he did not know what this vision wanted to show him' (verse 4). His exterior identification with the Crucified man did not take long in happening. Had Francis gone from being a man of prayer to becoming a visionary, and from a visionary to being someone gazed upon, now he became the receiver of the

---

[2] 1 Celano 94; 95. Translation from *Francis of Assisi: Early Documents. Volume I. The Saint*; 220-221 has been adapted for our purposes. The verse-numbers are ours.

wounds of the Crucified One. This transformation proceeded from
without to within. First Francis saw the Seraph at a certain distance. Then he saw the figure at close range. It was unbelievably
beautiful as well as being in a state of bitter suffering. Finally the
wounds appeared in Francis' hands, feet and side. What he had
beheld in his heart, emerged to the surface.

The way Celano highlights the Seraph's wings can create the
impression that Francis saw an angel. The beginning of the report
makes it clear however that he saw a *man*: 'a man, having six wings
like a Seraph'. Besides this, the word 'man' is qualified by the number 'one' (*unum*). The vision does not represent a number of Ser-
aphs like in the biblical vision of the prophet Isaiah, but of one single figure who is 'like a Seraph'. In the middle of the report (verses
5 and 6), the beautiful Seraph gazes lovingly upon Francis. At the
same time, Francis is intensely disturbed because this angelic figure is nailed to a cross. The greatest attention is given to the fact
that the figure is affixed to a cross (verses 2, 6 and 9). It is to be
remarked upon that Francis initially saw a man looking like a Seraph (verse 2), next only the Seraph (verses 5 and 6) and at the end
of the report once again a crucified man. The Seraph itself is no
longer mentioned (verse 9). It was this convergence of images that
especially amazed Francis.[3] Taken on its own, the vision of a Seraph – symbol of the burning love experienced in contemplation of
the highest order – was not unknown in those days. Completely
new for Francis was that between the wings of the Seraph, in the
glow of this heavenly figure, he saw a man affixed to a cross. How
could this glorious radiance be reconciled with the torment of
someone being crucified? Astonishment then, astonishment now.[4]

---

[3] Compare Charles André Bernard, 'La perception mystique visionnaire.' In:
Studies in Spirituality, 6 (1996); 168-193, 170 f. and 180.

[4] One may think of the similarity of form between Francis' vision and the
cross of San Damiano and of the metaphor of the serpent erected in the desert
(compare Numbers 21:9; John 3:14). Compare Dominique Gagnan, 'François au
Livre de la Nature. 10. La Parabole. Le Séraphin symbole royal.' In: *Études Franciscaines*, 26 (1976); 57-88.

Further on we will pause and dwell on the meaning of Francis' vision. First of all however, we will take a look at the 'Praises of God'. Soon after his vision, he wrote down this song of praise on a small piece of parchment in his own hand. On the other side of this parchment he wrote down a blessing, a personal word for brother Leo and drew a capital letter T. This parchment is kept in Assisi as a great treasure.

Praises of God

The text of the 'Praises of God' is reproduced here using our own division into three parts and our own division into numbered verses:

Laudes Dei Altissimi:

Praises of God, the Most High:

Pars I
1 Tu es sanctus Dominus
   Deus solus,
   qui facis mirabilia.
2 Tu es fortis,
3 tu es magnus,
4 tu es altissimus,
5 tu es potens,
6 tu pater sancte,
   rex caeli et terrae.
7 Tu es trinus et unus,
   Dominus Deus deorum.
8 Tu es bonum, omne bonum,
   summum bonum,
   Dominus Deus vivus et verus.

Part I
1 You are holy Lord God,
   the only One,
   Who does wonderful things.
2 You are strong,
3 You are great,
4 You are the Most High,
5 You are the Mighty,
6 You, holy Father,
   King of heaven and earth.
7 You are triune and one,
   the Lord God of gods.
8 You are the good, all good,
   the highest good,
   Lord God, living and true.

Pars II: Part II:
  9(1) Tu es caritas, amor,
10(2) tu es sapientia,
11(3) tu es humilitas,
12(4) tu es patientia,

  9(1) You are charity, love,
10(2) You are wisdom,
11(3) You are humility,
12(4) You are patience,

13(5)	tu es pulchritudo,	13(5)	You are beauty,
14(6)	tu es mansuetudo,	14(6)	You are meekness,
15(7)	tu es securitas,	15(7)	You are security,
16(8)	tu es quietas,	16(8)	You are stillness,

17(9)	tu es gaudium et laetitia,	17(9)	You are joy and gladness,
18(10	tu es spes nostra,	18(10)	You are our hope,
19(11)	tu es iustitia,	19(11)	You are justice,
20(12)	tu es temperantia.	20(12)	You are temperance,

21(13) Tu es omnia divitia nostra   21(13) You are all our riches
       ad sufficientiam.   that is sufficient.

22(14)	Tu es pulchritudo,	22(14)	You are beauty,
23(15)	tu es mansuetudo;	23(15)	You are meekness,
24(16)	tu es protector,	24(16)	You are the protector,
25(17)	tu es custos et defensor,	25(17)	You are the custodian and defender;

26(18)	tu es fortitudo,	26(18)	You are strength,
27(19)	tu es refugium,	27(19)	You are refuge,
28(20)	tu es spes nostra,	28(20)	You are our hope,

29(21)	tu es fides nostra,	29(21)	You are our faith,
30(22)	tu es caritas nostra,	30(22)	You are our charity,
31(23)	tu es tota dulcedo nostra,	31(23)	You are all our sweetness,
32(24)	tu es vita aeterna nostra.	32(24)	You are our eternal life.

Pars III: Part III
33 Magnus et admirabilis   33 Great and wonderful Lord,
    Dominus,
    Deus omnipotens, misericors   almighty God, merciful
    Salvator.   Savior.

Together with the Canticle of the Creatures, this is one of the most important spiritual texts Francis left to posterity. It is his prayer of gratitude after those extraordinary events in his life. Seldom has a mystic left us such a testimony so soon after the events. The Praises of God can therefore be compared to the famous 'Mémorial' by Pascal.[5]

The litany-form probably says something about the way in which Francis and his brothers prayed. When he offered this text to brother Leo, he told him that he had 'meditated in my heart' (2 Celano 49). For them *meditatio* undoubtedly held the meaning it had in monastic tradition: the muttered repetition of a text from the Scriptures.

There was Francis, marked with his Lord's wounds – what hasn't been said about this and how often hasn't he been depicted like this! It is therefore almost unbelievable that this unique testimony concerning the climax of his mystical life, we only possessed in a very mutilated form until only a short while ago. It was only in 1974, after having been subjected to modern x-ray techniques, that this prayer became accessible to us in a more or less reliable way.[6]

A Blessing for brother Leo

On the parchment, brother Leo made notes in red ink about the events which had occurred in September 1224 on Mount La Verna. In this testimony written by Francis' confidant in his own hand, he also mentions that the Seraph spoke to Francis:

> *'Two years before his death, the blessed Francis kept a forty-days' fast in the dwelling of Mount La Verna in honour of the Blessed Virgin Mary, the Mother of God, and of the blessed Archangel Michael, from the feast of the Assumption of the Blessed Virgin Mary until the September feast of Saint Michael. And the Lord's hand was upon him. After the vision and the words of the Seraph to him and the impression of Christ's stigmata upon his body, he composed these praises written on the other side*

[5] Written account of an extrordinary spiritual experience Blaise Pascal had on the evening of November 23rd,1654.

[6] Duane Lapsanski, 'The "Chartula" of St. Francis of Assisi.' In: *Archivum Franciscanum Historicum*, 67 (1974); 18-37.

of this sheet and wrote them in his own hand, thanking God for the kindness bestowed on him.
The blessed Francis wrote with his own hand this blessing for me, brother Leo.'

'May the Lord bless you and keep you.
May He show His face to you,
And be merciful to you.
May He turn His countenance to you
and give you peace.
May the Lord bless you, brother Leo.'

'In a similar way he made with his own hand this sign Tau together with a head.'

The Blessing, written by Francis in his own hand in black ink, can easily be read. Underneath the Blessing he wrote the Greek letter T (*tau*) with the drawing of a human head lying down. The bottom part of the vertical bar of the T rests on the mouth of the head. Surrounding this bar is a somewhat enigmatic series of Latin words. This Blessing, modelled on the blessing of Aaron (Numbers 6:24-26) is almost completely derived from the blessing which, besides being used on other occasions, was given in the service of penance and reconciliation on Holy Thursday.

The words surrounding the *tau*-sign are probably from the concluding formula of this liturgical blessing: 'May He bless you'. This blessing also echoes the entrance hymn of the Mass on the feast of the Exaltation of the Cross: 'We must boast about the cross of Our Lord Jesus Christ. In him is our salvation, our life and our resurrection, by whom we were delivered and set free. May God be gracious on us and bless us. May he let his face shine over us, and may he have mercy on us' (compare Galatians 6:14 and Psalm 67). The symbolic meaning of the Greek letter *tau* (in the Hebrew *taw*), also called 'sign' (*signum*) in the Christian tradition, has biblical roots: the chosen will bear this sign as a seal on their foreheads (Ezekiel 9:4 and Revelation 7:3). This sign was dear to Francis. He wrote it on the beams and walls of places of prayer.

In mediaeval times the *tau* was seen as a 'sign of salvation'. The Fraternity of Saint Anthony wore it on their habits. Amongst other things, they took care of those who had contracted leprosy or the deadly anthrax. Francis probably learned about the *tau*-sign from them. In medieval iconography the cross is often found in the form of a *tau*-sign, sometimes placed above a head, a skull and a human figure at the foot of the cross. In some images, Adam's skull and some bones are lying at the foot of the cross. This image was probably intended to convey two concepts. The first views the cross as the tree of life. The second is based on the legend that the cross was erected above Adam's grave.

In Francis' drawing however, a head, not a skull lies at the foot of the *tau*. Whose head is it? Adam's or Leo's? If this is a reference to the salvation of Adam, the father of humankind, Francis perhaps intended to portray the fact that Leo, like his 'father' Adam, could place his hope in the liberating power of the cross of the New Adam, Christ.

Francis' testimony: A neglected text

The parchment is 10 cm by 14 cm and made of goatskin. The Praises of God is written on the one side, the Blessing on the other. Leo folded the parchment twice, keeping the side with the Praises of God on the outside. He carried it on his person till his death in 1278 – probably as a talisman. He kept the Blessing from wear and tear by keeping it on the inside of the folds. The result was that the Praises of God soon became less legible. Later on, the document was considered a relic and is kept as such to this day.

So it is thanks to Leo that we can now, with a high degree of certainty, establish the authenticity of Francis's text, as well as the history of its origin. Unfortunately, we also owe it to him that the text of the Praises of God has, to a large extent, become illegible. Apparently he wanted to above all things preserve the Blessing he had personally received from Francis.

The parchment also bears other traces of great age. It has tiny little cracks, is flaked off at the edges due to the ravages of moisture and has blackened, especially at the bottom. The side on which the Praises is written has been repaired along the vertical fold using a piece of parchment a couple of centimetres in width. Due to this, part of the text can still not be read. Only after the parchment had been photographed with the help of ultra-violet light in 1974, did large portions of the text once again become legible, except for the words in the folds and on the bottom part of the parchment. It then became apparent that the mediaeval copies of the Praises did not always correspond to what had now become legible. Words and verses were missing. The repetition of a number of invocations had sometimes been left out. These manuscripts were the ones used by Kajetan Esser in 1976 in compiling the critical edition of Francis' writings. With them, he could fill in the gaps in the, now legible, text of the parchment. Even after the reconstruction of the text, there is still no consensus about the proper order of the invocations. Recently, researchers have made a new attempt at deciphering the writing.[7]

The Praises of God were written with no interruptions and its sixteen lines cover the entire page. The spaces between the lines left room for insertions which Francis made here and there. On the side of the Blessing, the cross-bar of the *tau* was drawn on the horizontal fold, the vertical bar on the vertical fold. Above and below the Blessing, which is quite legible, Leo made, as has been noted already, annotations in red ink. There is a striking contrast between Francis' large Roman letters, written unsteadily with his wounded hands, and the neatly written Gothic letters of his secretary.

---

[7] Kajetan Esser, *Die Opuscula des hl. Franziskus von Assisi. Neue textkritische Edition. Zweite, erweiterte und verbesserte Auflage besorgt von Engelbert Grau OFM*, Grottaferrata (Romae), 1989. Attilio Bartoli Langeli, 'Gli Autografi di Francesco d'Assisi (con una nuova edizione della Lettera di Spoleto).' In: *Frate Francesco d'Assisi. Atti del XXI Convegno internazionale*, Assisi, 14-16 ottobre 1993. Spoleto, 1994; 134-146; Enrico Menestò – S. Brufani (ed.), *Fontes franciscani (Medioevo francescano. Testi 2)*. Assisi, 1995; 45-51; Paul Paolazzi, 'Per gli autografi di frate Francesco: dubbi, verifiche e riconferme.' In: *Archivum Franciscanum Historicum*, 93, 2000; 3-28; Attilio Bartoli Langeli, *Gli Autografi di Francesco e di frate Leone*, Turnhout, 2000; 30-41; *Francis of Assisi: Early Documents. Volume I. The Saint*; 108-112.

The Praises of God: his testimony of the vision

The Praises of God comprises 33 invocations. Just as in his Canticle of the Creatures, the number 33 refers to the number of years of Jesus' life. All the verses, excepting the concluding one, begin with the address 'You are'. We can assume that Francis here worships God as He revealed Himself to him in his eye to eye encounter with the crucified Seraph. To a large extent, the invocations are borrowed from psalms and liturgical hymns.

Three parts can be distinguished:
• In the first 8 invocations, Francis acknowledges God as the Exalted One and at the same time as the most Near One, one and triune;
• These are followed by 24 invocations, indicating aspects of God's being;
• The last verse mirrors the first 8 invocations.

Part I: 8 invocations

1. You are holy
   Lord God, the only One,
   Who does wonderful things.
2. You are strong,
3. You are great,
4. You are the Most High,
5. You are the Mighty.
6. You, holy Father, King of heaven and earth,
7. You are triune and one,
8. The Lord God of gods.
9. You are the good, all good, the highest good,
   Lord God, living and true.

In using the address 'You are', Francis calls upon God as the One Who is Present. By repeating 'You are' he keeps this acknowledgement alive. Something of his understanding of the mystery of God can be discovered in the sequence of these eight invocations. As always in his prayers, God's sublimity comes first. He acknowledges God as the One 'Who does wonderful things'. This 'doing' is the only verb found in the Praises. The present tense perhaps signifies that Francis wished to say that God is 'doing' at every moment in time.

You are strong, You are great, You are the Most High, You are the Mighty: testimony of the awe of a person who, insignificant as he is, places his hope in God's protection. The biblical name 'Almighty' is one of the names for God which Francis associates with God's humility.

You, holy Father, King of heaven and earth: two of Jesus' prayers are echoed here – one from the high-priestly prayer: 'Holy Father' (John 17:11) and one from the Gospel according to Matthew: 'I praise you, Father, Lord of heaven and earth' (11:25). From other prayers of Francis we can also conclude that he greatly valued Jesus' own prayers.

Father, King: Francis preferably attributed the title of King to the Father. The title 'Christ King' is not to be found in his writings. This sixth invocation interrupts the rhythm of 'You are'. Besides this, it stands exactly at the centre of Part 1 and is comprised of *seven* words in the Latin text.

You are triune and one, the Lord God of gods: Francis praises the 'only Lord God' as the God who is three in one.

You are the good, all good, the highest good: this acknowledgement of God's self-revelation as the 'Good' was very familiar to him.

The concluding words, *Lord God, living and true* were known to Francis from the Roman canon of the Mass. He prayed these words at the end of each hour of the Office of the Passion: 'Let us bless the Lord God, living and true.' And he began his Christmas Psalm with: 'Exult in God our help – Shout to the Lord God, living and true, with cries of gladness' (Psalm XV,1 by Francis).

Seeing them in this light, the first eight verses of the Praises of God refer to God's approach to humanity: the holy One 'Who does wonderful things' (verse 1) makes himself known in Christ as 'the living and true God'.

Part II: 24 invocations in six verses

In this part Francis continues with the summing up of God's attributes. The form in which he does this is so different compared to the eight invocations in Part I that we have decided to regard this as a separate Part II. Following the structure of the Latin rhyme-schemes we have divided the 24 invocations of Part II into stanzas of four. One exception is the stanza made up of the eighteenth, nineteenth and twentieth invocations, none of which rhyme. In our sequence, this is the fifth stanza. There are some aspects of Part II as a whole which catch the eye and which we will deal with here as 'technical details':

- The fifth and sixth invocation are repeated in the fourteenth and fifteenth invocation: 'You are beauty, You are meekness'.
- The thirteenth invocation: 'You are all our riches, that is sufficient' is striking because of its length. In the Latin, this verse is comprised of 7 words. It forms the centre of Part II. In this way it mirrors the centre of Part I where the regularity of 'You are' was interrupted by 'You, holy Father, King of heaven and earth' (in the Latin also 7 words). One could say that the riches of all the previous and following invocations is concentrated in: 'You are all our riches, that is sufficient'. The word 'riches' forms the focal point.

Insertions

In the manuscript, the word 'love' (*amor*) is written above 'charity' (*caritas*). Francis evidently inserted this word afterwards. Why? Together with others, we share the opinion that the well-known song '*Ubi caritas et amor, Deus ibi est*' (Where charity and love are, there is God) resonates here. Already in Francis's time, it was sung in the liturgy of the washing of the feet on Holy Thursday.[8]

---

[8] Compare 1 John 4:18. In *Documents I,* Théophile Desbonnets and Damien Vorreux observe: 'L'Ubi caritas est sans doute une réminiscence de la Liturgie du Jeudi-Saint'; 30. The first line of this hymn is: 'Ubi caritas et amor, Deus ibi est'. If it is true that this hymn is echoed here, considering Francis' addition of *amor*, then the sequence is: 'You are charity, love'.

The fact that Jesus washed the feet of his disciples made a great impression on Francis and he mentions this relatively often in his writings. Even on his deathbed he insisted on having this passage from the Gospel read out to him (John 13:1-17).

He also inserted the tenth invocation 'You are our hope' afterwards. It remains intriguing as to why he did so and why exactly at this spot, for further on he had already written this same invocation (invocation 20). Besides this, it is strange that he deviates from the usual sequence of the divine virtues: *faith*, *hope* and *charity*. The theme of hope did however resonate strongly in the liturgy of the Exaltation of the Cross. Was this the only reason for this insertion and deviation? There is also the fact that there are exactly 33 Latin words between both invocations 'You are our hope'. All this may seem rather artificial to the reader, but Francis' reference to Jesus Christ using the number 33 can be demonstrated in different places in his writings.

A litany of names for God

In addressing God using virtues (or powers) Francis stands within a tradition which goes back to the desert fathers. They held the notion that when we entrust our thoughts and feelings to God, He lives in us and works in us with his powers. He works in us from within. In Francis' Praises of God, human virtues are understood as being God's gifts *as well as* referring to His being. Some of these virtues can also be found in other texts by Francis. Other virtues which were important to him like 'poverty', 'simplicity' and 'purity' do not appear in the Praises.

Springing from his own personal religious experience, this litany of names can only be heard by others with diffidence. We shall never be capable of making this prayer into our own, although it can invite us to search our own hearts and to pronounce our own names for God corresponding to our own experiences. A prayer conceived in this way can help us develop an understanding of God's unique presence in every one of us.

In what follows, we will try to gain understanding of the invocations within the context of Francis' writings, the report about the vision and the biblical-liturgical sources which nourished his prayer-life.

First stanza

1. You are charity, love,
2. You are wisdom,
3. You are humility,
4. You are patience,

In his vision of the Crucified One, Francis perceived the glow of His limitless love. First Francis wrote down 'charity' (*caritas*), and afterwards then added 'love' (*amor*). Where in his writings he speaks about 'in the charity which is God', Jesus' words 'abide in my charity' (John 15:9) are echoed. But when he considers God's love being an indwelling power, he chooses the word 'love'. 'Charity' and 'love' are names for the Holy Spirit. This opens the series of 24 invocations of Part II with the acknowledgement that it is Love itself which awakens love and brings the heart of man to worship.

'Patience' and 'the power to bear' are undoubtedly understood by Francis as being Christ's pre-eminent power. In view of the central place which 'bearing' and 'being patient' both have in his spirituality, it seems he was especially moved by this power. God's 'love' and 'wisdom' did not shirk from the self-emptying and humility of both crib and cross. And in the Eucharist, He reveals His 'humility', which lies beyond all comprehension, 'in the shape of bread'. In a letter to all his brothers, Francis wrote:

'O wonderful loftiness and stupendous dignity! O sublime humility! O humble sublimity! The Lord of the universe, God and the Son of God, so humbles Himself that for our salvation He hides Himself under an ordinary piece of bread!'[9]

---

[9] *Francis of Assisi: Early Documents. Volume I. The Saint,* 'Letter to the Entire Order' 27-28; 118.

Second stanza

5. You are beauty,
6. You are meekness,
7. You are security,
8. You are stillness.

'Beauty' and 'meekness' may remind us of the report about the La Verna-vision. It relates that Francis was touched by 'the kind and gracious look with which, as he saw, he was gazed upon by the Seraph. The Seraph's beauty was beyond 'imagination'. But the fact that the Seraph was fixed to the cross and the bitter suffering of that passion thoroughly frightened him. Could he not have rather described his experience with the words from Psalm 45: 'You are the most beautiful of men, (...) ride on for the cause of truth and to defend the meekness of the right'?

In those days this psalm was considered to be a song about Christ's mystical union with the Church. It was often used in contemplating the Song of Solomon. These two invocations (repeated in the fourth stanza) may well be an indication that the mystical tradition surrounding the Song of Solomon was not only known to Clare, but also to Francis. The fact that it is this very psalm which Francis quotes is also significant, seeing that in the same mystical tradition the above-mentioned verse from Psalm 45 is related to the figure of the 'Suffering Servant' from Chapter 53 of Isaiah.[10] Clare also associates this psalm with the suffering Christ:

> 'Your Bridegroom, more beautiful than the children of mankind, was made the least of men for your salvation, despised, beaten and many times scourged all over his body, dying on the cross in the midst of anguish itself; O (...) gaze, consider, contemplate, longing to imitate.' (Second Letter to Agnes of Prague 20)

In the passage from the Letter to the Faithful about the union of the believer to the Triune God, Francis also mentions the 'beauty'

---

[10] *Light Shining Through a Veil*; 131-132.

of the Bridegroom. Here 'beautiful' is also followed by words which
convey the meaning of 'meekness':

> 'O how holy, consoling, beautiful and wonderful to have such a
> Spouse! O how holy and how loving, gratifying, humbling, peace-
> giving, sweet, worthy of love, and above all things desirable it is to
> have such a Brother and such a Son: our Lord Jesus Christ, Who laid
> down His life for His sheep and prayed for us to His Father.'[11]

Considering that the Seraph was crucified, we can see that, just as
with Clare, this 'bridal mysticism' is united to a 'mysticism of the
cross'.

'You are security, You are stillness: this is the prayer of one who relies
on God entirely. Surrendering oneself to this 'security' creates room
for the 'stillness' of contemplation. In the monastic tradition, 'stillness' has the meaning of contemplation. Stillness is also a word for
the 'peace' which Francis wished for brother Leo in his Blessing.
In the Christian tradition, peace and 'stillness' are seen as gifts of
the Holy Spirit.

Why does Francis associate God's beauty and meekness, here
and in the fourth stanza, with names expressing security and protection? The French historian Le Goff has pointed out the connection between beauty and light in the Middle Ages.[12] In those
days darkness was incomparably more threatening that we can now
imagine with all our excess of artificial lighting. He points out 'the
search for the security of light' in those days and remarks that 'light
was beauty; it gave security'. The Franciscan theologian, Bonaventure (1217-1274) states: 'what bears light possesses the most
beauty'.

This reference to the conditions of life in Francis's days is confirmed by the fact that the word 'beautiful' occurs in the Canticle
of the Creatures precisely in those places where the poet sings the

---

[11] *Francis of Assisi: Early Documents. Volume I. The Saint,* 'Later Admonition
and Exhortation', nos. 55-56; 49.
[12] Jacques Le Goff, *La civilisation de l'Occident médiéval.* Paris, 1984.

praises of 'Brother Sun', of 'Sister Moon and the Stars', and of
'Brother Fire'. Clare also alludes to this theme of light and beauty
in her Third Letter to Agnes of Prague: 'the One at whose beauty
the sun and moon wonder' (verse 16). This fascination for the
beauty of light was in those days – see the Gothic cathedrals – certainly fed by the wish to banish the chaotic darkness as much as
possible by orientating oneself to a radiant and beautiful order. For
those living in the Middle Ages, the God of the intimate Union
(Psalm 45) was the Same as He Who would secure the eventual
completion of creation-out-of-chaos, in spite of life's uncertainty.

Third stanza

  9. You are joy and gladness,
 10. You are our hope,
 11. You are justice,
 12. You are temperance.

Joy and gladness: biblical and liturgical echoes also resonate here.
The juxtaposition of 'joy and gladness' was well-known to Francis
who had prayed Psalm 51, the psalm of penance, a countless number of times: 'Let me hear joy and gladness'. What Celano recorded
about his vision, 'he greatly rejoiced and was much delighted', can
probably be heard here. Here the visionary 'gives back' his experience of joy to Him Who is its source. Connected to this, it is interesting to note that Francis combines 'gladness' with 'poverty' in
some of his writings. We are reminded here of Admonition 27.
There, after 'humility' and 'patience' and before 'stillness' (rest) and
'meditation', we can read: 'Where there is poverty with joy, there
is neither greed nor avarice.' And in his Psalm for the Advent, the
words 'may the poor see and rejoice, seek God and your soul shall
live' have a central place (Psalm XIV, 5 by Francis).
    Our hope, justice – You are our hope: This invocation (which
Francis inserted afterwards) contains an irregularity when compared to the structure of the majority of the invocations: 'Our' is
mentioned here for the first time. 'Our' which he uses seven times

in the Praises of God, certainly refers to Francis' recognition of the fact that he felt united to the entire community of the faithful in his prayer. The juxtaposition of 'hope' and 'justice' can also be found in the prayers and songs for the feasts of the Finding of the Holy Cross (May 3rd) and the Exaltation of the Holy Cross (September 14th). In them, the Cross of Christ is called 'weapon of justice for the salvation of the world'. In his Office of the Passion, Francis prayed: 'In you, Lord, I have hoped (...) in your justice free me and rescue me' (Psalm XII, 1 by Francis).

Justice, temperance – Traditionally 'temperance' and 'justice' belong to the four capital virtues. Of the other two, 'strength' (*fortitudo*) is mentioned in the fifth stanza. 'Prudence' is not mentioned at all, however earlier on 'wisdom' is. 'Temperance' refers to the power people have to restrain themselves out of respect for what is frail. It has a place between 'too much' and 'too little' and reorders the relationship between God and man which was disturbed through the original sin of self-appropriation. As a name for God it means His respect for the measure and frailty of our material state. We recall the report of Francis' vision: 'two wings covered the Body of the Crucified One.' Who else could do this other than He Who is respecting 'Temperance' Himself?

You are all our riches, that is sufficient: the thirteenth and central invocation

Whom is Francis addressing with the words 'You are all our riches, that is sufficient'? A clue may be found in 'that is sufficient'. In Admonition 1 he namely cites the Apostle Philip's words to Jesus: 'show us the Father and He will be enough for us'. Jesus then says to him: 'Philip, whoever sees me sees my Father as well.' Francis is probably alluding to this when he wrote this invocation under the impression of the vision he had just had. We also recall what the Letter to the Ephesians calls 'the boundless riches of Christ' (3:8).

The fact that Francis is indeed addressing Christ here, is confirmed by the Earlier Rule of 1221. There he says while praying to the Father about Jesus: 'Who always satisfies You in everything, through Whom You have done so much for us. Alleluia' (Earlier Rule 23, 5).

Fourth stanza

14. You are beauty,
15. You are meekness,
16. You are the protector,
17. You are the custodian and defender.

After once again addressing God as beauty and meekness, Francis highlights God's concrete protection. With 'the protector' and 'the custodian and defender' he praises God as the One Who is near to us. 'Beauty' offered security in Francis' day. We have already noted this in our commentary on the second stanza. The conjunction of 'beauty' and 'meekness' refers to the quality of the protection and the defence: namely the love of humanity which he saw in the burning love of the crucified Seraph. One of the themes of the feast of the Exaltation of the Cross is the protection given by Christ's cross.

Fifth stanza

18. You are strength,
19. You are refuge,
20. You are our hope.

The theme of protection is more internalised in this stanza. Those psalms which bring to mind the symbolism of protective wings resonate here. In them, the merging of 'strength', 'refuge' and 'hope' are also striking. For example in Psalm 18:1-3: 'I love you, O Lord, my strength. The Lord is my rock, my fortress, and my deliverer, my God, my rock in whom I take refuge, my shield, and the horn of my salvation, my stronghold.' In the next Chapter we shall dwell on why this stanza differs from the others in length.

Sixth stanza

21. You are our faith,
22. You are our charity,
23. You are all our sweetness,
24. You are our eternal life.

'Our' unites this stanza with the last-mentioned invocation: You are our hope. 'Our' means: God is 'the Saviour of all Who believe and hope in Him and love Him' (Earlier Rule XXIII, 11). The trio 'hope', 'faith' and 'charity' (cherish) reminds us of Francis' Prayer before the Crucifix: 'Give me true faith, certain hope, and perfect charity'. He prayed this after having heard the commandment from the image of Christ in the church of San Damiano: 'Francis, go rebuild My house; as you see, it is all being destroyed.' Later on, Celano viewed what happened in this little church as being connected to the vision and the stigmatisation. 'From that time on, compassion for the Crucified One was impressed into his holy soul. And we honestly believe the wounds of the sacred Passion were impressed deep in his heart, though not yet on his flesh (2 Celano 10).

You are all our sweetness. Here Francis addresses God in a fashion which is based on the sense of 'sweetness' he experienced in the vision of the Seraph. His biographer tells us that Francis 'enjoyed the anointing of the Spirit' and that he could not hear 'the love of God without a change in himself' (2 Celano 196). In spite of the fact that this prayer is based on an intensely personal experience, Francis writes *our*. In recollecting the vision, he must have been profoundly conscious of his union with the suffering members of the Body of Christ, the Church. His Testament also contains a reference to a similar taste-experience: 'And when I left them (the lepers), what had seemed bitter to me was turned into sweetness of soul and body.' In this process of transformation, his sense of taste was altered completely. Once again, the oldest hymns from the liturgy of the Exaltation of the Holy Cross can be heard here: Christ, affixed to the Cross, by drinking the 'bitter gall' has enabled us to once again taste the 'sweet fruits' of paradise.

You are our eternal life: here texts are echoed from the Gospel according to John, where 'eternal life' is the pre-eminent gift of the Holy Spirit, the Giver of Life. In this final invocation, this gift is alluded to as being the final reality.

The six stanzas in the form of a cross

In the vision, as Celano described it, the wings of the Seraph formed a cross. Two wings were raised up, two were stretched out and two covered the body of the Crucified One. Does the Praises of God mirror this arrangement of the wings? Our answer is yes.

We have seen that verse 13, with 'our riches', forms the heart of part II. Stanzas 3 and 4 constitute the frame-work to this: just as the third stanza begins with a five-word invocation (verse 9), the fourth stanza concludes with a five-word invocation as well (verse 17). We could discard this as being insignificant, were it not for the last two invocations (verses 23 and 24) of the series of 24, which also number five words each. Moreover, as we have already noted, in stanzas 5 and 6 the word 'our' (*nostra*) also occurs 5 times.

One wonders whether Francis had some special purpose with these verses of 5 words each, and precisely in those places. In Francis's time, the number 5 referred, among other things, to the 5 wounds of the Crucified One.[13] Now, if we attempt to group the 6 stanzas we distinguished in Part II of the Praises of God as three pairs on the basis of the number 5, we discover the shape of a cross:

• Stanzas 1 and 2: the wings extending above the head form a kind of canopy that does not veil the head. Perhaps the invocations in these stanzas call to mind Francis' astonishment on seeing the radiant and suffering Seraph – and the fact that he gazed upon him lovingly.

---

[13] Cf. *Francis of Assisi: Early Documents. Volume I. The Saint*; 281, Celano 114: 'It presents to the eyes of faith, that mystery in which the blood of the spotless lamb, flowing abundantly through the five wounds, washed away the sins of the world.' See: *Light Shining through a Veil*; 105.

- Stanzas 3 and 4: the out-stretched wings stand for the arms of the Crucified One. At both ends there are five words (verses 9 and 17), which may indicate his pierced hands.
- Verse 13: 'You are all our riches, that is sufficient.' Could Francis have had Christ's opened heart in mind? Seven words in Latin – a reference to the fullness of the Spirit.
- Stanzas 5 and 6: the wings covering the body have a protective and concealing function. At the bottom end, the two invocations of five words each (verses 23 and 24) seem to indicate Jesus' two wounded feet.

Symbolism of the wings

It was after he had had the vision of the six-winged Seraph that Francis wrote the series of names of God. Of these six wings, two were extended upwards, two were out-stretched and two covered the body of the Crucified One.

In the Bible and also in the religious literature of the Middle Ages, the effective action of God's powers is often symbolized by wings. Sometimes these wings appear in conjunction with flames.[14]

Francis' contemporaries were also familiar with this symbolism. The Three Companions states: 'he said... I must be simply like a dove, flying up to heaven with the feathered strokes of virtue' (63). Celano also uses this metaphor in an account of how Francis died. Reflecting on the vision on Mount La Verna, he interprets the two wings extending above the Seraph's head as a symbol of a life which is exclusively turned to God. The two out-stretched wings refer to the act of flying, symbolising our two duties 'to our neighbour, refreshing the soul with the word of God and nourishing the body with material assistance'. The remaining two wings symbolise the covering up with remorse of the nakedness of a body that has been stripped of one's own merits. This happens regularly as it is stripped bare whenever sin breaks in (compare 1 Celano 114). In Bonaventure's writings, the symbolism of flames combined with that of

---

[14] *Respectfully Yours*; 251.

wings is unmistakable: 'he (Francis) saw a Seraph having six wings, fiery as well as brilliant.'[15]

A cross in the structure of Part II of the Praises of God

	stanza 1: 1. You are charity, love, 2. You are wisdom, 3. You are humility, 4. You are patience.	
	stanza 2: 5. You are beauty, 6. You are meekness, 7. You are security, 8. You are stillness.	
stanza 3: *(5 words in the Latin text):* 9. **You are joy and gladness,** 10. You are our hope 11. You are justice, 12. You are temperance.	*verse 13:* **You are all our riches,** **that is sufficient.** *(7 words in the Latin text)*	*stanza 4:* 14. You are beauty, 15. You are meekness, 16. You are the protector, 17. **You are the custodian and** **defender:** *(5 words in the Latin text)*
	stanza 5: 18. You are strength, 19. You are refuge, 20. You are **our** hope	
	stanza 6: 21. You are **our** faith, 22. You are **our** charity, 23. 'You are all **our** sweetness,' 24. 'You are **our** eternal life.' *(Twice five words in the* *Latin text; and 5 times 'our')*	

[15] *Francis of Assisi: The Founder.* The major Legend of Saint Francis', Chapter XIII: 3; 632.

Mary and the Church

If Part II of the Praises is read 'from the bottom up', then the sequence of the words 'life', 'sweetness' and, a little further up, 'our hope' should be taken note of. These words are namely to be found in the 'Greeting to Mary' which Francis was most probably acquainted with: *Salve Regina (mater) misericordiae, vita, dulcedo et spes nostra* (Hail holy Queen (mother) of mercy; our life, our sweetness, our hope). Mary was the pre-eminent image of the Church for Francis. In the Salutation of the Blessed Virgin Mary he says: 'Hail Lady, holy Queen, holy Mother of God, Who are the Virgin made Church.'

Part III: the thirty-third and final invocation

33. Great and wonderful Lord, almighty God, merciful Saviour.

This final invocation is comprised of 8 words in the Latin (8 invocations in Part I; 24 invocations in Part II). This number corresponds to the number of 8 invocations in Part I. In Francis' time, the number 8 referred to amongst other things, God's initiative and to the resurrection of Jesus Christ.

This thirty-third invocation resumes several of God's attributes which were mentioned in Part I: 'wonderful' and 'great' and does so almost in the reversed sequence in this verse 33: 'great and wonderful', demonstrating the connection between Parts III and I.

Christogramme

'Lord God' is mentioned 3 times in Part I and once in the concluding verse (Part III, verse 33). The first words of the Praises 'You are holy' – an allusion to God's sublimity – can be connected to the last words 'merciful Saviour', which describe God's descending approach. The first and the concluding verse form a vertical line. This line runs through verse 6 (Part I) and verse 21 (Part II, verse 13) which are both comprised of 7 words in the Latin.

'Father, King' are the two central words of Part I. 'Our riches' are the two central words of Part II and refer to Christ, as has already been noted:

'You holy FATHER, KING of heaven and earth';
'You are all OUR RICHES, that is sufficient'

Besides this, there are two diagonal lines, which can be connected to each other cross-wise: from the words 'wonderful' (verse 1) and 'great' (verse 3) across to 'great and wonderful' (verse 33). Together with the vertical line mentioned above, these two diagonal lines form a Christogramme which is concealed like a watermark in the text of the Praises. As remarked upon earlier in this book, the initial letters of Jesus Christ are I and X in the Greek.

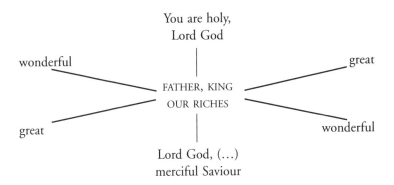

The Praises of God differs from other prayers by Francis in that it does not end with a doxology to the Holy Trinity. All the same, this prayer completely relates to the Triune Mystery:
• The *Father* is the only one of the three divine Persons who is mentioned by name.
• The *Son* is invoked as 'our riches' and the name of Jesus Christ is woven into the text as a monogram.
• In concurrence with the number-symbolism of the time, the 24 invocations of Part II allude to the creative power of the *Holy Spirit* in the faithful.

Francis' Praises of God can be compared to an artistically woven miniature, as can Admonition 27, which shall be dealt with in the next Chapter. Both these texts confirm the fact that in the Middle Ages 'where religious matters were concerned, the utmost beauty was striven for' (Frits Van Oostrum). All the same, the question may arise as to whether these reports about a heavenly vision, written high up on a mountain-top and far away from normal everyday life, can be related to the issues of our day and age.

Everything depends on how we define 'issues of our day'. It is evident that no directions for life-improvement can be found in the Praises. Although if one is prepared to receive this prayer as what it essentially is – a testimony on how it was given to Francis to understand who God is – then it is more up to date than any modern action-programme whatsoever. For, just like Admonition 27, it alludes to the Source which inspires us to meaningful action. Those who limit 'doing' to deeds of action will have to discover for themselves that every attempt to open up in prayer to God is in itself an incomparable and extreme act. An act which can only be accomplished with God's help and which exactly in this way can become the fertile ground for a life-style built on solid foundations.

'My secret is mine'

The occurrences on Mount La Verna were disconcerting to Francis. The brothers who were there with him at the time noticed his bewilderment only too well. Their questions as to what had happened caused Francis grave doubt. Could he really tell others what had occurred in a direct and unconcealed manner? Usually, in matters concerning his prayer-life, he would say: 'My secret is mine.' But now he realised that in the long run it would be impossible to keep especially the stigmata, which had followed upon the vision, hidden. In the end when he asked some of the brothers for their advice. Brother Illuminatus responded:

> 'Brother, you should realize that at times divine sacraments are revealed to you not for yourself alone but also for others. You have

every reason to fear that if you hide what you have received for the profit of many, you will be blamed for burying that talent.'[16]

Impressed by these words, he self-consciously and hesitantly told the brothers what he had seen. However, he did not tell them what the Seraph had said, and so maintained the stance he had taken in Admonition 28, which concluded his collection of Admonitions:

'Blessed is the servant who stores up in heaven the good things which the Lord shows to him and does not wish to reveal them to people under the guise of a reward, because the Most High Himself will reveal His deeds to whomever he wishes. Blessed is the servant who safeguards the secrets of the Lord in his heart.'

---

[16] *Francis of Assisi: Early Documents. Volume II. The Founder*, 'The Major Legend of Saint Francis', Chapter XIII, 4; 633.

7. A veiled account of his vision at La Verna: Admonition 27

Admonition 28, with which we ended the previous Chapter, belongs to a broad tradition of mediaeval literature which spoke of intimate spiritual experiences in very guarded terms. When such reticence was deemed necessary, various literary genres would be applied as cloaks and veils, as we have already noted in the Introduction. It is important to keep this in mind when reading Francis' poems which, of course, were based on such experiences. And *could* he have written in any other way after his vision on Mount La Verna?! After God had revealed Himself to him as the respectful One Who Conceals, then, in Francis' eyes, the concealment of his experience must have been required more than ever. As far as we know, he therefore did not leave us any direct account of his vision, although he did understand that the vision was not only meant for himself. He fulfilled his task to both 'safeguard the secrets of the Lord in his heart' as well as to proclaim them, by reporting his vision in a 'sealed' fashion. He did so in The Praises of God and in connection to this, also in Admonition 27.

Admonition 27 has a unique place in the pathway to learning of the 28 Admonitions. Its form deviates from that of the other Admonitions as well as from all of Francis' other writings. Using a popular literary genre of the times, it sketches the contradictions between certain virtues and vices.[1]

---

[1] Damien Isabell O.F.M. examines each of the virtues and vices in the light of Francis' writings and other sources on him. See: 'Admonition XXVII and the Content of the Ministry to Spiritual Direction.' In: *The Cord, A Franciscan Spiritual Review*, 38 (1988); 4-18; idem: 'The "Virtues" in Admonition XXVII of the Writings of Francis of Assisi and their Usefulness in Spiritual Discernment.' In: *The Cord, A Franciscan Spiritual Review*, 38 (1988); 35-57.

All the same, we shall try and demonstrate that Admonition 27 also contains a reference to his vision on La Verna, just as The Praises of God does. Why did he give his account in the form of a poem? He must have realised that poetry is particularly suitable for the cloaking of references to whatever transcends human understanding, though which can nevertheless be faintly discerned. By interweaving various elements (sound, rhythm, rhyme, double-entendres etc.) poetry enables us to evoke more than the mere sum of its parts. Because a poem, being 'condensed', is more or less a closed entity, it offers protection against disrespectful curiosity.

A poem

Based on the rhyming (in the Latin) we have divided the text into two stanzas. The irregularities in this poem are striking. The apparent 'weaving flaws' have been printed in small capitals.

Stanza 1

> 1. *Ubi caritas* EST *et sapientia,*
>   *ibi nec timor nec ignorantia.*
> Where there IS charity and wisdom,
> there is no fear or ignorance.

> 2. *Ubi est patientia et humilitas,*
>   *ibi nec ira nec pertubatio.*
> Where there is patience and humility,
> there is no anger or disturbance.

> 3. *Ubi est paupertas* CUM *laetitia,*
>   *ibi nec cupiditas nec avaritia.*
> Where there is poverty WITH joy,
> there is no greed or avarice.

Stanza 2

4. *Ubi est quies et meditatio,*
   ibi NEQUE *sollicitudo* NEQUE *vagatio.*
Where there is rest and meditation,
there is NEITHER anxiety NOR restlessness.

5. UBI EST TIMOR DOMINI AD ATRIUM SUUM CUSTODIENDUM,
   IBI INIMICUS NON POTEST HABERE LOCUM AD INGREDIEN-
   DUM.
WHERE THERE IS FEAR OF THE LORD TO GUARD HIS COURTYARD,
THERE THE ENEMY CANNOT HAVE A PLACE TO ENTER. (compare
Luke 11:21)

6. *Ubi est misericordia et discretio,*
   ibi nec superfluitas nec induratio.
Where there is a heart full of mercy and discernment,
there is no excess or hardness of heart.

- Verse 5 differs both in form and length: it contains two lines of eight words each, whereas the other five verses have two lines of five words each (in the Latin).
- In verse 1, 'is' (*est*) is in a different place than in the other verses.
- Verse 3 has 'with', (*cum*) whereas the other verses have 'and' (*et*).
- Verse 4 has 'neither...nor' (*neque...neque*), whereas the other verses have 'no...or' (*nec...nec*).

A poem's irregularities may reveal the poet's ineptitude, but a poet who has proved his ability elsewhere may deliberately 'build in' irregularities in order to alert the attentive reader to a deeper meaning. We believe that the composer of the Canticle of the Creatures purposely wove irregularities into Admonition 27. These give access to a much deeper meaning than this poem, when seen only as a didactic poem on vices and virtues, does at first sight.

   In order to discover the significance of these irregularities, we shall unfold the new perspective this text offers step by step. We are aware of the fact that this detective work will demand a great deal of patience from our readers, but feel we may ask this of them seeing that the results are surprising as well as enriching.

The fifth verse as a 'key'

Our starting point is the most remarkable irregularity within the poem: the length of verse 5. What did Francis intend by this? Does this interruption of the rhythm perhaps offer us a key to a deeper meaning?

In this verse Francis' quotes almost literally from the Gospel according to Luke 11:21. 'When a strong man, fully armed, guards his castle, his property is safe' (literally: 'in peace'). Where the Gospel reads 'fully armed', Francis wrote 'fear for the Lord'. (Or did he mean 'fear of the Lord' = 'the Lord's fear'? Both translations are possible.) Evidently he was alluding to a fear or reverence which is of a completely different nature than the 'fear' he rejected in verse 1. But why did he cite exactly this verse from Luke?

It is a fact that the eleventh Chapter of Luke, from which this verse is taken, contains many elements which in several ways touch on themes from Admonition 27 and The Praises of God. In this Chapter, for example, 'a sign from heaven' is asked for. Francis must have experienced his mysterious vision as a heavenly sign – and then perused the bible for texts about a sign from heaven. Luke's Chapter 11 is one of these, besides for example, passages from Revelation, the Song of Solomon and Malachi.[2]

The question remains as to why Francis substituted the words 'strong man, fully armed'. Maybe he was inspired by Cassian, the monk who brought over the wisdom of the desert fathers to the West in the fifth century CE. His texts often functioned as a kind of 'prayer book' for many a monk.

We believe that Francis, on his many journeys, must probably have heard texts by Cassian is some abbey or other. If, when composing Admonition 27, he had had Cassian's commentary on Luke 11:21 at

---

[2] *Respectfully Yours,* Chapter 7; 278 ff.

the back of his mind, this could have suggested the substitution of 'strong man, fully armed' by 'fear of the Lord'. Cassian namely sees a connection between Luke's 'fully armed' and the 'fear of God':

> 'For if a strong man – that is: our spirit – guards his house well armed and fortifies it with the fear of God right to the most distant corners of his heart, all his possessions – that is: the fruit of his asceticism and virtues which took up so much of his time – will be in peace. But if someone comes who is stronger than he, and who defeats him – especially the devil who makes him agree with those thoughts – then the latter will rob him of his entire equipment in which he had put his trust – that is: constantly keeping in mind the Scriptures and the fear of God – and he will divide as spoils whatever he possessed – that is: the merits of his virtues which he allows to turn into the opposite vices.'[3]

Cassian's connection between the Gospel-text about the 'strong man, fully armed' and the theme of the 'fear of God' is remarkable. He understands the 'strong man' as being 'our spirit' who 'guards his house well armed' and who lets 'all his possessions (...) be in peace' when he 'fortifies (...) with the fear of God (...) (the) most distant corners of his heart'. Francis also associates the 'fully armed' man with the 'fear of the Lord', although he gives the 'fear of the Lord' a much deeper significance. He is namely also concerned that the virtues mentioned not be changed into the opposite vices.

The fear of the Lord

In the fifth verse Francis obviously wished to emphasise the traditional *fear of God*. What did he have in mind? What does he write about this theme elsewhere? An important text can be found in Chapter 17 of the Earlier Rule of 1221:

> 'It (the Spirit of the Lord) strives for humility and patience, the pure, simple and true peace of the Spirit. Above all, it desires the divine

---

[3] Jean Cassien, *Institutions Cénobitiques*. Texte latin revu. Introduction, traduction et notes par J.-C. Guy. (*SC*, 109). Paris, 1965, Chapter VI; 13; 278.

fear, the divine wisdom and the divine love of the Father, Son and Holy Spirit' (verses 15-16).

This is one of Francis' texts concerning the mystery of the Trinity. So to see, he connects 'divine fear' with the Father, 'divine wisdom' with the Son and 'divine love' with the Holy Spirit.

In associating 'wisdom' with the second Person of the Holy Trinity, he follows an old Christian tradition. In his Letter to the Faithful he explicitly follows this tradition when he states: 'the Son of God, the true wisdom of the Father' (verse 67). Also following a time-honoured tradition, 'love' stands for the Holy Spirit. Elsewhere in the Earlier Rule, Francis associates 'love' and the Holy Spirit: 'through the charity of the Spirit, let them serve and obey one another voluntarily' (Chapter 5:14).

The words 'divine fear' remain a puzzle. Of course, the 'fear of the Lord' is well-known from the Scriptures and tradition, but there it concerns man's reverence for God. It is however clear that in the text quoted from the Earlier Rule, that 'divine Wisdom' and 'divine Love' indicate names for respectively the Son and the Holy Spirit. But 'divine fear' usually seems to refer not to the Father, but to the attitude of the faithful who have reverence for the Father. Or did Francis intend here to call the Father 'divine Fear'? Meaning here of course, 'divine Reverence' or 'divine Awe'. We wish to take this last interpretation seriously, because there are texts by the Greek Fathers which leave room for this unusual interpretation.[4]

If we read the triad in verse 15 parallel to that in verse 16, then the virtue of 'humility' can be related to the Father, that of 'patience' to the Son and that of 'peace of the spirit' to the Holy Spirit. The parallel structure of both verses is then:

Verse 15:	*Verse 16:*	
humility	divine Fear	Father
patience	divine Wisdom	Son
peace	divine Love	Holy Spirit

[4] John Chrysostom (347-407 CE) in: *PG,* 53, column 70.

We shall deal with 'humility' as a reference to the Father further on. In The Praises of God, Francis addresses God as the Patient One: 'You are patience'. One of Francis' first brothers, Giles of Assisi, left us the following saying: 'The spirit rests in humility; patience is her daughter.' If 'humility' refers to the Father for Francis, then 'patience' being a reference to the Son, is supported by Giles. The fact that 'peace' is a name for the Holy Spirit for Francis, is evident from a number of places in his writings.

A comparison of Admonition 27 with the Praises of God

We have seen that a litany of 24 invocations lies at the heart of The Praises of God. This can be sub-divided into 6 stanzas of mainly four verses each. We have also seen that the presence of divine powers was often symbolised by wings in the Christian tradition. Could the six verses in Admonition 27 perhaps refer to the 6 wings of the Seraph of Francis' vision? Which similarities are there then with Part II and Part III of the Praises? We shall compare Admonition 27 and these parts of the Praises:

Praises of God	Admonition 27

Part II
1. You are CHARITY, love,
   You are WISDOM,
   You are HUMILITY,
   You are PATIENCE.
	1. Where there is CHARITY and WISDOM, there is no fear or ignorance.
	2. Where there is PATIENCE and HUMILITY, there is no anger or disturbance.

2. You are beauty,
   You are meekness,
   You are security,
   You are STILLNESS (*quietas*).
	See verse 4: rest (*quies*)

3. You are JOY and gladness,
   You are our hope,
   You are justice,
   You are temperance.
	3. Where there is poverty with JOY, there is no greed or avarice.

You are all our riches that is sufficient. 4. You are beauty, 　You are meekness, 　You are the protector, 　You are the custodian and defender.	4. Where there is REST (*quies*) and meditation, there is neither anxiety nor restlessness.
5. You are strength, 　You are refuge, 　You are our hope.	5. Where there is fear of the Lord to guard his courtyard, there the enemy cannot have a place to enter.
6. You are our faith, 　You are our charity, 　You are all our sweetness, 　You are our eternal life. Part III: Great and wonderful Lord, almighty God, MERCIFUL Saviour.	6. Where there is a heart full of MERCY and discernment, there is no excess or hardness of heart.

The fifth verse of Admonition 27 and the fifth stanza of the Praises of God

As we have seen, Francis substituted Luke's 'strong man, fully armed' with 'fear for/of the Lord'. In the Praises, 'You are strength' stands between 'You are the protector, You are the custodian and defender' and 'You are refuge'. These are all names that evoke the same image as in verse 5 of Admonition 27: an image of the guarding of a domain, in order that an enemy power may not enter. Now, The Praises of God was written while Francis was still under the impression of the vision of the Crucified One, whose body was covered with two wings. Did he perhaps have this vision in mind while composing Admonition 27? In this case, 'his courtyard' (*atrium*, verse 5) would designate this protected and guarded Body. Regarding this, it is important to realise that in the symbolism of the church-building in Francis' times, the 'courtyard' (*atrium*) often referred to the Body of Christ.

The connections we have postulated between the fifth stanza
and the fifth verse as well as to the vision of Christ may be unexpected, but they are a possibility. How should the 'fear of the Lord'
be understood then? These words could designate the protective
wings of the Seraph. And as has already been said, some texts from
the monastic tradition speak about the 'fear of God' in the sense
of God's reverence. 'Fear' could then be a designation for one of
the names of God the Father, and could then indeed be translated
as the 'reverence of the Lord'.

The first two verses of Admonition 27 and the first stanza of the
Praises

The deviating first verse of Admonition 27 is: 'Where there is
charity and wisdom, there is no fear or ignorance'. In contrast to
the other verses, in the Latin text '*is*' is placed directly after 'charity' instead of after 'where'. It has been correctly pointed out that
the hymn for the Holy Thursday liturgy is echoed in this first
verse: '*ubi caritas est et amor, Deus ibi est*' (where charity and love
are found, there is God).[5] Our interpretation of why this verse is
an exception, is that Francis put the word 'is' here in the same
place as in the hymn because he wished to refer to the way Jesus
washed the feet of his disciples on their last evening together. Our
interpretation is supported by the first verse of Part II of the
Praises: 'You are charity, love'. Why did Francis insert 'love'
between the lines of the Praises, where he had already written
'charity'? A plausible solution is that also there he was reminded
of the hymn for Holy Thursday.

---

[5] Théophile Desbonnets et Damien Vorreux. *Saint François d'Assise, Documents et Premières Biographies*. Paris, 1968. Deuxième édition revue et augmen-
tée. Paris, 1981; 30; cf. also Gregory the Great, 'Liber Responsalis, Ad Manda-
tum' (a text for the ceremony of the washing of the feet on Holy Thursday): 'Ubi
est caritas et dilectio, ibi sancta est congregatio, ibi nec ira nec indignatio [Where
there is love and affection, there is the holy community, there is neither anger nor
indignation],' *PL*, 78, columns 849 and 766.

In the first stanza of the Praises, the sequence is 'charity, love', 'wisdom' and then 'humility' and 'patience'. Comparing the first stanza to the first two verses of Admonition 27, we see that the same virtues appear here in pairs. The idea has occurred to us that the interweaving of these virtues by Francis had a special significance for him and that there is perhaps a connection between both texts.

Codes in Admonition 27 and in The Praises of God

Other similarities between Admonition 27 and The Praises of God are numerological, but therefore of no less significance.

- In verse 3 'with' is an irregularity. In the verses 1, 2, 4 and 6 the virtues are namely connected using 'and'. This also raises the question whether this difference is only a coincidence. The word 'with' is the 24th word in the Latin text of the Admonition counted from the top down. The central part of The Praises of God also has 24 invocations. In Francis' times, the number 24 designated the universal action of the Holy Spirit and the praise of God.[6]
- The fifth stanza in the Praises is irregular. The fifth verse of Admonition 27 is also irregular. The fact that all the lines of Admonition 27 consist of 5 words in the Latin, except for the fifth verse, is also remarkable. In Francis' times the number 5 could also refer to the 5 wounds of the crucified Jesus.
- The fifth verse of Admonition 27, which in our provisional interpretation deals with God the Father's protection of the Body of His Son, has two times 8 words. The number 8 traditionally symbolised Jesus' resurrection. But why should the fifth verse speak about the resurrection? Our answer is that the amazing thing about Francis' vision was that the crucified Lord appeared as the Living One: anguish and joy intermingled.
- Another irregularity in Admonition 27 is the use of the words 'neque...neque' ('neither...nor') in verse 4. This seemingly

---

[6] *Respectfully Yours,* see: Appendix: The Symbolism of Numbers; 397-404; *Light Shining Through a Veil*; 106.

insignificant variation is nevertheless food for thought. The second *neque*, before *vagatio* ('restlessness'), turns out to be the *twenty-eighth* word counting *from the bottom up*. Long before Francis, the number 28 designated the Church for ecclesiastical writers.[7] It was regarded as being a perfect number: it is the sum of its divisors and also of the whole numbers 1 up to and including 7. The fact that Exodus 26:2 gives the required length of each curtain of the tent of the tabernacle at 28 cubits, certainly also played a role in this number being used as a reference to the Church.

Mary in Admonition 27 and in the Praises of God

In The Praises of God, the number 28 also plays a certain role (this number can be found by counting the words of stanzas 5 and 6 from the bottom up in the Latin) in connection with an allusion to the hymn addressing Mary, the '*Salve Regina*'. This connection is no coincidence. Francis owed this to the tradition which saw Mary as the prototypical image of the Church.

Regarding all of the above, it is quite understandable to ask why the Latin words are counted from *the bottom up*. This can be explained if one realises what the feast of the Assumption of Mary (August 15th) meant to Francis. He began his retreat in La Verna on this feast-day in 1224. The ascending movement which is conveyed by the concept *assumption*, is expressed in the arrangement of the words of Admonition 27 and of the Praises, especially if one reads both these texts *from the bottom up*. The fact that Francis received his vision on or sometime around the feast of the Exaltation of the Cross also made a deep impression on him, for this feast is also characterised by an *ascending* movement – namely the ascension of the Crucified One Who is also the Exalted or Risen One.

---

[7] Heinz Meyer, *Die Zahlenallegorese im Mittelalter. Methode und Gebrauch.* München, (1975); 155; *Bedae Venerabilis Opera*, Pars II, 2A. *Corpus Christianorum*, Series Latina, 119 A; 46-47.

In connection to this, it is interesting to take note of certain associations between Admonition 27 and the texts from the liturgies celebrating feasts of the Virgin which Francis prayed from his prayer-book. In the divine office for the feast of Mary's Assumption on August 15th, a passage from the Song of Solomon (6:10) has an important place. This passage concerns a heavenly sign: 'Who is this that looks forth like the dawn, fair as the moon, bright as the sun, terrible as an army with banners?' Obviously, the Church-in-prayer traditionally saw Mary in the splendour of the Easter Christ, her Orient.

In Francis' times, at matins on the feast of Mary's Nativity (September 8th), a sermon by Innocent III was read in which he commented on this text from the Song of Solomon. After dwelling on Mary as 'the dawn' – he calls her 'the end of the vices and the origin of the virtues' – he goes on at length to associate her with the words 'fair as the moon'. Then he carries on to say:

'Chosen like the sun. In the sun, two things are commended: its splendour and its glow. Because it shines, it is a sign of wisdom. Because it glows, it is a sign of love. (…) So Mary is the chosen one inasmuch as she shines and glows like the sun. It is through wisdom that she shines, it is through love that she glows. For the Holy Spirit came upon her, and the power of the Most High overshadowed her. The Holy Spirit is the love, of whom is said: "God is Love." And the power of the Most High is the wisdom, of which we read: "Christ is God's Power and God's Wisdom." Listen to Mary who asks out of wisdom: "How can this be, since I have no husband?" Listen to her who answers out of love: "Behold, I am the handmaid of the Lord, let it be done to me according to your word." Listen to the wisdom in Mary: Mary is said to have kept all these words, and to have collected them in her heart. Listen to the love in her: "My soul magnifies the Lord, and my spirit rejoices in God, my Saviour".'

• Some details in this text deserve our attention: Innocent III emphasises Mary as being 'the end of vices and the origin of virtues'. Admonition 27 also deals with vices and virtues. The words 'love' and 'wisdom' in the first verse of this Admonition form a pair, just as in Innocent's sermon. The same holds for The Praises of God.

- He calls the Holy Spirit 'love' and Christ 'wisdom'. This is important in view of the interpretation of the virtues in Admonition 27 that we shall present below.
- He also writes. 'Listen to the wisdom *in* her (Mary) (…). Listen to the love *in* her.' Wisdom and love are therefore indwelling powers just as in Admonition 27 with its repeated: '*where…, there…*'. The Praises of God also considers the virtues to be indwelling powers. The fact that Francis wrote 'You are *our…*' demonstrates this from our point of view.

Names for the Divine Persons

The similarities between The Praises of God and Admonition 27 are also intriguing for another reason. It is clear that in Part II of the Praises, Francis addresses God with the names of virtues: 'You are charity' etc. Now the first four virtues from the Praises also occur in Admonition 27: 'charity', 'wisdom', 'humility', 'patience'. Further on in this Admonition, 'joy' and 'rest' can be found which are also used in the Praises as names for God. These similarities raise the question as to whether these virtues can also be considered as names for God in Admonition 27. This could mean that this Admonition could also perhaps be understood by us as a veiled account of what Francis was told by the Seraph in his vision.

We have already noted that in Chapter 17 of the Earlier Rule of 1221, the word 'love' refers to the Holy Spirit and 'wisdom' to the Son. In this way, other virtues mentioned in Admonition 27 could each refer to one of the Persons of the Holy Trinity. We are aware of the fact that many will consider this interpretation – which is our own – as rather astonishing. To explain this, we shall therefore make a short tour of discovery through Francis' writings. A comparison of certain texts will help enable us to fathom the deeper meaning of Admonition 27. We shall restrict ourselves to the most important clues.

Supposing that each of the virtues mentioned in Admonition 27 could indeed be regarded as being a name for one of the Persons of the Trinity: which Persons are then specified?

Love and wisdom
We have already noted that 'love' in the Christian tradition stands for the Holy Spirit and that Francis also associates 'love' with the Spirit. 'Wisdom' designates the Son. Regarding this, see the earlier mentioned citation from the Letter to the Faithful: 'they do not have spiritual wisdom because they do not possess the Son of God, the true wisdom of the Father' (67).

Patience and humility
'Patience' stands for the Son. 'Humility' stands for the Father. We base this on the parallel between the verses 14-16 of Chapter 17 from the Earlier Rule: 'The Spirit of the Lord, (…). It strives for humility and patience, the pure, simple and true peace of the Spirit. It desires the divine fear, the divine wisdom and the divine love of the Father, Son and Holy Spirit.'

Poverty with joy
'Poverty' stands for the Father. The central passage from the Later Rule of 1223, Chapter 6,4 can confirm this: 'This is that sublime height of most exalted Poverty.' Our interpretation is that here, just as in that Chapter, 'Poverty' refers to God the Father.[8]

'Joy' stands for the Holy Spirit. In our interpretation we follow the tradition which attributes the 'anointing with the oil of gladness' to the Holy Spirit (Psalm 45:7).

Rest and meditation
'Rest' stands for the Holy Spirit. In Francis' writings 'resting' occurs in connection to the Spirit. 'And the Spirit of the Lord will rest upon all those men and women who have done and persevered in these things and It will make a home and dwelling place in them.' (Second Letter of the Faithful, 48). It is part of the Christian tradition that 'peace' and 'rest' are attributed to the third Person of the Holy Trinity.

---

[8] See: *Respectfully Yours,* Chapter 5, 188 ff and Chapter 4; 168.

Initially it may appear arbitrary to associate 'meditation' (*meditatio*) – which in all of Francis' writings only occurs here – with the Son. This is however supported by the New Testament which designates the Son as Word, Wisdom and Truth. Besides, as we shall see, in unfolding the regularity of the structure of Admonition 27, this interpretation presents itself as a matter of course.

Fear and his courtyard
'Fear' and 'his courtyard' can also be understood as being names for God. 'Fear' stands for the Father and 'his courtyard' can, as we have already remarked upon, designate the Body of the Son. The fact that in verse 5 Francis substitutes Luke's words 'a strong man, fully armed' with 'fear of the Lord', has the extra effect of creating a regular structure in the series of names for God which he has summed up. It will shortly become clear as to why.

Mercy and discernment
'Mercy' stands for the Father. Jesus' words: 'Be merciful, just as your Father is merciful' (Luke 6:36) supports our interpretation. It also appears to be confirmed by the regularity, or rhythm of the poem.

'Discernment' stands for the Holy Spirit. In this interpretation we follow the time-honoured tradition which considers 'discernment' or 'sensitivity' to be a gift of the Holy Spirit.

A pleasing regularity
If the virtues in Admonition 27 are understood as being references to the Persons of the Holy Trinity as we have suggested, then in both stanzas practically the same regularity can be found. Only in the verses 2 and 5 are the references to the Father and to the Son reversed. The fact that this reversal is significant will become evident when we deal with the Christogramme which is woven into the text.

Stanza 1:

1. Where the Holy Spirit is and the Son,...
2. Where the Son is and the Father,...
3. Where the Father is with the Holy Spirit,...

Stanza 2:

4. Where the Holy Spirit is and the Son,...
5. Where the Father is and the Son,...
6. Where the Father is and the Holy Spirit,...

What do the vices refer to?

The justification of our interpretation of Admonition 27 as a veiled account of Francis' vision of Christ coupled with sometimes surprising designations of the Persons of the Trinity, making use of virtues, requires an answer to the above-mentioned question. Don't the vices form an inexplicable ballast in our interpretation? And why it is exactly *these* vices or weaknesses which are mentioned?

To start with, we must note that the vices are summed up here as not being present: 'there is no (...) or (...)'; 'there is neither (...) nor (...)'; 'there the enemy cannot have a place'. These negations raise the question: what is present then? Where the vices could have been present, an open space has been created by their absence.

We suppose the following: where in a certain verse two vices are mentioned as not being present, this creates an open space for the Person of the Trinity who is not mentioned in that verse. For example, where verse 2 says: 'Where there is patience and humility, there is no anger or disturbance.' We interpret the first half therefore as: Where there is the Son and the Father. Then the second part is interpreted as: there is the Holy Spirit.

This interpretation is rather less strange than it may initially seem. This becomes clear if we check the contexts in Francis' writings in which 'anger and disturbance' (verse 2) or other similar concepts occur. These two vices then indeed appear to be countered by the action of the Holy Spirit.[9]

---

[9] See: Chapter 3, Peace: God's Gift and Theodore Zweerman, 'Jesus' Word: "Blessed are the Peacemakers...." in the Interpretation of Francis of Assisi.' In: *Greyfriars Review* 9:1 (1995); 39-60. Compare in the Later Rule 7,3: 'they must be careful not to be angry or disturbed at the sin of another, for anger and disturbance impede charity in themselves and in others.'

A key to verse 1

> 'Where there is charity and wisdom, there is no fear or ignorance.'

A certain amount of amazement is due where verse 1 is concerned. Why did Francis write something so plainly evident? Of course there is no ignorance where there is wisdom! And that perfect love casts out fear is to be found in the First Letter of John (4:18). Or did he have an underlying meaning in mind? We seem to have found a key in the Gospel according to Matthew. In Chapter 21, the chief priests and the elders of the people are asked by Jesus as to whose authority he is acting upon:

> 'Jesus said to them, "I will also ask you one question; if you tell me the answer, then I will also tell you by what authority I do these things. Did the baptism of John come from heaven, or was it of human origin?" And they argued with one another, "If we say, 'From heaven', he will say to us, 'Why then did you not believe him?' But if we say, 'Of human origin', we are afraid of the crowd; for all regard John as a prophet." So they answered Jesus, "We do not know." And he said to them, "Neither will I tell you by what authority I am doing these things."'

The vices of 'fear' and 'ignorance' are referred to here in Matthew: 'we are afraid' and 'We do not know.' The point being made in this passage is that Jesus' interrogators are trying to avoid the correct answer. It is implicitly given in verse 23: 'Who gave you this authority?'. For the reader who is a believer, there is only one possible answer: Jesus' Father. The underlying meaning of verse 1 is therefore: 'Where there is the Holy Spirit and the Son, there is the Father.'

A key to verse 3

> 'Where there is poverty with joy, there is no greed or avarice.'

In the second half of Psalm XIV of Francis' Office of the Passion which he composed for Advent, he cites the last part of Psalm 69:33-37:

'May the *poor* see and *rejoice*,
seek God and your soul shall live. (…).
They will dwell there and acquire it by *inheritance*.
The descendants of God's servants will *possess* it
and those who love His *Name* will dwell there.'

The words 'inheritance' and 'possess' have their negative counterparts
in greed and avarice (Admonition 27,3). This however does not yet say
much about what is present in the space which is created by the absence
of 'greed' and 'avarice'. The key lies in the last line of Psalm XIV: 'those
who love His Name will dwell there'. Now, in Francis' series of Psalms
for the Office, the praising of the Name occurs only from Psalm VII
on, in which he calls upon us to honour the Son as the Risen One. The
Name of the Son is also concerned in the context of Psalm XIV (the
coming of Christ). This interpretation is confirmed by the parallels in
the contents of verses 5 and 6 in Chapter 6 of the Later Rule:

'Let this (the most exalted Poverty) be your *inheritance* which leads
into the land of the living. Giving yourselves totally to this, beloved
brothers, never seek anything else to *possess* under heaven for the
Name of our Lord Jesus Christ.'

The underlying meaning of the third verse of Admonition 27 is therefore: 'Where the Father is with the Holy Spirit, there is the *Son.*'

Anxiety: a key to verse 4?

'Where there is rest and meditation,
there is neither anxiety nor restlessness.'

This verse evokes the story about Martha and Mary in the Gospel
according to Luke 10:38-42. Mary sits at the feet of the Lord. She
is listening: an image of quiet attentiveness. Regarding Jesus' answer
to Martha: 'You are worried and distracted by many things', the
Latin text which Francis knew contains the word *sollicita* (anxious),
which is the same word *sollicitudo* (anxiety) found in this verse.
The Gospel according to Matthew offers an answer to the question
as to who is able to remove this anxiety:

'But if God so clothes the grass of the field, which is alive today and tomorrow is thrown into the oven, will he not much more clothe you – you of little faith? Therefore do not worry (*solliciti*), saying, "What will we eat?" or "What will we drink?" or "What will we wear?" For it is the Gentiles who strive for all these things; and indeed your heavenly Father knows that you need all these things' (Matthew 6:30-32).

In the Earlier Rule Franciscus exhorts all his brothers to 'put aside every care and anxiety (*sollicitudine*), to serve, love, honour and adore the Lord God with a clean heart and a pure mind in whatever way they are best able to do so, for that is what He wants above all else. Let us always make a home and a dwelling place for Him Who is the Lord God Almighty, Father, Son and Holy Spirit' (Chapter 23,26-27).

Is Francis saying in Admonition 27,4 that 'rest and meditation' stand for the contemplative life and 'anxiety and restlessness' for the active life? He tells us loudly and clearly that quiet attentiveness is necessary in all that we undertake just as much in our work as in our interior prayer-life. The 'One' is necessary: the 'understatement' which is a pseudonym for the Holy Spirit. This 'Rest' protects us from excessive care and worry which can cause confusion and inner chaos. In more contemporary terms: 'Rest' protects us from channel-surfing (on TV) and flitting from the one place to the other. There is a report telling us how Francis usually meditated: 'His memory took the place of books (...). He said this was a fruitful way to read and learn, rather than to wander (*evagari*) through a thousand treatises' (2 Celano 102). In Admonition 27 he also connects 'anxiety' and 'restlessness' (*vagatio*). In this verse we can therefore hear the echo of the following: Where there is the Holy Spirit, there is also the Son and the Father.

A key to verse 5

'Where there is fear of the Lord to guard his courtyard, there the enemy cannot have a place to enter.'

The irregularity of the fifth verse does not mean that it does not refer to two of the three Persons of the Trinity like the other verses do. This is because 'fear of the Lord' can, as has already been said, refer to the Father and 'his courtyard' to the Son. Could we therefore read here: 'where the Father is and the Son, there is the Holy Spirit'? Let us once again consult Luke 11:21. 'When a strong man, fully armed, guards his castle, his property is safe' (the Latin translates literally as: in peace). 'Peace' is a name for the Holy Spirit for Francis. He does not however adopt Luke's positive second half of this passage: 'his property is safe'. Just as in the other verses of this Admonition, here he uses a negative formulation: 'there the enemy cannot have a place to enter.' The question is then: who does have a place to enter? The answer could be: the Holy Spirit. The underlying meaning of the fifth verse of Admonition 27 is then: 'Where the Father is and the Son, there is the Holy Spirit.' It is the Holy Spirit who takes the place of the enemy.

And the last words?

> 'Where there is a heart full of mercy and discernment,
> there is no excess or hardness of heart'.

The end of the Gospel according to Mark offers us a key to the term 'hardness' (*induratio*). It reads as follows: 'Later he appeared to the eleven themselves as they were sitting at the table; and he upbraided them for their lack of faith and stubbornness (*duritiam cordis*), because they had not believed those who saw him after he had risen' (Mark 16:14). After these words Jesus orders them to proclaim the good news and He returns to his Father. 'Hardness' appears to mean the unwillingness to discern; not 'seeing with the eyes of the Spirit'; and closing our eyes to the needs of our neighbours. This also clarifies what Francis wished to say in his first Admonition: 'Therefore children, how long will you be hard of heart (*gravi corde*)? Why do you not know the truth and believe in the Son of God?' (verses 14-15). If these final words of Admonition 27 result in the reader's opening himself for God's Son, then the last verse could mean: 'Where there is the Father and the Holy Spirit, there is also the Son'.

A reference to the Holy Trinity

Applying this key to every verse – for verse 2 see page 187 – the underlying meaning of Admonition 27 can be seen as:

1. Where there is the Holy Spirit and the Son, there is the Father.
2. Where there is the Son and the Father, there is the Holy Spirit.
3. Where there is the Father with the Holy Spirit, there is the Son.
4. Where there is the Holy Spirit and the Son, there is the Father.
5. Where there is the Father and the Son, there is the Holy Spirit.
6. Where there is the Father and the Holy Spirit, there is the Son.

Certainly not a very spectacular message! The Christian dogma of the Trinity has always been understood this way. However, the full significance of our interpretation of the contrast between the virtues and the vices only clearly appears when verse 5 is associated with Luke 11:21, namely as the designation of the protection which the Father gives to the Body of his Son, the Church. And also by determining that the specific names for the Persons of the Trinity in Admonition 27 are valuable clues to the way Francis understood the Trinitarian mystery.

Christ and the Church: a mutual indwelling

In as far as Admonition 27 is a description of a tension between virtues and vices, it deals with the way in which God is actively present *in* man. According to the monastic tradition: in the heart of man. God's indwelling is evident from the virtues or powers which he bestows on a person. This interpretation of the space to which is alluded by Admonition 27 – every verse contains the words 'where'/ 'there' – is not weakened by understanding the virtues as being names for the Persons of the Trinity. In our interpretation, the heart of man is also a place of dwelling. This awareness of God's indwelling can also be seen when Francis for example asks his brothers:

> 'In the holy love which is God (…) to serve, love, honour and adore the Lord God with a clean heart and a pure mind in whatever way they are best able to do so, for that is what He wants above all else. Let us always make a home and a dwelling place there for Him Who is the Lord God Almighty, Father, Son and Holy Spirit' (Earlier Rule of 1221, Chapter 22,26-27).

Our interpretation of Admonition 27 however also supposes that every believer is embodied in the protected Body of Christ, the Risen One. In other words: Gods indwelling in the Church is realised by his indwelling in each and everyone of the faithful, while the believer himself dwells in Christ, God-with-us. This mystery of mutual indwelling is clearly spoken of in the New Testament. Francis' vision can therefore also be understood from the perspective of New Testament passages concerning the relationship between Christ and the Church. A mutual indwelling is implicit in the 'great mystery' (Ephesians 5:32) of the relationship between Bridegroom and Bride: the Church is embodied in the risen Lord. And He lives, freed from the limitations of time and space, in and with His Church. The faithful live in God and God lives in their heart. In his own way, Francis says what Christ said to Teresa of Avila: 'Soul, you must search for yourself in Me, and you must search for Me in yourself.'

Jesus Christ: Alpha and Omega

Francis repeatedly wove the biblical symbolism of the letters *A* and *O*, as designations of Christ, into his texts. We have already mentioned this in connection to the Canticle of the Creatures in Chapter 2. This play on the letters *A* and *O* can also be found in his Salutation of the Virtues.[10] The same is the case for Admonition

[10] *Respectfully Yours*; 151; 172.

27, which in our interpretation presents the new Man, as he appeared to Francis on Mount La Verna. In the Latin original, the virtues and vices in the first half of the Admonition all end with the letter *A*, except for the irregular verse 2. The virtues and vices in the second half all end on the letter *O*, except for verse 5.

The poem presents a pleasing harmony: the 'positive' half of every verse is equal to its 'negative' counterpart (in the Latin always five words; in verse 5 each time eight words). Altogether these lines contain two times 33 words. In Francis' times, the number 33 referred to Jesus Christ, who became man, died and rose: the new Adam.

Christogramme

The connecting lines between the names for the Father and the Son in the irregular verses 2 and 5 together form the letter X. If this letter X is joined to the line running figuratively from the virtues ending with an A (first stanza) to the virtues which end with an O (second stanza), the total result is a Christogramme:

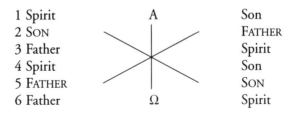

1 Spirit	A	Son
2 SON		FATHER
3 Father		Spirit
4 Spirit		Son
5 FATHER		SON
6 Father	Ω	Spirit

Much has already been discovered in our comparison of Admonition 27 with The Praises of God: the crucified and glorified Christ as the One who lives with and in his Church, together with and in everyone who searches for him. Francis' vision is apparently made up of different layers of meaning. It is full of tensions: sadness and joy at the same moment for the amazed visionary; the 'at once' of the suffering and glorification of the Crucified One. It is especially surprising that both Jesus *as well as* the Church are presented and that Francis associates the Church with the assumption of Mary. All this should especially be seen in the perspective of salvation-history. The risen Lord, freed from the vicissitudes of a temporal life, is nevertheless closely united to the fate of his people. In the vision of the Seraph, Francis saw the interconnection of past, present and future: this is the Spirit of love who remained inviolable even in Jesus' manner of dying, and through Whom He could, after having risen, remain inspiring the Church.

Names for the mystery of God

Francis was not a theologian by profession. He had however developed a strong theological intuition through his meditation. The word 'intuition' receives its original meaning in Francis, insofar as he lets us know in his accounts what he *saw* on Mount La Verna. Together with what he *heard* (could this perhaps have been the names of the divine Persons used in the Praises and in Admonition 27?), his vision can reveal much about the basis of his spirituality.

The Holy Spirit

In our interpretation of Admonition 27 the Holy Spirit, the One Who inspires the Church, is mentioned first. This is the case in each of the two stanzas. This special function of the Holy Spirit as an 'opener', can also be seen in Part II of the Praises: there the first name is 'love'. In the passage from Chapter 17 of the Earlier Rule, which gave us a key to discovering the names of the divine Persons Francis had in mind, it is also the 'Spirit of the Lord' which reveals these names. In the Second Letter of the Faithful (verses 48-53), the Holy Spirit 'opens' in a different way. This text, which many consider to be Francis' most mystical piece of writing, deals with the indwelling of the Holy Trinity in the hearts of the faithful:

> 'And the Spirit of the Lord will rest upon all those men and women who have done and persevered in these things and It will make a home and dwelling place in them. And they will be the children of the heavenly Father, Whose works they do. And they are spouses, brothers and mothers of our Lord Jesus Christ. We are spouses when the faithful soul is united by the Holy Spirit to our Lord Jesus Christ.

> We are brothers, moreover, when we do the will of his Father who is in heaven; mothers when we carry Him in our heart and body through love and a pure and sincere conscience; and give Him birth through a holy activity, which must shine before others by example.'

That the action of the Holy Spirit was of primary importance to Clare and Francis, is recorded in their Rules: 'Let them pay attention to what they must desire above all else: to have the Spirit of the Lord and Its holy activity.' This was the very source of their lives. Does this mean that there is a contrast between Francis' relationship to Jesus Christ – Whom he calls 'all our riches' in the Praises – and his life with and through the Holy Spirit? Nothing is less true. The Holy Spirit is given by Christ to the faithful and through His Spirit he remains intimately united to His Church. Without Francis' conviction that Christ lives with and in His Church for all times, his spirituality threatens to become a 'Church-less' spiritualism – or become a 'Spirit-less' Christocentrism, which would have a biased fixation on a Jesus who lived an exemplary life in Palestine, who died and then rose again. It is true that Francis thought of Jesus primarily as the one who served and washed the feet of his disciples. But this certainly does not mean that his view of Jesus was narrowed down to his life then and there. Jesus Christ as God-with-us, united for all times with His Church, forms the heart of his faith.

The Holy Spirit who Francis – as can be seen in Admonition 27 and the Praises – knew to be inspiring 'Love', 'Joy', 'Gladness', 'Rest' and 'Discernment', is indispensable to being able to see Christ in His divine essence (also evident in Admonitions 1 and 8). The names which Francis designated to Christ in Admonition 27 can only have been inspired by the Spirit. It is also this same divine Inspiration Who helps Francis in understanding the mystery of the Father.

God the Son

It is hardly necessary for us to add anything concerning the names which Francis gave to Christ in Admonition 27 – 'Wisdom',

'Patience', 'Meditation and 'Courtyard'. When researching their biblical origins, it became clear that each of these names offers much insight into the mystery of Christ's Person. Two aspects of the names for God's Son may be mentioned here:

- Each of these names refers to feminine traits. This is especially true for the designation of Christ as 'Meditation'. This recalls Mary who 'treasured all these words and pondered them in her heart' (Luke 2:19; compare Admonition 28). In the First Testament, 'Wisdom' is personified as 'Lady Wisdom'. In the Middle Ages the word 'Courtyard' was, as we have already noted, one of the names for the Church as the Body of Christ. Feminine characteristics were attributed to the Church during mediaeval times. The meaning of 'bearing like a mother' for Francis, leads us to surmise that he also attributed motherly traits to 'Patience'.

- The names 'Wisdom' and 'Patience' denote the powers which were acknowledged by Paul to be in the Crucified One, namely 'wisdom of God' and 'power of God' (1 Corinthians 1:24). This dimension of wise foolishness and strong weakness is undoubtedly echoed in the names which Francis uses for the Son. Without His 'power to bear', the wisdom of the cross cannot be understood in faith. 'Wisdom' became the 'Master' when He washed the feet of His disciples on the eve of His suffering, and especially when He became a pupil in the school of suffering: 'Although he was a Son, he learned obedience through what he suffered' (Hebrews 5:8).[11]

God the Father

The names with which Francis designates the Person of God the Father in Admonition 27, deserve special attention. Not only

---

[11] For the meaning of 'patience', see Damien Isabell O.F.M.,'The "Virtues" in Admonition XXVII of the Writings of Francis of Assisi and their Usefulness in Spiritual Discernment.' In: *The Cord, A Franciscan Spiritual Review*, 38 (1988); 35-57; 38-41.

because they are a valuable witness to his understanding of the pre-eminently Concealed One, but also because they assist us in discovering how his spirituality is rooted in this understanding of the Most High. These names induce amazement, especially if we consider the usual 'images' for God. In speaking about the Father, the pre-eminent Origin, Francis is himself also original. Especially in referring to the Father as 'Poverty' and as 'Fear' or 'Reverence', he opens up perspectives which, it is true, were previously not completely unknown, but all the same are exceptional, even in our day and age.

The names for the Father in Admonition 27 are: 'Humility'; 'Poverty'; 'Fear' or 'Reverence' and 'Mercy'. The following considerations we have based on the supposition that Francis continuously reflected upon the experience of God's action he had known in his active and meditative life. Using the biblical tradition, we shall endeavour to taste the fruits of these reflections of his.

Humility

Francis experienced the Father as a mystery of 'Humility' or 'Meekness'. It is astonishing that he used exactly this concept of lowness in referring to the Most High! In their searching for the Origin of 'Humility', Christians are led by how Jesus showed himself to be. As the Way to the Father, He is the Image of the Father who searches for us first. The humility which characterises the Eternal One, is revealed in the humility of Jesus.[12]

---

[12] Compare: François Varillon, *L' humilité de Dieu*. Paris, 1974; Romano Guardini, *The Lord,* London 1963[6]; 321-328, 326 f.; J. Macquarrie, *The Humility of God. Christian Meditations*. London, 1978; J.-B. Freyer, *Der demütige und geduldige Gott. Franziskus und sein Gottesbild – ein Vergleich mit der Tradition*. Romae 1989. François-Xavier Durrwell, *La résurrection de Jésus mystère de salut*. Paris, 1982[11]. Alexander Gerken, *Theologie des Wortes. Das Verhältnis von Schöpfung und Inkarnation bei Bonaventura*. Düsseldorf, 1963, Chapter 5: ‚Die Demut Gottes'; idem, 'The Theological Intuition of St.Francis of Assisi'. In: *Greyfriars Review,* 7 (1993); 71-94.

One of the names which Francis gave to the Son is 'Patience': the endurance of the 'Lamb of God'. Bearing in mind his brother Giles' intuition that 'patience' is the daughter of 'humility', we suppose that Francis could have considered Christ as 'Patience', borne of 'Humility', which is the Father Himself. In The Praises of God, Francis prays: 'You are Humility' and then 'You are Patience'. To borrow a word from Christian Bobin: God is the Highest, as well as the 'Deepest'.[13] This expresses the descending movement which the 'Word of the Father' experienced in the incarnation:

> 'The most high Father made known from heaven through His holy angel Gabriel this Word of the Father – so worthy, so holy and glorious – in the womb of the holy and glorious Virgin Mary, from whose womb He received the flesh of our humanity and frailty.' (Second Letter to the Faithful, 4)

For Francis, Christ's incarnation meant that He accepted our human existence to the very utmost: the offering of himself on the cross. To what extent God went in becoming all things human, is however not only apparent in the incarnation, then and there, from the crib to the cross: his extreme approach is also continuously seen in the Church, where Christ is present in his word and sacrament. Here, God's loving Humility consistently reveals itself, even deep down in our human defects (compare Admonition 1).

When in Francis' days it was obvious that the Church was direly in need of reformation, he did not put his trust in either hard conservatism or hard reform-action, but rather in the 'soft' power of Christ who reveals himself *in* weakness. With his non-moralising message, Francis wished to lead people into this mystery of Christ's self-emptying, which continues in the fallible and failing Church. This is how God's transforming Love reveals itself in Humility. The fact that Francis was deeply conscious of God's humility, has also been suggested by Nguyên-Van-Khanh:

---

[13] Christian Bobin, *Le Très-Bas. Paris, 1992.*

'The Son became man (...) to reveal the Trinity, which gives itself to its creation. In other words, to reveal the *humble Trinity*.'[14]

Poverty

Who did Francis consult when he denoted the Father as 'Poverty'? This is not clear, but it is a definite fact that in the bible 'humility' and 'self-emptying' are closely connected. This is also true for the writings of Augustine, but if we are correct, the word 'Poverty' is not used by him as a name for God. However this is the case in Clare's writings, where 'Poverty', profoundly united to 'Humility' and 'Love', is one of the three names for God.[15] Exactly in the middle of the Later Rule, Francis wrote the following words, pregnant with mystery:

> 'This is that sublime height of most exalted poverty which has made you, my beloved brothers, heirs and kings of the Kingdom of Heaven, poor in temporal things but exalted in virtue (verse 4).[16]

Our interpretation of 'Poverty' being here a reference to God the Father, is confirmed by our interpretation of 'Poverty' in Admonition 27, and vice versa. It is remarkable that exactly at the centre of Part II of The Praises of God it says: 'You are all our riches, that is sufficient'. In the previous Chapter we argued that this invocation is addressed to the Son. The contrast between these two central designations, namely 'Poverty' and 'Riches', can be understood through the difference between the view of God as the Giver and of Christ as His Gift to the world. As pure Giver, the Father is united to the Son who has emptied Himself as an Image of the

---

[14] Norbert Nguyên-Van-Khanh, N., *Le Christ dans la penseé de Saint François d'Assise d'après ses écrits*. Paris, 1989; 139 (italics by the author).

[15] Cf. Hermann Schalück, *Armut und Heil. Eine Untersuchung über den Armutsgedanken in der Theologie Bonaventuras*. München 1971; Emmanuel Levinas, *Transcendance et intelligibilité, suivi d'un entretien*. Genève, 1984; 56 ff; idem, *A l'heure des nations*. Paris, 1988 (in it the study: „Judaïsme et Kénose", 133-151); *Light Shining through a Veil;* 62-63;

[16] *Respectfully Yours,* Chapter 5, pag. 190.

Father. And thanks to the Son's complete gift of Himself, the Church recognises all her Riches in Him: namely the riches that the Son receives from the Father and gives to the Church. Limitless generosity, total self-giving: this is what the name 'Poverty' for God seems to mean for Francis and Clare.

Has this understanding of the Father as Poverty completely disappeared in our times? Some witnesses demonstrate that this is not so. There are for example the words by Abbé Pierre which echo his Franciscan formation:

> 'What I felt penetrating me ever more profoundly in the reading of this passage from the Gospels, led on by Saint Francis, was the discovery that the greatest greatness of the Eternal One, revealed to us in the most radical way in Jesus, is that He is, in His very own way, the poorest of the Poor (…). The Eternal One is poor, and this means to say: insufficient-unto-Himself, like all Love is.'[17]

Among present-day theologians we mention Maurice Zundel. Also influenced by Francis, he closely associates God's 'poverty' and his 'humility'. Zundel also points out Francis' notion of the 'identity of the Trinity and poverty'.[18] The Dutch theologian Oepke Noordmans also deserves to be mentioned here.[19]

Reverence

We suppose that for many, especially 'Reverence' or 'Awe' as names for God are surprising. What could be more natural than that the believer, in view of the frailty of mankind, respects God's majesty

---

[17] B. Chevallier interroge L'Abbé Pierre. Emmaus, ou venger l'homme en aimant. Paris, 1980, 30.

[18] Maurice Zundel, Je parlerai à ton coeur, Éditions Anne Sigier, Sillery (Québec), 1990; Vie, mort, résurrection, Éditions Anne Sigier, Sillery (Québec),1995; idem Pèlerin de l'espérance, Éditions Anne Sigier, Sillery (Québec), 1997; Marc Donzé, La pensée théologique de Maurice Zundel, pauvreté et libération. Genève – Paris, 1980; 81; 144. On Zundel, compare also Dictionnaire de Spiritualité, part XVI, column 1665-1669.

[19] Oepke Noordmans, Verzamelde Werken. Deel VIII: Meditaties. Kampen, 1980; 276 f.

and approaches this mystery with reverence? God's sublimity which was especially revealed in the Son's descending, evokes this awe. But could the reverse be postulated? God's 'Respect' or 'Reverence' for man? Francis is not afraid of attributing reverence to God the Father.

What are his motives for this? We will give an answer by posing some questions. Could the person, in respecting his neighbour who is just as vulnerable and essentially inviolable as he himself is, not also then in this attitude of reverence be an image of his Creator? Could the rich sensitivity which is the positive centre of all our vulnerability and frailty, not also be a reference to Him who created us in this way?

Is Francis unique in his designation of God as 'Reverence' in Admonition 27? There is not much known about texts he may have read or heard which could have suggested this idea to him. We do however know that this designation is not completely unknown to the Christian tradition. And besides this, 'fear of the Lord' is considered to be a fatherly moment. Perhaps Francis was inspired by spiritual writers in forming his understanding of the mystery of God the Father as being the mystery of Reverence. It is a fact that John Chrysostom (347-407 CE), in regarding that 'purest fear of God' which was manifest in Jesus Christ, developed the idea that Jesus' respect for his Father – as mentioned in the Letter to the Hebrews which calls him a pupil in the school of suffering – was so immensely awesome, that God therefore revered Him with Respect.[20]

If all is well, our (faintest) understanding of this reverence of the Father to the Son, will already be the great awakening of our 'Fear of God', namely our reverence for Reverence.

Francis and the virtue of reverence

There is a story from which we can conclude that the virtue of reverence or fear was held in great esteem by him – that he indeed

[20] John Chrysostom (347-407 CE) in: *PG*, 53, column 70.

saw it as the essential condition for the acquisition of all the virtues. This story, which can be retraced to brother Leo, is about a brother who had seemed to be a very holy man and who left the brotherhood. In the story, Francis plays the role of the master who tests his students' theses:

> 'One day, brother Leo and some other brothers were walking on a road with Francis, and they asked the saint why the above mentioned brother had left the order. And he replied: 'I want to give a lecture, and to place before myself some points of discussion, that is: to answer them and to resolve them. Let no one speak to me till I have finished.' And first he said: 'Humility,' twice or thrice; 'Purity,' 'Temperance,' 'Poverty,' and other virtues, each of them several times. And at each of them he said to himself: 'Do you know it well?,' and he answered: 'Yes.' But at the end of the discourse he said several times: 'Reverence.' And when he asked: 'Do you know that?' he answered: 'No.' And again he exclaimed, repeating it several times: 'Reverence.' And he asked himself the question: 'Do you know that?,' and kept replying: 'No.' And he exclaimed even more often: 'Reverence.' And at last he replied with great difficulty: 'Yes.' And he added: 'Without reverence, man amasses virtues in vain; but only a few possess it, so that one can hardly learn it.' And in conclusion he said: 'Because of a lack of reverence, this virtue-rich brother fell and left the order.'[21]

Custodian and protector

We wish to relate our interpretation of 'fear of the Lord' in Admonition 27,5 (as a reference to the Father Who is the custodian and protector of his 'courtyard', the Body of the Son) to what was expressed in Francis' vision by the protective wings of the Seraph. In The Praises of God, this protection was expressed in the invocations: 'You are the Protector; you are the custodian and defender; you are strength; you are refuge.'

---

[21] Livarius Oliger, 'Descriptio codicis S. Antonii de Urbe.' In: *Archivum Franciscanum Historicum,* 12 (1919); 380, no. 54.

In the Bible and in the Christian tradition, 'fear of the Lord' also appears to refer to fatherly protection. The reference to fatherhood in connection to protection can be found in Francis' dream about the mother-hen, from which we have already quoted in Chapter 5. According to his biographers, Francis interpreted the dream as follows: He saw himself above all in a motherly role. But his new brotherhood was also in need of a father-figure, which was lacking in his person. That is why he asked Pope Honorius to 'give him one of the cardinals of the Church of Rome as a pope (*papa*) to his order'. The pope granted his request and, as the story continues, 'gave the Lord of Ostia as a father to the blessed Francis, by naming him as *protector* of the order'.

Mercy

The last words of the final verse of The Praises of God are: 'merciful Saviour'. The word 'merciful' also appears in the last verse of Admonition 27. As has been said, in our interpretation of this Admonition, 'merciful' refers to the Father. Jesus' words 'Be merciful, just as your Father is merciful' (Luke 6:36) is based on one of the names which refer to the Eternal One in the First Testament: the Merciful One. The way in which Francis speaks about merciful behaviour in the introduction to his Testament and in his Letter to a Minister, suggests that tender empathy lay at the heart of his understanding of mercy.

Saviour

Did Francis also have the Father in mind regarding the invocation 'merciful Saviour' in The Praises of God? Then 'Saviour' would here especially denote the Father as the one who brings history to completion. Some liturgical texts which Francis knew well, indeed refer to the Father as the Saviour. For example, the hymn '*Media vita*' calls God the 'merciful Saviour'.[22] The context makes it clear that it is the Father who is referred to here.

---

[22] *Sancte Deus, sancte fortis, sancte misericors Salvator, amarae morti ne tradas nos* (Holy God, holy strength, holy merciful Saviour, lead us not into bitter

As it seems, the conclusion and introduction to the Praises are harmonised: in both parts God the Father is called upon – Origin and Destiny. As the 'merciful Saviour', the Father is the bearing Womb, the definite Protection. To say it in human terms: motherly and fatherly at the same time.

The continuation of Christ's suffering in the Church

One of the fascinating aspects of Francis' vision on Mount La Verna is his simultaneous experience of anguish and joy, both for the One whom he saw, as well as for himself. Christ appeared to him as his Sympathiser and Fellow-Sufferer. In their commentaries on Paul's vision of the Church as the Body of Christ, church-fathers have interpreted the mystery of the Church and Christ being two-in-one, as that of the 'total Christ' and as the continuation of the incarnation in humanity on its journey through history. Is this continuation also the continuation of Christ's suffering? For as the Risen Lord he is intimately united with his Body, the Church. The fear of doing injustice to the glory of Him who overcame death forever, combined to notions about God not being able to suffer, made many a theologian wary of speaking about the continuation of Christ's suffering. Nowadays, theologians are however more restrained in viewing God as immovable or static. Isn't the notion of this continuation of Christ's suffering forced upon us when we consider Christ's words to Saul: 'Why do you persecute *me*?' (Acts 9:4) And what if we really let what he says in Matthew 25:40 sink home: 'Just as you did it to one of the least of these who are members of my family, you did it to me'? If we can say that Christians suffer in union with Christ, does this not also mean that Christ suffers with them? Like Augustine says: 'Christ toils in you, suffers thirst and hunger in you, is still tormented in you. He still dies in you.'

---

death). This prayer, attributed to Notker Balbulus († 912), was sung at the *Nunc dimittis* during compline. Sometimes this prayer was also used as a magical formula in times of calamity.

When Francis meditates on the greatness and degradation of man in Admonition 5,3, he writes: 'And even the demons did not crucify Him, but you, together with them, have crucified Him and are still crucifying Him by delighting in vices and sins.' In doing so, maybe he was recalling the word from the Letter to the Hebrews (6:6): 'since on their own they are crucifying again the Son of God'. Whatever the case may be, the imagery of Francis' vision of the glorified Suffering One who is at the same time the suffering Glorified One, is confirmed by the addition of 'you (…) are still crucifying Him' in Admonition 5. This does not have to mean that we should hold a pessimistic view of salvation-history. It does, however, entail a realistic acknowledgement of how profoundly the risen Saviour is united to sinful man.

The fact that Francis in his Praises prayed seven times 'You are *our…*', obviously expresses his recognition of the fact that Christ revealed himself as one of us, as the Sympathiser. In seeing the 'unimaginable beauty as well as the bitter suffering' of the Crucified One, Francis saw the mystery of God-with-us-through-all-times.

Francis the Mystic

Jesus Christ, the crucified and risen Lord, united with his Church: this is the core of the veiled account which Francis bequeathed to us about his vision on Mount La Verna. This union of Christ and his Church had already occupied his heart for his entire life.

The period of meditation in seclusion on Mount La Verna only intensified all he had experienced. What is however new, is that the marks of Christ's wounds expressed on the outside what he had felt burning on the inside since his encounter with Christ in San Damiano: the love for his Love (compare 2 Celano 10).

The man praying in front of the crucifix in San Damiano is the same person as the mystic who bore witness to his vision. His activities during the intervening years – taking care of lepers, being a popular preacher, inspiring his brothers, being God's acrobat, a friend of animals, praying in caves and hermitages, a maker of peace, and so forth – these were all inspired by this love. The words that Christ addressed to him in that little church of San Damiano, 'Go and repair my House', meant both the repairing of dilapidated churches as well as of the universal Church in which Christ the Crucified and Risen One lives as our Fellow-Sufferer for all ages. In following him so radically, Francis became the pre-eminent seeker of God.

8. Francis: flexible and tough

'We wish to read the signs of the times,
yet with the wisdom of the Scriptures.'
(Cardinal Danneels)

In our 'thought-experiment' in the Introduction, we mentioned the 'Letter to the Rulers of the Peoples'. In it, Francis emphasises certain things using a mixture of meekness and boldness which typify him. The fact that this mystic, as sick and weak as he was, wished to send a letter to those in power, says a lot. Intimately united to Christ, whose wounds he carried in his own body, he remained concerned with all that was happening around him. His letter starts off with two powerful exhortations: 'My Lords, do not forget that you will die' and 'my Lords, do not forget that God is still around'.

A Letter to the Rulers of the Peoples

1. Brother Francis, your little and looked-down-upon servant in the Lord God, wishes health and peace to all mayors and consuls, magistrates and governors throughout the world and to all others to whom these words may come.
2. Reflect and see that the day of death is approaching.
3. With all possible respect, therefore, I beg you not to forget the Lord because of this world's cares and preoccupations and not to turn away from His commandments, for all those who leave Him in oblivion and turn away from His commandments are cursed and will be left in oblivion by Him.
4. When the day of death does come, everything they think they have shall be taken from them.

5. The wiser and more powerful they may have been in this world, the greater will be the punishment they will endure in hell.
6. Therefore, I strongly advise you, my Lords, to put aside all care and preoccupation and receive the most holy Body and Blood of our Lord Jesus Christ with fervour in holy remembrance of Him.
7. May you foster such honour to the Lord among the people entrusted to you that every evening an announcement may be made by a messenger or some other sign that praise and thanksgiving may be given by all people to the all-powerful Lord God.
8. If you do not do this, know that, on the day of the judgement, you must render an account before the Lord Your God, Jesus Christ.
9. Let those who keep this writing with them and observe it know that they will be blessed by the Lord God.

The tone of the letter is prophetic. In appealing to the sense of responsibility of those in power, he offers them the choice between blessing and curse, life and death. This letter is no exception. Even his Canticle of the Creatures resounds with the serious note of Jesus' beatitudes and warnings of woe. Without restraining himself in any way whatsoever, the *poverello* points out the Almighty's commandments. His deep awareness of his own smallness obviously did not inhibit his sense of mission.[1] Just as the Canticle of the Creatures ends with praises to God for 'our Sister Bodily Death', so this letter begins with a call to the rulers to be mindful that the day of their own death is at hand. Francis is quite antagonistic here and does not mince his words in confronting the powerful with their ultimate powerlessness, referring to God and his commandments. 'Forgetting death' and 'forgetting God' stand side by side. Just like the prophets, Francis does not shirk from pointing out the very worst to the rulers – the total separation from God, only to

[1] Leonhard Lehmann, 'The Letter of Saint Francis to the Rulers of the Peoples: Structure and Missionary Concerns.' In: *Franciscan Digest* IV (1991); 25-62.

then surprisingly refer to the Eucharist, sacrament of Christ's presence. Evidently this Letter was written for Christians.

Founded on the Gospels

Francis' feet are firmly planted on the message of the Gospels here: the letter reflects part of Jesus' Sermon on the Mount. This is obvious from the comparison with the passage on the birds and the lilies (Matthew 6:19-34), a text which exegetes have often called 'the Franciscan passage'. Some parallels meet the eye. Jesus' rejection of a certain type of worrying is used literally by Francis. The impossibility of serving God as well as Mammon (let us recall the might of the economy) induces Francis to sharply criticise a godless life. Jesus' words: 'Strive first for the kingdom of God and his righteousness' are echoed in Francis' advice to put cares and worries aside. It is true that Jesus' reference to misguided worrying ('you of little faith') is missing, but his insistence on receiving the Bread points to the open-attitude which is essential to all faith. Generally speaking, the question which permeates Jesus' entire message also resonates in this letter: 'What are you looking for? What do you desire?' (compare John 1:38; 18:4; 20:15). Francis fathoms their deepest motivations and calls forcefully for a reorientation of their lives: which meaning or nonsense characterises their lives? In brief: his subject is spirituality.

In the twentieth century the poet Rilke also established this narrowing of views due to this forgetfulness (namely the death of God): In a letter which he wrote over a year after the start of World War One (this moment in time is of course not unimportant), he speaks of this. After, as he said, death and God had been 'expelled' and 'driven out' and had become something 'of a lower order' and become 'something else, (...) the ever smaller cycle of what only happens here accelerated; so-called progression became an event in a world captured within itself, which, whatever poses it may strike, had forgotten that it from the very start would eventually be overtaken by death.'[2]

---

[2] Rilke wrote (November 1915): R.-M. Rilke, *Ueber Dichtung und Kunst.* Frankfurt, 1974; 65-71; 68.

Forgetful of death and forgetful of God

The heart of the matter is therefore Francis' recognition of our mortality as well as of his recognition of God as the source of life. *The recognition of our mortality*: meaning the recognition of the limits of our power and possibilities; of the confines of everything we can make and manage, can buy and manipulate. It is the ancient wisdom of the Greek 'know yourself' and that of all great religions. This wisdom understands finality and transience. It has a central place in the Canticle of the Creatures. In this bubbling Song of Praise, which summarises Francis' spirituality, Francis is a crystal clear realist who refuses to cherish illusions about our material state and fragility. It is no coincidence that his final words in this song are 'in great humility'. So, from the bottom up, with both feet on the ground, he sings out his Song of Praise. Clearly, meekly and boldly.

The recognition of the 'living and true God'

The 'living and true God' is infinitely greater than we are and the One to whom everyone is accountable. Francis was above all a man who recognised others, a man of respect and of reverence. This reverence is expressed in his endlessly repeated prayer 'who are You and who am I?', just as much as in the special emphasis he places on God as the 'merciful Saviour' – God as the Saviour of the risen Lord *as well as* God, the Saviour of humanity. Saviour: the ultimate fulfilment of our desire for a home and fruitfulness. Living in hope is a living that is oriented towards the ultimate redemption by the Merciful One.

This letter therefore deals with man's incontestable mortality and with our Origins and Destiny. This may be true, but is it also an inspiring message? It certainly is, but only if we keep in mind that Francis was not only a visionary who realistically accepted the limits of being human. He was above all a creative man who, without arrogance, possessed a great magnetism because of his inspired boldness and the open-mindedness belonging to a man who had nothing to lose and who expected everything from God. It was precisely this freedom which enabled him to deal in a positive way with the vulnerability and frailty we all have. Gratefully accepted frailty and vulnerability – heralds of and witnesses to our mortality – it is these that turn out to be the great talents which Francis made the most of.

The limits to what is 'makeable'

The most important things in our life and in society are those which cannot under any conditions be *made*, produced or bought. *Forgiveness* is given – or not. It cannot in any way be forced or produced. Also the *inner peace and joy*, of which Francis gradually learned the secret, could not independently be made by him. At most, he could open himself up to it in hope

Why are recognition, affection, forgiveness and inner peace not able to be bought or produced? Why are they for this reason costlier than gold? Not because we mortal makers only have limited power and a finite production capacity at our disposal. Even if these were to be infinite, then recognition and forgiveness would still not in any way be able to be forced or planned. This is because the most valuable thing we know of is *freedom*: a very vulnerable freedom, which precisely because of this frailty is so valuable.

There is a good reason that Christians, together with the first Letter of Peter, may speak of 'the precious blood of Christ' (1:19), which cannot be paid for in gold or silver. 'Precious blood': extremely costly, given in freedom, the powerful vulnerability of the pre-eminent Giver, which appealed greatly to Francis. He repeatedly used the word 'precious' when he spoke about the care with which the faithful should approach the Eucharist.[3]

After the catastrophe of Good Friday, the Risen Christ did not reproach the disciples (John 20:19-23). He didn't put them to shame. He recognised them in the covenant which he himself did not break. And then he wished them peace. And in the end he

---

[3] *Francis of Assisi: Early Documents. Volume II. The Founder*; 'The First Letter to the Custodians', 56; 2-6; 'Letter to the Clergy', 52; 11; 'The Testament', 124; 10-12.

gave them the power to forgive. Recognition, real peace and forgiveness: three values which we cannot fabricate ourselves. The words that Jesus said to his disciples on that occasion 'receive the Holy Spirit', contain an encouragement: receive the power to receive, to be open and to be hospitable. In other words: receive the Spirit of communication and real contact. The freedom to be there for others is real freedom: hospitality.

Everything that makes life really worth while belongs to the order of what you may receive: always unearned, always experienced as a surprising gift, as mercy. This goes for Francis and Clare, and no less for us, modern or post-modern as we may be.

The infectiousness of goodness

Why was Jesus' attentiveness to our need for simple recognition, for forgiveness and for inner peace so important for Francis? Why did he in his turn try to be the same with everyone he met: from the highest lords – the pope and the sultan – down to the 'worthless and despised, the poor and weak, the sick, the lepers and beggars along the way'? (Earlier Rule, 9,2 and further)

Because he himself had received unearned attention from Christ, when he recognised in the leper who kissed him his own Lord Jesus and had felt his forgiving love: 'And afterwards I delayed a little and left the world' (Testament 3). He no longer had a choice. He had experienced the most valuable thing that can be experienced, namely being loved in spite of all. He was infected by this immense acknowledgement of his dignity *in* all his indignity, and therefore became infectious to all he met. For however infectious evil may seem, the infectiousness of goodness is greater. It is certainly no less gripping. And isn't it this very infectiousness of goodness which still appeals to us in Francis?

The fundamentalism of hard cash

The value of our vulnerable and frail freedom deserves all our attention in this day and age. For nowadays the urge to produce has become greater than ever. This ever accelerating production-process is mirrored in riches which have swollen proportionately to it – however only for a very small percentage of the world's population. Besides, this huge capacity to produce is based on a special type of 'fundamentalism': the fundamentalism of hard cash. Whoever, frail as he is, is called to compassion in following in the footsteps of Jesus and Francis and Clare, must nowadays deal with the extreme *hardness* of the present-day market-economy. In spite of the fact that in these days of information technology all kinds of 'flexibility' and 'adaptability' have become the slogans of the day on the labour-market, this hardness has not diminished.[4] What is forcing itself upon us is a flexibility which is fiercely assertive. In the harsh light of this dominant steely mentality, the shielding and protection of this free vulnerability seem to have become ridiculous. What can the acknowledgement of 'good vulnerability' do in the face of an economic structure in which hard criteria have become a matter of course?

Now, after his conversion, Francis' life-style was given durability through his very own type of inflexibility. We must endeavour to view the hardness of Mammon together with Francis' own toughness. Why the rat-race in order to gain possessions, then and now? Because people realise all too well that their existence is vulnerable, dependent and unstable. Possessions mean security: a certain amount of independence and a means of support, in spite of our instability. Indeed, it appears to be this simple. And it is a good thing as well; but only on the condition that this security does not degenerate into a kind of protection at the cost of others and excluding them. This exclusion, being an obstacle to true community, is one of the reasons why Francis is so fiercely against the tendency towards self-appropriation and against the placing of oneself above others. This is why service to others has such an important place in his way of life. Long before the important twentieth-century philosopher Emmanuel Levinas pointed out the priority of

---

[4] Compare Richard Sennett, *The Corrosion of Character: The Personal Consequences of Work in the New Capitalism*. W. W. Norton, 1998.

the other as being the cornerstone of ethics, Francis had done so using the same biblical source: he had seen how the hard mentality of self-appropriation at any cost had driven an endless amount of victims to the margins of Assisi.

The hardness of Mammon

Is it a coincidence that these days the word 'hard' is more often heard in everyday-language than it used to be? 'Hard action', 'hardened criminals', hard currency', 'hardened journalism', 'hard porn', hardware', 'hard drugs': as if it has to be hammered into us that nothing can stand on its own without first being hardened up. In contrast to this, things which are tender in our perception are often disqualified as being 'soft' or 'weak'.

In the background, the idol Mammon basks in glory. This name can be translated as 'our Support', 'the Unshakeable', 'the Principle Matter' (and, if you will, 'our Capital'). This idol offers its services to all who are in search of absolute and solid certainty – the security of hard currency –, to only shortly afterwards hold all who have accepted its services clenched in an iron grip. For the moment this hardness may disguise itself on the labour-market as flexibility, but this does not mean it is no less hard. All things frail and vulnerable seem to be sacrificed to it. Crises in the agricultural sector emphasise that even the strongest animal is defenceless against the power of modern technology – especially when it is harnessed in the endless striving for profits.

Tender and tough

What was this solid ground, this exceptional 'hardness', that Francis had discovered, so that he even dared to consider an expedition into the hard world of greed, accompanied by only a few penniless brothers as disciples of the Son of Man? In his conversion he had learned to recognise and accept the limits of human life. This was fundamental. These limits he had above all learned to see and respect in the tender skin of a man, however disfigured this leper may have been – no, precisely because he was so disfigured. But isn't this the world turned upside down? For what could be more vulnerable and tender than the skin, or the retina of an eye, or an ear-drum? Can any resistance, any obstinacy be found in these?

Or could Francis from then on only think and live differently because he had seen in the skin and membranes of a fellow-human an inviolable reality: a moral force with an unwavering cry for respect? In the Earlier Rule of 1221 he writes about the face of Christ. He does this in connection to what he calls 'the right of the poor' (this is the right of the weak which must never give way to the so called 'right' of the strong). He continues with:

> 'Let them not to be ashamed and remember, moreover, that our Lord Jesus Christ, the Son of the all powerful living God, set His face like flint (Isaiah 50:7) and was not ashamed (…) Alms are a legacy and a justice due to the poor that our Lord Jesus Christ acquired for us' (Earlier Rule 9,4 f.).

'Set His face like flint': the most tender and vulnerable, being the hardest and toughest; an amazing unyieldingness, an amazing strength, an amazing foundation for the alternative life-style of this disciple of Jesus Christ.

These days, Francis is often spoken of as being a bringer of peace and reconciliation. And rightly so, because this was the core of his life's mission: bringing peace through servility. However we should keep in mind that he was only capable of reconciliation because the foundation he stood on was irreconcilable. This trusty servant of the 'meek and humble at heart' was, just like his master, in a certain way absolutely inflexible. On no account did Francis wish to kow-tow to the ruling system of money-making and career-planning. It was exactly on the basis of this inflexibility that he was capable of bowing down before any pariah he came upon, and in doing so bowing down before the Son of God who identifies Himself with the most vulnerable.

Inflexible: intolerant?

Recently the scope of tolerance has been a lively topic of discussion. No wonder, now that it has become apparent that living in a multicultural society – at a national as well as global level – has its own demands. In this new situation, the question may be raised whether Francis' inflexibility towards certain practices also means that he should be deemed intolerant. In a certain way he was. For his honest compliance and tolerance were based on an unwavering foundation of what he deemed holy; just as his work for reconciliation was only possible on the basis of his being irreconcilable in a good way: his conviction that his essential values could not be used as bargaining chips.

It is in questions such as these concerning the demarcation lines between tolerance and intolerance that the heart of Francis' spirituality lies. It is namely no coincidence that the value we have translated as bearing which was so important to him is often translated as tolerating. The task to bear or tolerate what is difficult or sometimes even terrible, must have also evoked the question for him as to how far he should go in his bearing or tolerance. What could he – indeed what must he – take upon himself in all reluctance? And what could not be accepted under any conditions whatsoever, because it would completely go against the evangelical lifestyle which determined his own way of life as a disciple of Jesus Christ? Which convictions and practices must he therefore reject in principal as not to be tolerated? And – just as important – in what way should he express his rejection?

His principal rejection of different views and practices did not mean that he always wished to combat these in concrete. For his tolerance was neither indifferent nor fanatical. Standing on the solid rock of Jesus' identification with the oppressed and poor, an indifference which accepted everything was not an option in his eyes. For a relativism such as this (which is nowadays sometimes presented under the guise of tolerance) would mean that he would not be considering the genuine otherness of his fellow-humans and everything that this stood for, as well as his own values, in a serious way. But he was also not characterised by a fanaticism which views different beliefs and practices as intolerable and which therefore wishes to deprive others of the possibility to lead their own lives. His journey to the Sultan, right across the front-lines, made it clear that he distanced himself from the crusaders who were bent on removing their opponents.

The issue is *how* he desired to deal with what he considered reprehensible in the lives of others. Regarding this, the conclusion of Chapter 17 of the Earlier Rule is typical. Here he uses words which were initially intended to be an open end to the whole Rule: 'When we see or hear evil spoken or done or God blasphemed, let us speak well and do well and praise God Who is blessed forever' (verse 19).

Inflexible towards everything that threatened peace and reconciliation, Francis apparently wished to guard himself and his brothers from behaviour which as a reaction to evil, would have been determined by that evil. He had learned from his Master how one's own life can then threaten to become poisoned by what nowadays is called resentment or rancour. The evil would only spread even further. For Francis, 'speak well and do well' presumes the indispensable action of the Holy Spirit with whom he above all wished to remain united.

However what if the confrontation with those who thought and lived differently was unavoidable? People like Francis who travelled around preaching, could be sure to expect confronting encounters such as these. And all the more when, as was often the case, he came across faction-fighting and feuds. We already mentioned in Chapter 1 what he saw as being his and his brothers' duty in such cases: neither glossing over, nor accepting injustice. And again and again that frank and respectful double call: to duly honour God and to start a new life in repentance. In this way, this tough preacher would do anything to promote a voluntary conversion of his audience's ways.

Living amongst Muslims

A special situation did however arise when some brothers felt called to go and live as missionaries amongst 'the Saracens (Muslims) and other non-believers'.[5] The authorities of the brotherhood were

---

[5] Jan Hoeberichts, *Francis and the Islam*. Quincy, 1997.

obliged to give them permission to do so. The question was however, whether a mission like this didn't mean a greater chance (whether of one's own choice or not) of dying as a martyr. Francis foresaw this possibility and in the Chapter in the Earlier Rule about missionary activity he wrote:

> 'For love of Him, they must make themselves vulnerable to their enemies, both visible and invisible, because the Lord says: "Whoever loses his live because of me will save it in eternal life"' (Earlier Rule, 16,11).

He follows this passage with a series of quotations from the Gospels regarding the prescribed attitude during persecution. Following in Christ's footsteps and having inflexibility toward a persuasion based on other principals can in extreme cases indeed mean sacrificing one's life. Francis is very clear about this. It is however very striking that in the same Chapter he offers a second possibility for living between people of other faiths and creeds:

> 'As for the brothers who go, they can live spiritually among the Saracens and non-believers in two ways. One way is not to engage in arguments or disputes but to be subject to every human creature for God's sake and to acknowledge that they are Christians. The other way is to announce the Word of God, when they see it pleases the Lord, in order that (unbelievers) may believe in almighty God, the Father, the Son and the Holy Spirit, the Creator of all, the Son, the Redeemer and Saviour, and be baptized and become Christians because no one can enter the kingdom of God without being reborn of water and the Holy Spirit' (Earlier Rule 16, 5-7).

Regarding the first way, Francis avoids all action that could lead to conflict – even if it were 'only' to be arguing or debating. Therefore no 'holy-war' mentality. His choice for tolerance towards people of other faiths takes the shape of bearing or enduring the burdens which are inherent to a self-imposed inferior position. Francis' willingness to subordinate himself was probably prompted by his respect for the Muslim belief in the almighty God, Creator of heaven and earth. This tolerant respect meant an acceptance of what he had discovered to be true in the other. His willingness to

subordinate himself, presumed a clear appeal to Muslim hospitality. Without arriving with a show of power and theological arguments, he hoped simply to be received as a fellow-human and to
be tolerated. All the same, this choice for a radical form of tolerance was no hindrance to his being a witness through his way of
life and, if questioned, to admit to being a follower of Christ. His
own beliefs and way of life stood firm.

Sensitive to the vulnerability of all living things

Does Francis' inflexibility show us what our duties are in our modern world of neo-liberalism? Yes it does, but only if we do not
immediately start planning points of action which have to be
implemented as soon as possible. What we are about to say, may
sound ridiculous. All the same, we feel that in a world which is
dominated by the shallow and indifferent no-nonsense mentality
of a steely and cold flexibility-economy, our first duty is towards
the preservation and development of our sensitivity to the vulnerability of all living things. This is sensitivity towards the invaluable
dignity of all that cannot be measured or produced or which is not
considered to be of economic importance – but this does not mean
that they have less of a claim to our admiration and respect. It is
an attitude of being sensitive towards the own special dignity of
what is vulnerable, and of being inflexible precisely in this sensitivity. For in this way we can, together with Francis and Clare,
become pupils of Christ who was the most vulnerable and most
deeply Wounded One, and who, by accepting and enduring his
frailty, became the Cornerstone – 'the Rock who followed' his people (Acts 4:11; 1 Corinthians 10:4).

A gift of the Holy Spirit: discretio

This most precious gift, this sensitivity that enables us to discern
and to judge correctly, this *discretio* was the foundation of Francis'
prayer-life and efforts. This is where the real basis is to be found.
We too must be aware not to let this sensitivity be dethroned by

any trendy fashion or by any advertising campaign whatsoever; for this sensitive *discretio* is another name for the Holy Spirit. The Spirit about which Francis wrote to his brothers: 'Let them pay attention to what they must desire above all else: to have the Spirit of the Lord and Its holy activity' (Later Rule 10,8).

This sensitivity appreciates the endless diversity of our fellow-creatures: for everyone's unique face as well as for the face of 'our sister, mother earth' whose face has these days become so badly disfigured. When this sensitive *discretio* starts to bloom, our own vulnerability and dependence on the primary conditions of survival remain what they were. And all the same, our vulnerability is then no longer something which is in the first place held to be negative, but is rather a different word for the beautiful capacity to enter into contact by picking up life-signs from others and to communicate with them. Whoever thinks that it is beneath the dignity of our autonomy to be dependent on air, food and essential affection may try and see how long he or she can stand this kind of independence! Thank God there is a 'good' dependence: we live by it and we are revived by it. In much the same manner, it is only thanks to the instability of our existence that we can literally and figuratively move ourselves and can represent others.

Beauty: source of genuine spirituality

Sensitivity and perception are also the roots of all creativity in the arts and thought. They are closely related to that indispensable intuition which enables us to discern the genuinely new and unexpectedly beautiful amongst the 'matter-of-factness' and endless *faits accomplis* which hem us in. In the Titus Brandsma Lecture 2000 at the University of Nijmegen, Cardinal Danneels spoke about the opportunities for a spiritual reawakening in these times of efficiency, commercialisation and utilitarian thinking. In his forceful plea to once again recognise beauty as a source of genuine spirituality, he also said:

> 'Beauty heals us of the wounds which pure economic, utilitarian and technical thinking cause. (...) It cannot be reconciled to the

violence and fever of haste. (…) It leads us into the realm of para-
doxes through its symbolic language which synthesises, binds and
unites.
Speaking to young people about God as truth or as the original
image of perfection, makes them stop listening rather quickly. (…)
We have not made use of the many paths to God which lie in the
endless images of beauty that can be found in our churches, muse-
ums, literature and theatre. Bach's Passions contain a 'dimension of
revelation' which few – including young people – are able to resist.
And not only because of their musical perfection. They offer something which comes from above.'[6]

Our word 'ethical' can be directly traced to the Greek word for the
'sensitivity' which enables us to discern what is beautiful and good.
Artistically blessed or not, everyone can learn to open themselves
to the beauty of God's creation. In this quiet attentiveness they can
escape from the constraint imposed by lives solely based on utility
and efficiency. During the lengthy and torturous roll-calls in concentration-camps, the sunrises and sunsets were often an inalien-
able source of consolation for the inmates. But everyday life also
has its own various forms of constraints and being 'occupied'.

Where so much shallowness is forced upon us by rapidly changing labour-relations, this is of primary importance. Not to speak
of the moral indifference which, according to the parallel statements of Adorno and Pasternak, were at the root of the atrocities
of the totalitarian regimes of the twentieth century.

'Originally from'

In a time in which a blizzard of impressions from the media is
overwhelming us, it is urgently necessary to cultivate a sensitivity
towards values which seemingly do not count when viewed from
an economic perspective. This snow-storm feels even more bitterly
cold, now that many have become spiritually homeless. How often

---

[6] Godfried Danneels. *Is een oude honger terug? Schoonheid als bron van spiritualiteit.* Nijmegen, 2000; 30 f..

can people be heard saying: 'I used to be a Catholic', or 'I used to
be a Baptist'. People do not feel completely (or not at all) at home
with the institutions of their youth – as far as these still remain
standing. Followers of Francis also know this feeling. The far-reaching upheavals in the Church and society have not passed them by.
This displacement is however not only distressing. For many of us
it meant being liberated, learning to speak out and becoming self-
assured in our actions. The freedom of God's children has been
given more opportunities. How could Jesus' proud words 'the children are free' have been forgotten? (Matthew 17:24-27; compare
Romans 8:21). The crisis which has become apparent in these feelings of displacement, also offers the opportunity to arrive at a new
consciousness of the great 'home' of God's creation: the space we,
as responsible partners, may share with our fellow-creatures.

Introspection and dialogue are indispensable in learning to
understand the signs of our times and for making a fresh start.
This is actually how the Earlier Rule of 1221 came into being: a
continuous dialogue by the brothers, who shared their experiences
with one another, sifted through them and, by placing these in the
light of the Gospel, managed to discern the good from the bad.
Francis and Clare only managed to become prophets by their continuous introspection and learning through experience and through
the dialogue they held with each other and with others. Being people who meditated, they became exceptionally good at reading and
understanding the Scriptures, society in their days and their own
experiences in life. They experienced their vocation as a twofold
mission: What was the challenge of their times? And in what way
did this situation force them to read the Holy Scriptures? We can
recognise this in the words of Cardinal Danneels which head this
Chapter: 'We wish to read the signs of the times, yet with the wisdom of the Scriptures.' By being alert to contemporary events *and*
by steadily contemplating God's illuminating Word, they could
comprehend God's promise of salvation throughout all the winds
of change in whatever direction they were blowing. Because whatever the day and age, it all comes down to proclaiming and giving
God's help, in spite of all the numbness and blindness and in spite

of all the dazed and lost looks. In intensely experiencing their loving relationship with the living Lord and by identifying themselves with his unshakeable and tender affection for people, they managed to see things in proportion, liberating themselves by laughing things off – and in this way they could learn to understand the signs of their times.

Signs of the times

When Jesus spoke about understanding the signs of the times, he compared these to how people interpret the weather. The signs of the times are just like the signs of changing weather. They demand interpretation. Regarding this, it is interesting to note that the French and Italian languages have the same word for time as for weather: *le temps* and *il tempo*. The Italian word *tempo* has a third meaning which has been borrowed by other languages. It can also mean 'rhythm' or 'measure'. On its own, 'rhythm' can mean a quiet rhythm. It is however typical of our times and society that this word 'tempo' has usually come to mean a 'quick' or 'accelerated' *tempo*. For many, this atmosphere of haste is breathtaking. Is it a coincidence that hyper-ventilation is a modern condition? The question as to who is beating this fast rhythm is of course not often raised. What is the motivation behind this ever increasing fever? It is a cold fever, a cold activity, which led the poet Huub Oosterhuis to use the image of 'fire that gives no warmth'. This feverish excitement is forcing its way into all aspects of life.

Who is beating this rhythm? This question cannot be seen separately from the position the idol Mammon has acquired. In the rich areas of North America and Europe it is probably the pre-eminent sign of the times that we no longer 'have time' and that our experience of time has become ever more pressurised. Living in the era of information technology is to live with a different concept of time than before. Because of technical developments, 'time' often manifests itself as 'compressed time' (Moltmann). Information can be at one's fingertips with lightning speed. By just pressing a couple of buttons, enterprises can exert their influence. But, thank

God, accounts of atrocities in seemingly far-away places can also reach us quickly by e-mail. The world's conscience can also be roused much more quickly than ever before.

Numbness and keeping things in the dark

The twentieth century was characterised by wake-up call after wake-up call. The AIDS-disaster threatens to become a new plague-epidemic and to depopulate large areas of Africa and Asia. One could expect that our vigilance would have increased in proportion to this. However we are confronted with the paradoxical fact that the use of sedatives and drugs has increased tremendously: legally via the pharmaceutical industry, and illegally via all kinds of criminal circuits. On top of this is the numbing and distraction caused by an endless, often untasteful, stream of amusement-programmes. Many people are 'workaholics' and often have to be, seeing the increased pressure of work. It isn't easy to escape from this collective 'acceleration' and from the rapid alternation of impressions. One can even become addicted to this by channel-surfing. There are those who are 'only' addicted to noise and to the unstoppable stream of empty words. There have never been so many ways to numb ourselves and addicts have never had it so difficult.

Our increased tempo of living and our attitude towards time as being compressed has caused our bodies, which have their own 'clock', to vehemently protest. 'Brother mule' stubbornly refuses to be harnessed to the yoke of our ever increasing haste. Our bodies protest with fatigue and concentration-problems every time we change time-zones. Cows that are milked also protest when summer- and winter-times are introduced. 'Stress' is probably mostly due to our feeling of being stuck between our own experience of time flying at an ever increasing pace and our body's experience of time, refusing to be bossed around. Our body has its own time-span for learning and growing. The body's wisdom, which speaks its own language, cannot be denied without impunity.

The value of duration for Francis

What does the wisdom of Francis and Clare have to say about all of this? Of course they could not have guessed at the 'digital revolution'. All the same, some basic aspects of their spirituality are of great importance regarding the wisdom concerning our bodies, including the wisdom and perception of time of the bodies of others. We have the 'virtues of duration' in mind.[7] This seemingly old-fashioned expression calls to mind virtues such as faithfulness, loyalty, patience, the ability to mourn and to thank. Francis' basic attitudes can be heard here. All these, then as well as now, imply a certain duration of time. 'Giving back' presumes a memory that can thankfully look back in time. And 'bearing' is pregnant with the notion of living in the duration of time and enduring things.

The acknowledgement of the everlasting value of the virtues of duration, once again implies a toughness which is the watermark of genuine humanity. An unshakeable attitude which can stand up to the hardness of hard cash. The word 'duration', just like the French word *durer* and the German *Dauer*, are derived from the Latin *durus* which means 'hard'. Our perception of the durability of things, includes the notion of an inflexibility which will not give way to any acceleration in tempo whatsoever. 'Duration' also means: what doesn't blow around in the wind; what isn't like chaff, but is 'planted by streams of water' (Psalm 1:3).

The far-reaching solidarity which characterises the life-styles of Francis and Clare, therefore has everything to do with what they considered to be genuinely solid. That is: firm, stable and able to be counted on. Solidarity as a 'virtue of duration' means that people offer each other stability and assistance in 'time which is fleeting'. And isn't this 'instability of time' precisely exacerbated in the compressed time of information technology, which incites us to be ever more hasty? The call to engage with others also implies working with the lonely, for whom time seems to crawl along at a snail's pace.

---

[7] Paul van Tongeren, *Over het verstrijken van de tijd. Een kleine ethiek van de tijdservaring.* Nijmegen, 2002; 90.

Out of tune with reality?

It may perhaps seem out of tune with reality to give so much attention to sensitivity and the inflexible feeling for time that our bodies have. It is a daring move to want to live with and for 'the softer
powers'. Can this be done by children of the Enlightenment and
the digital revolution? Is it not true that we live in the 'up-market
area of the global village'? What we recognise as imperishable and
thoroughly positive in all that is fragile and vulnerable, appeals to
us on the one hand, but at the same time we tend to recoil before
the evident superior force of an economic system which encompasses the world and triumphantly carries on as it pleases. We hear
biblical prophets like Isaiah saying 'Here I am!'. But like Jeremiah
we tend to stick to: 'Who am I, that I should be able to do this?'

Peace is the way

These well-known doubts do not have to embarrass or paralyze us.
The values we wish to stand up for are not only looming far away
upon the horizon. The essential values of spirituality are like the
wisdom of the saying which could be seen painted on a wall of the
Moses and Aaron Church in Amsterdam: 'There is no way to
peace; peace is the way'. This amounts to observing the valuable
initiatives and activities which are already present in our world.
'Peace is the way.' Just as there is no way to freedom; freedom is
the way. And just as there is no way to a good life according to the
Gospels, because this good life, inspired by the Gospels, *is* the way.
Sensitivity, solidarity with the weakest, courageously bearing and
persevering: this is the mission. All the good things in our world
– even though they call to be expanded upon – show us the way
we must travel.

    Whoever wields an absolute criterion as far as this is concerned,
under the motto of: 'everything or nothing' is playing a dangerous
game. The result will then quickly turn out to be: 'our life is not
everything, far from it, therefore it is nothing'. However whoever
looks with Francis' respectful eyes, will be able to say: 'It is certainly

not everything which we make of it. But it is also not nothing! And who are we to snuff out a glowing pit? It is all too clear which sparks should be fanned.'

However, whoever thinks he or she is capable of travelling 'the way of peace' on their own steam does not belong to the circle of Francis, Clare and their followers. We have already remarked upon the special significance of the words 'Love', 'Peace' and 'the most holy Will' in the Canticle of the Creatures – references to the Holy Spirit, 'the pointing finger of the All Highest'. For 'love', 'peace' and 'the will of God' are pseudonyms for the mystery of the 'Helper' whom Jesus promised us.

Slow down

One of the signs of our times is that more people than ever before are finding their way to contemplative monasteries and meditation centres. In the midst of all the haste surrounding them, they come to reflect upon what is truly of importance in their lives. Contemplation amounts to slowing down and considering the experiences and issues which can barely receive attention in their busy lives; and with both feet firmly planted on the ground, away from all heightened activity, to listen in the silence to what is perhaps being spoken from elsewhere. For this essential truth cannot be made or produced. Being touched belongs to another order: that of the affective basis of our existence which is threatened by an excess of planning and efficiency. Above all, it amounts to being receptive to what comes from 'the beyond'.

Even if Francis didn't have the faintest idea about the hecticness of our society, he too was confronted with the task of combining a life full of activity with the restfulness of contemplation. The fact that he did not find this task easy is apparent from Clare's advice on how to deal with this. A life of contemplation appealed so strongly to him that he wondered whether he should not devote himself solely to this. Or should he stick to Jesus' call to go out and proclaim the Gospel which had set him ablaze with enthusiasm at the beginning of his conversion. From her own experience Clare knew of Francis' special talent to proclaim to others about how Christ inspired him. Her advice amounted to continuing the combination of active life as well as making time for contemplative prayer.

The 'art of living' which characterises Francis, was indeed made up of this double vocation. Even these days it can become clear to what extent lonely contemplation must have appealed to him if one visits the highly situated hermitages and caves in the Rieti-valley where he withdrew himself from time to time. During his life as a celebrated 'man of God' the silence and majesty of the pristine natural surroundings must have meant a great deal to him. His words are typical: 'Where there is rest and meditation, there is neither anxiety nor restlessness' (Admonition 27,4)

For those who, affluent or not, live with worries and distractions, these words are food for thought. Francis did not only meditate in deserted spots. Also while he travelled around preaching he must have undoubtedly meditated on his days-long journeys, inspired as he was by the traces to be found of the Creator in nature. His biographer tells us that he saw a reflection of God's goodness in all that was beautiful: of the live-giving Foundation and Cause (compare 2 Celano 165). And in giving back to God, he was, as his biographer remarks: 'not as much a man of prayer, but totally and entirely prayer itself' (2 Celano 95). In the seclusion of her cloister, Clare too urged her sisters who worked outside the cloister:

> 'When the most holy mother used to send the serving sisters outside the monastery, she reminded them to praise God when they saw beautiful trees, flowers and bushes; and, likewise, always to praise Him for and in all things when they saw all peoples and creatures' (The Acts of the Process of Canonization 14,9).

Nowadays people rightly ask whether the appeal of monasteries and meditation centres should not be supplemented by a spirituality for everyday life. How can people who are completely taken up by the cares and worries of work and family give form to an authentic spirituality for their own lives? A deepened motivation and orientation of their lives is precisely at issue here: in order that they are not lived, but can try and give form to their relationship with the Faithful One in a thankful and receptive way.

Many people try and make time for meditation in their own homes and surroundings, without desiring or being able to take on a monastic way of life. They are however conscious of the fact that meditation, wherever it is practiced, is only authentic and viable if done with an attitude of receptiveness. Everything revolves around the respectful attention which is called alertness in the Gospels:

> 'Beware, keep alert; for you do not know when the time will come. It is like a man going on a journey, when he leaves home and puts his slaves in charge, each with his work, and commands the doorkeeper to be on the watch' (Mark 13:33-34).

Being a 'doorkeeper' in one's own life – this it what it is apparently all about. This means that we must deal with the huge number of impressions which reach us – and sometimes come flying at us – in our everyday life in a discerning way; to be able to shut ourselves off from what is strange to our innermost nature. And above all to open ourselves up to what can really still our hunger for true life.

Where can this 'doorway' or 'gateway' be found? The functioning of our senses is central to the basis of every kind of spirituality – whether sought for in monastic silence or in hectic everyday life. These are the 'gateways' through which we can become attentive – whether at home or whilst travelling. Therefore exactly in those spots where a human being is most vulnerable and fragile – the retina, the eardrum, everywhere we are most sensitive: this is where what we cannot produce ourselves presents itself to us. And what we cannot do without. What we remarked upon earlier on in this book about Francis' sensitivity, is also true here: as poor as he was – and because he was poor – this sensitivity constituted his immense riches.

Living in attentiveness

Being a 'doorkeeper' amounts to living in attentiveness:

'Whoever lives in attentiveness does not only possess a well-formed power of observation, but also the emotional quiet and space to use it. He has sufficient quiet to remain standing in what is happening now and not to run ahead, and is sufficiently 'tidied up' not to keep ruminating on the past.

Attentiveness can perhaps best be described as a middle-way between on the one hand forgetfulness and carelessness, and on the other an obsessive tendency to not only wish to see all that happens, but also to want to control it. *Letting* things happen, but all the same being present, this is attentiveness.'[8]

How can one acquire this attitude of attentiveness towards life? The answer is: by making room for reflection and prayer on a regular basis. Perhaps this leads to another question: prayer, all very good and well, but how do you do that? A clear and direct answer cannot be given. There is no general method which seamlessly fits everyone's character.[9]

Individual shades are important, but also the realisation that prayer should be done in secret. When Francis prayed he avoided making any show of it whatsoever. The intimacy with God was too fragile and precious for him to do otherwise. These days, much of what is actually not suited to being revealed stands in the glare of media attention. For certain types of plants, harsh sunlight is deadly. Those of us living in the era of 'emotion-TV' and 'reality-TV' must beware of 'nakedly' showing off our innermost experiences and emotions, because the general tendency to desire more and more is also applicable here.

Sociologists say that we are living in an 'experience-society'. 'Experience?' The elderly Cardinal Newman remarked that he no longer experienced any emotions in his prayer. The time for this had apparently passed by. Jesus also often prayed in 'the desert', in apparent lifelessness. Modern Christians who often live in a

---

[8] Paul van Tongeren, *Over het verstrijken van de tijd*; 90.

[9] Chester P. Michael and Marie C. Norrisey, *Prayer and Temperament. Different Prayer Forms for Different Personality Types.* Charlottesville, Virginia 22902, 1984.

spiritual no-mansland must, in all this desolation, once again meditate on the desert – which the Bible portrays as the place of first
love – and learn to have faith over and against all temptations.

Prayer: art of living

For prayer silence is indispensable. For in silence the realisation
germinates that the essence of the Mystery can no longer be put
into words – just as the essence can 'only' be found in the white
surrounding purified words on paper. This realisation does not
make searching for the right word superfluous: sanctified words
can evoke the Ineffable. This 'evocation' is what all works of art can
bring about: amazement and gratitude – and sometimes the recognition of the Creator. Just like the works of great theologians are
the results of their prayer. In this way every authentic prayer is an
expression of the art of living of this unique person – however poor
this prayer may perhaps seem to him.

'Evocation' may remind us that praying and singing together on
a regular basis is desirable. Singing together, with silent intervals,
gives the heart the opportunity to resonate. And in periods of spiritual emptiness when words no longer mean anything, singing
together is a chance to 'listen with the lips' as the Dutch song-
writer Willem Barnard once said. For just as there is a way from
inside to outside – from the praying heart to the singing mouth –
there is also the way from outside to inside – from the lips singing
along to the empty heart. Sometimes this way is opened in a surprising fashion.

Like beggars with empty hands

Gestures are also important in our prayer-life. What is expressed by
the body resonates in the soul and vice versa. Empty hands express
receptiveness. The simple gesture of opened hands can evoke the
realisation of our neediness as creatures. In this opening gesture we
recognise God as the Generous One, Who knows what we are in
need of. Prayer entails: asking again and again, perseverance, just

like in Jesus' parable of the friend who knocked in the night (compare Luke 11:9-13 and 12:30).

To pray is to grow in the realisation of our own poverty and trust. Here we may recall the famous, but also high-spirited words of Thérèse of Lisieux: 'On the evening of my life I will appear before You with empty hands… I will only be able to offer You my desires.'[10] Now that the trappings of a traditional Catholic way of life have disappeared, we can embrace the high-spiritedness and trust which are echoed in these words of Thérèse. Opening our empty hands in the freedom of being children of God. Praying for the ability to pray, thankful for being allowed to thank and blessing because we are allowed to bless. And always, before we say anything, there is the sighing of the Spirit from below. Praying in such a way is so simple that it quietens us. Our task is to regularly open our hands for what cannot be organised or made. To pray to be able to be touched by the One who knows how to touch. It is true: when this 'being touched' happens in a crisis, it can be extremely difficult. All the same, a crisis such as this, which is always unexpected and unwanted, can bring about the opening which we require at a certain moment to continue to grow.

In remembrance of Him

We have not discussed the second half of the Letter to the Rulers of the Peoples. In it, Francis points to the mystery of the Eucharist in a surprising fashion. What does this mean? That he places his brotherly call – also to us Moderns or Post-Moderns who still call the shots in this world – in a special perspective. He starts his letter by saying: 'Reflect and see that the day of death is approaching. With all possible respect, therefore, I beg you not to forget the Lord (…)' In other words: 'Do not forget that you are made of earthenware, fashioned out of clay. And do not forget God's Breath of Life, the inspiration you cannot do without.' However this call

---

[10] Thérèse de Lisieux, *Correspondence générale*. Editions du Cerf & Desclée De Brouwer, 1972-1973, LT 218.

is placed in a special light when Francis places it in the spotlight of 'receiving the most holy Body and Blood of our Lord Jesus Christ with fervour in holy remembrance of Him (...)'. 'In remembrance of Him' is the opposite of forgetting our good material state and of forgetting the Only One who may truly be called good. It is as if Francis calls us: 'Do not forget how it was the Powerful One who pre-eminently revealed Himself in our mortal existence with all His sensitivity. Remember that his Son became flesh, became bread. In the Eucharist our human fragility is transformed by Him into his most precious gift. God also entrusts this gift of Himself to you in the breaking of bread. In it you will find the power to be people after his own heart.' It is no wonder that Francis, exactly in his texts about the mystery of the Eucharist, emphasises *discretio*: the sensitivity to be able to discern.

Francis' First Admonition – as we have already seen in Chapter 3 – offers us words of encouragement. They deal with God's hiddenness and with the Holy Spirit Who helps us to somewhat realise the mystery of our origins and destination in the man Jesus and in his eucharistic gifts. The concluding words of this Admonition may be an encouragement for those who realise that they are confronted with a tough mission in these times which are characterised by a fading notion of God: 'And in this way the Lord is always with His faithful, as He Himself says: 'Behold I am with you until the end of the age.' Via Francis, this promise by the One Who Lives with us for all times can be heard across the landscape of our Modern and Post-Modern Era.

What Francis was inspired by?

Francis: marked by the wounds of Jesus. Artists have often portrayed him in this fashion: in ecstasy, his hands raised up high, staring up at heaven. Sometimes these wounded hands appear to have taken on a more protective attitude, as if to say: 'It is not about me. Look at Him who became the poorest and least of all people for us. I desired to be his servant.' Humble, poor and at the same time joyous, he pointed towards Christ, touched by the mystery of God's descending love and by that respectful hiddenness of God in His Servant, Jesus. This is what inspired Francis' spirituality.

God's humility and poverty: perhaps this is *the* intuition of the 'illiterate' Francis. Illiterate, but also a theologian in the fullest sense of the word: 'he knew the poor, crucified Christ' (2 Celano 105). Humility: not many words sound so old-fashioned and unacceptable. And it *is* old-fashioned. And at the same time completely new. For it evokes the mystery of the Other, the Eternal One. And it points towards the supreme possibility to be open to Him.

In an image in the cathedral of Chartres, Jesus and the first human can be seen standing side by side: the 'new Adam' and the 'old Adam'. Their faces are alike, as if they were brothers. Their expression is one of desire and expectation. There is something inartificial about them, something naïve and vulnerable. And all the same they are hopefully – against all odds – looking out for another world.

In order to place ourselves – we modern, adult and autonomous humans – together with Francis next to them, one thing is necessary: to ask God for a 'second naivety'. Not as a regression into infantile behaviour, but rather as the simplicity which transcends our hectic and stubborn way of life. This naivety could very well be called a second diffidence. This diffidence, which embarrasses all inattentiveness, is an essential part of Francis' inheritance. For Diffidence, just like Humility and Poverty, was for Francis another name for the mystery of God.

Bibliography

Reference Works

Biblia Sacra. Juxta Vulgatam Clementinam. Divisionibus, summariis et concordantiis ornata. Romae-Tornaci-Parisiis, 1927.
Dictionnaire de Spiritualité, ascétique et mystique, doctrine et histoire. Paris, 1932 ff.
Holy Bible, New Revised Standard Version, Anglicized Edition with Apocrypha, Oxford, 1998.
Migne, J. P. *Patrologiae cursus completus.* Series latina, Paris, 1844/64. Paris, 1932 ff.
Novum Testamentum, Graece et Latine. Eberhard Nestlé et Kurt Aland. Editio XXII. Stuttgart, 1964.
Sources Chrétiennes. Série des textes monastiques d'Occident. Paris, 1941 ff.

Sources on Francis and Clare of Assisi

Claire d'Assise. Écrits. Introduction, (texte latin, traduction, notes et index. Marie-France Becker, Jean-François Godet, Thaddée Matura). *Sources Chrétiennes, 325,* Paris, 1985.
Clare of Assisi. Early Documents. Ed. and trans. Regis J. Armstrong O.F.M. Cap., (revised and expanded). St. Bonaventure, NY, 1993.
Dicta beati Aegidii Assisiensis. Quaracchi, 1939². *The Golden Sayings of the Blessed Brother Giles of Assisi.* Ed. Paschal Robinson. Philadelphia, 1907.
Fontes Francescani. Edizioni Porziuncula, (a cura di *Enrico* Menestò e di Guiseppe Cremascoli, Emore Paoli, Luigi Pellegrini, Stanislao Da Campagnola). Apparati di Giovanni M. Bocalli, Assisi, 1995.

Francis of Assisi: Early Documents. Volume I. The Saint. Edited by Regis J. Armstrong, O.F.M. Cap., J.A. Wayne Hellmann, O.F.M. Conv., William J. Short, O.F.M., New York – London – Manila, 1999.

Francis of Assisi: Early Documents. Volume II. The Founder. Edited by Regis J. Armstrong, O.F.M. Cap., J.A. Wayne Hellmann, O.F.M. Conv., William J. Short, O.F.M., New York – London – Manila, 2000.

Francis of Assisi: Early Documents. Volume III. The Prophet. Edited by Regis J. Armstrong, O.F.M. Cap., J.A. Wayne Hellmann, O.F.M. Conv., William J. Short, O.F.M., New York – London – Manila, 2001.

Opuscula Sancti Patris Francisci Assisiensis. Denuo edidit iuxta codices mss. Caietanus Esser O.F.M., (Bibliotheca Franciscana Ascetica Medii Aevi, Tom. XII), Grottaferrata (Roma), 1978.

PRINTED ON PERMANENT PAPER • IMPRIME SUR PAPIER PERMANENT • GEDRUKT OP DUURZAAM PAPIER - ISO 9706

N.V. PEETERS S.A., WAROTSTRAAT 50, B-3020 HERENT